THIS IS MY LIFE

THIS IS MY LIFE

The highly entertaining autobiography of a favourite TV presenter...

Eamonn Holmes is one of the most popular TV presenters in the UK, but his life and career have been roller coasters of highs and lows. At the age of 21 he was the youngest ever anchorman in Irish television, but when his show was axed his uncertain future prompted crippling panic attacks. When his beloved father died, Eamonn decided to make a clean break and take a job on a new morning show, GMTV. The rest is history. Here he talks candidly about his co-presenters, the guests he has loved and loathed – and his own burning ambition.

THIS IS MY LIFE

by

Eamonn Holmes

Magna Large Print Books
Long Preston, North Yorkshire,
BD23 4ND, England.

3419380

British Library Cataloguing in Publication Data.

Holmes, Eamonn
    This is MY life.

    A catalogue record of this book is
    available from the British Library

    ISBN 0-7505-2604-1
    ISBN 978-0-7505-2604-3

First published in Great Britain in 2006 by Orion Books
An imprint of the Orion Publishing Group Ltd

Copyright © Eamonn Holmes 2006

Cover illustration © Trevor Leighton by arrangement with GMTV

Published in Large Print 2006 by arrangement with
Orion Publishing Group

Magna Large Print is an imprint of Library Magna Books Ltd.

Printed and bound in Great Britain by
T.J. (International) Ltd., Cornwall, PL28 8RW

To Declan, Rebecca, Niall and Jack.
I hope that I am as good a parent to you as
my mum and dad were to me.

Acknowledgements

To anyone who feels they should have been mentioned and wasn't – my apologies. There are reasons for everything – in this case, mostly to do with space. But if I forgot you or a significant event, I am going to blame Amanda Harris for editing you out.

Having said that, I would like to thank:

Maria Malone, whose idea all of this was, and who had to listen to me incessantly droning on, even by phone during her holiday.

Amanda Harris, whose judgement is so wise for one so young, and to everyone at Orion for having the faith to publish.

Luigi Bonomi, whose infectious enthusiasm made me believe I could write this book.

Bill and Caroline McFarlan, for their support, friendship and wisdom.

Anna Moorby, my wonderful PA, for keeping my office running and making all the important decisions whenever I was off being an author.

Caroline Hollinrake, my other wonderful assistant, who, even though heavily pregnant, sorted out my vast collection of family snapshots and put some order into them.

Vince O'Sullivan – driver extraordinaire – who had to, between destinations, live with me dictating this text when he should have been listening to the radio. It's a good job he's hard of hearing. Thank you for your tolerance, Vince, and thank you for getting me everywhere on schedule, even on the odd occasion when I run late!

Ruth, for her love and support, and for distracting Jack every time he wanted to come into the office and play with Daddy.

My brothers, Leonard, Brian, Colm and Conor, who have had to live with me too often being a talking point in their lives – thank you for putting up with it, boys.

My mum, Josie, for having me and naming me Eamonn – I couldn't have done it without you! I also couldn't be the man I am without your guidance and standards.

My dad, Leonard – I always knew you were important, Dad, but now I know why. I never made it as a carpet fitter but I still strive to do a job the way you would want it done. I can hear you saying, 'If a thing's worth doing – it's worth doing well.' I hope you can see this book from Heaven and think I did just that.

To anyone who has bought this book – I am humbled, thank you.

And finally, let's not forget the late, great Eamonn Andrews, who provided me with not only a name but also a career path to follow.

Contents

What's In A Name?

It was my mum's idea to call me Eamonn, after the TV presenter Eamonn Andrews, who hosted various sports programmes as well as *What's My Line?*, *Crackerjack!* and, most famously, *This is Your Life*. He was telly's first all-rounder.

Eamonn Andrews, good-looking, genial, charming, was, outside Guinness, Ireland's best-known export to Britain and the country's most successful broadcaster. Mum adored him. Perhaps she hoped by naming me after him I'd grow up to be like him, and if she did she may well have unwittingly set me on the path to a broadcasting career because I'm convinced that some of Eamonn Andrews rubbed off somewhere.

Television has always fascinated me. When I was little more than a toddler, Mum says I would sit glued to the box saying, 'One day, I'm going to be on that.'

'Yes, yes, son, sure you are,' she'd say, naturally never believing it.

There are not many of us about – Eamonns, that is – not on television anyway. There's the poet rap artist who got to number one in the charts – Eamon – but he's only got one 'n'. Outside that I pretty much have the field to myself, just as Eamonn Andrews did in the fifties, sixties and seventies.

For better or worse, like Gazza, Becks, Jordan and Pelé, there's only one of me on the telly, which means that people tend to remember the name – even though some can't quite get to grips with the spelling or the pronunciation. David Bowie's wife being one.

'Eamonn,' said I, as I introduced myself, smiling and holding out my hand.

The exotic creature in front of me frowned. 'E-man,' she said.

I tried again. 'A-mon,' I articulated, working my lips around the vowels and syllables to try to help her out. She was from Somalia after all.

The supermodel shook her head. I wasn't sure where I was going wrong. I was just trying to be friendly. It must be my accent, I thought – I'm not getting through here.

'Aye-monn,' I slowly repeated, beginning to sound like a mooing cow.

'Em-an,' she bluntly retorted.

Iman was my star guest on GMTV that day and I didn't want to annoy her. Her arrival in the studio, flanked by a mini entourage, had produced a flurry of excitement. It certainly would have been hard to miss her. She's about nine feet tall and a striking woman, a beauty who clearly turns heads wherever she goes. And at that moment her pronunciations were turning mine.

Enunciating more clearly – 'A-MOON,' I said, 'like as in space.'

At this she freaked. 'Im-anne,' she snapped. 'My name is Iman!'

Bloomin' hell. 'I know what your name is – I'm

14

just trying to tell you mine!'

So much for putting guests at their ease.

I've now had a career in TV that spans more than twenty-five years. That's not bad going; not quite as long as my namesake, but getting there.

So, Mum, you got it right when you decided to name me Eamonn – Amen to that!

ONE

The New Lodge Road

People have got used to seeing me early in the mornings, so much so that over fifteen years at the BBC, GMTV and Sky News they assume I've got used to getting up early. Believe me, you never get used to getting up at 3.30 a.m.! As I get into my car at 4 a.m. I thank God for my driver, Vince. However early I'm up, he's been up earlier. Even when I'm early, I'm late. It's always a rush to be prepared physically and mentally for that 6 a.m. appointment with the camera. Then again, life started out that way for me. I was born too early for my mother's birthday despite being two weeks too late for my own...

I came into the world plain Eamonn Holmes on 3 December 1959, in the Mater Hospital, Belfast. It was very nearly 4 December, but my mother could hold on no longer, despite the pleas and encouragement of the nurses to do so. You see, 4 December was my mum Josie's

15

birthday, and they all thought it would be a lovely thing if I was born on the same date. As it turned out, we missed synchronising by just fifteen minutes. Although I didn't get to share her birthday, I did get to share her star sign of Sagittarius and most of her characteristics, including looks, a placid temperament and knock-knees. Well, I got the knock-knees anyway.

Mum and my dad, Leonard, had been married for eleven years at this stage, with one other son, my brother Leonard Paul, who was four years old. Holding on during her birth pangs would have been the last thing on Mum's mind. It had taken seven years to conceive Leonard junior and, following that, Mum had suffered a miscarriage and then almost lost me four months into her pregnancy.

Now that number-two son had finally arrived, they were faced with the dilemma of what to call me. I would have thought some saint's name to whom Mum had prayed for my safe delivery may well have been top of her list, and she did indeed cast her eyes upwards for inspiration. But, appropriately, they only got as far as the television set, appearing on which was the heavenly form of then Irish TV pin-up Eamonn Andrews.

Mum put it like this: 'I looked at him, and looked at you, and you had the same lovely wavy black hair that he had.'

My path in life must surely have been determined from that moment on.

For the first eight years of that life, home was a red bricked terraced council house on the New Lodge Road, in Belfast. Number 161. Our front door opened straight onto the street. It may have been public pavement but it was outside our door and, like most of our neighbours, we claimed it as our own, complete with the old gas lamppost that was part of it. It must have only been six feet wide but it was ours to play hopscotch on or for my mum and dad just to stand there and talk to the world going by. Those were the days when people tended to take a bit more responsibility for what was around them. It may have been the council's duty to sweep the street, but as far as my mum and plenty more like her on the road were concerned, this was their bit of land and it was up to them to keep it clean. I remember to this day her technique of kneeling on a mat, scrubbing brush in hand, dipping into a big bucket of soapy water. The result was a beautiful arc of suds, the exact span of her arm. Then would come the bucket of clear water and everything was rinsed spotless.

You stepped from our glistening pavement into a narrow hallway. To the right was a small front parlour. In fact, everything was small, but perfectly formed. The parlour was what was termed 'the good room' and was rarely used except at Christmas or funerals. Behind that was our living room, complete with fireplace and, under the staircase, the 'coalhole'. In previous years, that's where coal would have been kept but, for us, it mostly held an assortment of shoes and welly boots or water boots as we call them in Belfast. Did it rain more in those days or were water boots just part of every child's kit in the early sixties? Not a winter went by that me and my brothers weren't fitted up for a new pair – always black. Our duffel coats hung in the coalhole as well – again, always black, with big wooden toggles.

The living room led on to what was known then as a scullery – a kitchen in today's parlance. The toilet was in the yard, the walls of which my dad kept impeccably whitewashed, with the edges black-tarred. Upstairs, there were two bedrooms. There wasn't a bathroom: we bathed in a pink baby bath in the living room.

My mum was incredibly house-proud, always cleaning. Everything was spotless, including us. Some people compete with their neighbours in terms of having a better car or nicer curtains. With Mum the biggest sin was if we ever looked scruffier than anybody else's children. There was no excuse for filth, in her mind. 'Soap and water doesn't cost much,' was her mantra. No matter how bad a hand life dealt anyone, she always felt you could still look the part even if you weren't the part.

Nobody in the New Lodge had a garden. We'd play on what was known locally as the spare ground, an old Second World War bombsite a few doors down. It was nothing much, just a piece of wasteland where a couple of houses once stood, but we'd amuse ourselves digging up worms and using it as a dirt track for our Matchbox, Dinky and Corgi toy cars. Whatever the game, the result was the same: we would end up filthy! My mother would despair. 'Would you look at the state of your fingernails,' she'd say, exasperated, when we came home. Out would come the pink plastic bath and the scrubbing brush.

The New Lodge Road was a bustling place on which to live. It was a tight community of Coronation Street-type houses surrounded by shops. In these days of out-of-town retail developments and housing estates where so many of us are dependent on cars to get anywhere, think of the thrill it was to have shops across the road, to the right, to the left, and on almost every corner.

There was Giffen's the butcher, Morelli's ice-cream parlour, Hamilton's wool shop, the Nu-Look fish and chip shop, and the almost space-age launderette, where not only could you wash your clothes but you could wash yourself in a coin-operated shower cubicle. I'm pretty sure no house on the road had a bathroom so there was money to be made charging people for their wash and brush-up.

We had McKelvey's paper shop, a chemist's opposite, and beside that Torbett's, where you could buy warm bread and lemonade in little shot glasses at a penny, tuppence or thruppence. Shops were more magical back then. There were more smells, there were weights and measures – all sorts of brass weighing machines and glass receptacles – and lots of brands that have long since disappeared from our lives. Whatever happened to Spangles, Aztec bars, Fry's 5 Boys chocolate, Spanish Gold sweetie tobacco and even sweetie cigarettes?

There was a little theatre for plays and functions where way back then a young local lad called Ciarán Hinds was treading the boards. He went on to tread much more salubrious ones and appeared in a number of feature films including *The Phantom of the Opera* and *Calendar Girls*. Perhaps many of you will remember him most of all for his role as Julius Caesar in the BBC epic, *Rome*. There was even a cinema at the top of the road, the Lyceum, a marvellous Edwardian building. Add to that a number of pubs like Lynch's and the Plough and the Stars, and there was never any need to go anywhere else for anything. It was all there, all within a hundred yards of our front door.

The biggest thrill of all was the shop beside us – Katie Hughes's grocery store. Better still, her children, Thomas and Margaret, were our playmates. Although she was called Katie Hughes, she was actually Katie Morrison, married as she was to Tommy. There was a habit in those days of women being referred to by their maiden names. Not only that, they often addressed each other as Mrs This and Mrs That, however long they might have known one another, never ever using Christian names. Katie's shop was one big adventure. It smelled of soil, of fruit and vegetables, of beetroot boiling in her back kitchen before being sold on the front counter. Today it would probably be closed down by the Food Standards Agency but those were the days when few things were pre-measured or pre-wrapped. Things were weighed using big pounds and ounces scales, the fruit and veg was covered in soil, there were no carrier bags – you took your own shopping basket – and everything that had to be wrapped was wrapped in either brown paper or newspaper. The cabbages, cauliflowers, potatoes, lettuces, carrots, tomatoes, apples and oranges were all arranged in heavy sacks or lightweight balsa wood boxes. You could even buy your tea loose from a chest, and that wasn't the only thing that was loose. All this natural produce brought little visitors as well. Cockroaches, spiders and, worst of all – mice! To this day I hate mice and Katie Hughes's shop is to blame.

The fireplace in our house backed up against the wall where Katie stacked her potatoes – sacks and sacks of them. Obviously, there was some sort of hole where the little rodents could sneak through. The result was that 101 New Lodge Road often resembled a scene from *Tom and Jerry*. There were mousetraps with big lumps of cheese everywhere and best of all was something you wouldn't believe unless you actually saw it with your own eyes ... the coalhole door, behind which our water boots were stored, had one of those half-moon-shaped holes at the foot of it, the like of which you only seen in a cartoon. It was a real mouse hole and most of the little buggers lived in there. Sharing your home with a mouse is one thing – sharing your water boot with one is something else.

I must have been about four and Mum had just fastened me up in my duffel coat and put my gloves on. All that remained before I was ready to face the rain and the puddles were my boots. One foot went in no problem. The second faced an obstruction. My toes couldn't quite get in the whole way. What could be stopping them, I thought, as I turned the boot upside down? A big brown mouse was the answer! Out it darted and scarpered the way they do back into the coalhole. I've never worn a pair of wellies since without kicking them over in advance.

Granda Holmes died ten years before I was born, but I heard the stories about him. He was a respected figure on the Lodge Road, a coalman with a horse and cart. I believe the horse was called Shirley, and it was a name that lived on in our lives, as Daddy subsequently referred to his carpet van by the same name. I know it sounds strange but that van was so temperamental it definitely had a life of its own. He had to coax it to start, he had to coax it up hills, always with the encouragement, 'Come on, Shirley, come on, girl.' I tell you it would have been easier getting around on my granddad's horse and cart. As a boy, my dad would have gone with him on his rounds. I wasn't aware of huge deprivation in the area but people weren't always able to pay their bills. Both jobs and money were hard to come by and looking back I can remember hearing the adults talking, telling tales of how drink and gambling had ruined many a family. What I also recall is the less people had the more they seemed happy to share.

Granda Davy Holmes had a nature that he obviously passed on to my dad. He was quite easy-going about money – too easy-going. 'Pay me when you can,' he'd say. And if the customer expressed doubt he famously added, 'Sure, if you don't pay me, God will.' As anyone in TV contracts departments will know, it's a phrase I still use to this day!

In the end, it wasn't people's bad debts that caught him out, it was breathing in all that coal dust which ended not only his delivery round but sadly also ended his life.

I was still a baby, just a year old, when my second brother Brian was born. Three of us shared the back bedroom, me and Brian in a double bed, Leonard with a single bed all to himself.

I've no doubt my parents must have struggled to make ends meet at times with such young boys and that things can't have been easy, but we were always well fed and well turned out. I don't remember feeling cramped in our tiny terraced house, but clearly there can't have been much room, especially since we also had my dad's mum, Granny Ellen Holmes, who was ill with dementia, living with us for a while. Goodness knows how we all squeezed in.

I don't remember much about my Granny Holmes, but I do remember my last meeting with her. One day Brian and I got up with the larks. I was just four years old and Brian was three. No one else in the house had stirred yet, so off we went playing, tumbling down the stairs until a bit of horseplay ended up with us falling against the parlour door and ending up in the 'good room' itself. Inside, taking up most of the space, was a large box on legs. It had polished sides and shiny metal handles. Curious, we put our hands on the edges and slowly pulled ourselves up on our toes. Our little eyes peered over the edge to get the fright of our lives – Granny Holmes lying there, eyes shut, white as a ghost, dead! She was laid out in the parlour for the wake, though no one seemed to have remembered to mention it to us. I tell you, the shock of seeing her 'tattie bread' as we would say in Belfast scared the life out of us as well. Back up those stairs we went two at a time and straight under that candlewick bedspread until Mum and Dad came to wake us. That experience about summed up what living in such a close community was all about. The whole cycle of life to death was shared by all around. When Mum was pregnant with me and she had a threatened miscarriage at four months, little though he was, my four-year-old brother Leonard raised the alarm by running next door to Katie Hughes in her shop. Help was always at hand, people were there for each other, and never more so than at funerals.

TWO

Angel on My Shoulder

I've often been on my own in life, especially working away from home and family, but I've never felt alone. Even though I've been left to make so many decisions by myself I've always felt guidance and direction. It could be a sort of confidence, it could be because I'm a great believer in fate, or it could be because I feel an angel on my shoulder.

Granny Holmes may have been my first experience of a dead body, but that was only to prove to be my induction. Abhorrent or morbid it may seem to many of you now, but in sixties Belfast, Catholic children in particular were constantly brought to wakes to pay their last respects. Unlike today, where most people are 'laid out' in funeral parlours, the dead we visited were in the front parlour at home. You would never have needed an address for the wake house; it was always easy to spot.

In those days nobody had Venetian blinds. Windows were covered in paper blinds on a spring-loaded roller, pulled down by a tassel. It was always a big thing to go to the hardware shop to have them replaced. After two years or so the sunlight would turn them yellow and the hardware man would rip off the old paper and have replacements cut to whatever length you wanted tacked on to your existing wooden roller.

At the wake house every blind was drawn.

The scene was always the same: adults dressed in dark clothes huddled together speaking in whispered tones, one or two men outside the front door, having a smoke. You would never have seen a woman smoking in public: they were all inside. Maybe there would be wailing, maybe there would be laughing, maybe there would be prayers. The skill for us kids was to get in, pay our respects and out again before someone had the bright idea of saying the rosary. That was worse than seeing the corpse! Mum and Dad would pay their respects, though Dad was more of a funeral person than Mum. If the truth be told, I think it was because he quite liked all the socialising that went with them. Then someone from the bereaved family would come out with the line us kids would dread. 'Would the children like to say their goodbyes?' No, we bloody well wouldn't – but we had no say in the matter. Off we would be shepherded to gaze into coffin after coffin of aunts, uncles, neighbours, friends of Mum and Dad, acquaintances of Mum and Dad, and acquaintances of acquaintances of Mum and Dad. Granted, some of these occasions were very sad, but since me and my brothers were in the age range of between five and twelve during these experiences, they tended for us to be more scary than sad. Especially when some twisted old hag, usually with rosary beads in her hand, would suggest, 'Why don't you kiss Aunty/Uncle/Mr/Mrs goodbye?' Nowadays most kids would answer that with, 'Why don't you just piss off?' We didn't say that with our lips but our faces must have given the game away. Silently and without objection, but full of fear and trepidation, we did what we were told – touching the clasped hands of the deceased while placing a small kiss on the head. If you have never touched or kissed a dead body in a coffin, let me tell you they all feel the same – cold and hard. The difficult bit done, we were usually rewarded with a glass of lemonade, or 'mineral' as it was called.

In fact, when it came to soft drinks Northern Ireland was spoilt for choice. Not only were we famed for our mineral production with factories around the city but we had two types of lemonade – white and brown. Those were the

26

colours, incidentally. Generations of Ulster folk abroad would create confusion by asking for a vodka and white, or a whiskey and white. In England, bar staff would often mistakenly think we were referring to a brand of lemonade called White's, which does exist. The answer would come back, 'We haven't got any White's,' prompting us to add to the confusion by saying, 'Then brown will do.' Of course, they definitely wouldn't have any of that because we are the only ones who make it.

Drinking is an essential part of Irish Catholic wakes, which generally start with tea and minerals and quickly progress to stout and spirits. Even the priest works up a thirst after the prayers. Many may criticise us for the way we deal with death, but what's the choice? Bottle it up, deny that it has happened, not say your goodbyes, not share the tears and, with them, the memories that bring some laughter as well? There is no easy way to deal with bereavement but I'll settle for our way.

My mum's dad, Granda Fitzsimmons, died on 2 November 1955, long before I was even thought of. It must have been a terrible time of anguish and grief for my mum, having given birth to my eldest brother Leonard just three weeks earlier. All these years on, there's still a picture of my granda in his army uniform on her mantelpiece. Private Jack Fitzsimmons was a soldier with the Irish Guards. He left his job at the *Belfast Telegraph* to fight during the First World War after his brother was killed in action, only to suffer a terrible shrapnel injury himself.

Although he recovered, his war wound needed attention for the rest of his life.

When he died, the one piece of consolation my mother held onto was the fact it was All Souls' Night. All Souls' Night is a feast in the Catholic calendar that comes after All Saints' Day and Hallowe'en. The saints' day is 1 November, but 2 November is reserved for those passing between the physical world and the spiritual world. The priest who gave Granda Fitzsimmons the Last Rites told Mum that he died on the most special of days, when the gates of heaven are truly wide open and God is in a particularly welcoming mood. It appears that All Souls' Day is a bit like an open day for heaven with a lot of folk who have passed on coming out to take the hand of those who might fall prey to the lure of the devil, with words to the effect of, 'Hey, why don't you try out this heaven place – it's got great facilities.'

It means that come All Souls' Night most of those in the spirit world are on an evening out. In common with many people of her generation, my mother would pay heed to the tradition of leaving out a piece of food and a drink for any souls who would be wandering through our home. For us kids it was a scarier night than Hallowe'en. When we would come down the next day, sure as heck the glass of whiskey or water or the biscuit or sandwich would have a sup and a bite taken from them. A good few years were to pass before we realised that it must have been Dad doing what he did best as a practical joker. Thing is, after he died Mum continued to leave out the drink and the snack and come morning somebody had still had a little sample of both. I hope for her sake it's him that's doing it.

Always as a child I was aware of being surrounded by people. That doesn't happen so much nowadays. Families break up, communities break up, and an increase in living standards means fewer of us are dependent on those around us for help. Who now ever asks their neighbour for a cup of sugar or a half bottle of milk, or even to use the phone? They did when I was young. People are more independent, they are more affluent, families are smaller, and so often nursery schools take the place of grandmothers. I'm delighted to say that even in the brief few years that I was aware of her, nothing could ever take the place of my mum's mum, Granny Fitzsimmons.

Outside seeing her in her coffin, I've no strong recollection of my father's mother, Granny Holmes, even though she lived with us. Although my Granny Fitzsimmons lived a mile and a half away, all my grand-maternal memories revolve around her. I don't know if she was special or I was just special to her. Mum tells me I bear a strong resemblance to my Granda Fitzsimmons, which may have something to do with the closeness between me and Granny.

I was only six when she died but to this day I remember what her hair was like, what her glasses were like, how her hands felt, what her voice sounded like, what she wore, and even how she smelled. Funny how smells stay with you. There are attractive smells and clean smells, warm homely smells, comforting smells, and then there are all the opposite smells of people who however nice they might have been in your life you just remember for one thing – that they stank! Whether it was their breath, their body odour, their clothes, their feet or worse, all their redeeming qualities would be forgotten in place of their smell. My sense of smell must be heightened. My son Niall constantly reminds me that I am obsessed with how things smell, and recalls how after warning him and Declan they were not to eat in their beds, I raided the room saying, 'Who's been eating Wagon Wheels in here?' – Niall's point being, 'Wagon Wheels don't even have a smell and he can still smell them!'

Granny Fitzsimmons smelled of lavender water. Things like that stand out.

From Granny Fitzsimmons I could see where my mum got her standards of cleanliness – standards which have always remained important to me down through the years. I've always believed that a clean car goes better, and a clean house makes me feel right at home.

My best days were days when Granny collected me from school. Off we would walk from Holy Family Primary in Newington Avenue across the Limestone Road and into Alexandra Park to feed the ducks and swans. It was here one day that she told me, 'I have so many grandchildren but you are my favourite.'

At the risk of offending my many many cousins, she may also have told that to all of you, but I believed it. It made me feel special and increased my incredible affection towards her. When I remember that day now I think there was another reason she told me that. She was seventy years of age and by then she must have known she was dying of breast cancer. She'd had an operation the year before and was told she was fine, but it turned out the cancer had spread into her bloodstream and she was never really well again. As a six-year-old I wasn't made privy to how bad things were with her, except for one visit to her sick bed in the Mater Hospital. The next thing I remember is being told that she was dead, and the laying out of her body at her home where she lived with my aunt May and my uncle Tommy Banks in Cranburn Street.

Cranburn Street was the street beside St Malachy's College, in those days an elite Catholic grammar school which folk like us probably wouldn't aspire to. It was the breeding ground for Belfast's Catholic hierarchy, those that went into medicine, law and the priesthood. How ironic that one of the few pictures I possess of Granny Fitzsimmons has the college behind us. I look at that picture and it's as if she's saying, 'Don't worry, son, you'll go there one day too.'

Her wake was over the usual three days. Days of tears, prayers, laughter, smoking and drinking, more tears and more prayers, before she was laid to rest beside her beloved Jack, Granda Fitzsimmons. Granny was gone but she wasn't out of my life. I was always aware of her thoughts, her words, her guidance, always aware of her protection, of that little smell of lavender in the air. Was I mad? I don't think so.

Twenty-one years after her death, I was in the same room as the world-famous British medium

Doris Stokes, fifteen minutes away from a live transmission of the *Open Air* programme on BBC 1. My fellow presenter Patti Caldwell was to interview Mrs Stokes, who was the star of that day's show. Doris, though, pushed Patti aside and beckoned me to cross the room. She told me that she knew I wasn't due to interview her but she felt a presence around me more than anyone else there that day. She told me I had a guardian angel protecting me who was standing by my side right then. She then became more specific. 'Her accent is much much stronger than yours – she's hard for me to understand. But her name is Maggie and she says she's your grandmother.'

My grandmother's name was Maggie and although intrigued by what Doris Stokes was telling me, strangely, I wasn't particularly surprised. I always had that confidence that Granny Fitzsimmons was looking over and after me. Although the floor manager of the programme was now keen to get her into the studio in time for transmission, Doris quickly told me that Maggie had a message. It was very specific and was for 'the couple who were married with my ring'. This meant nothing to me, but as soon as the programme was over I phoned my mother and told her what had happened and the puzzle of 'the couple who were married with my ring'. Without pause for thought, Mum told me they were my cousin and godmother, Maureen, and her husband, Ray McGrady. The message I relayed to Maureen reduced her to tears, but at the same time gave her great hope.

Doris Stokes, the country's most acclaimed medium, was to be the first of her kind to tell me that my grandmother was my guardian angel, but somehow I didn't need anyone to tell me. I already knew.

THREE

Early Influences

In this celebrity-obsessed society of ours it seems that the plaudits often go to the least deserving people. But hey – that's showbiz! Real life is a much tougher place in which to pick up praise. One of the great pleasures of my working year is to host the National Teaching Awards for BBC2. Now these are the sort of people we should be holding up as role models for our kids. I hope like me you've had a teacher who has made a difference, someone who has helped you become the person you are today.

When I started Holy Family Primary School, I remember mum watching anxiously from the other side of the railings. Come lunchtime she was there to meet me. Actually, she had never gone away. She had been there the whole time, just in case I'd taken against my new sur- roundings and decided to make a run for it. It didn't happen then and it would never happen throughout my fourteen years of education at primary and grammar school. So much is made of the horrors of the state education system. Maybe I was lucky, maybe, as is often said, the standard is somewhat higher in Northern Ireland, but I can honestly say my school years were some of the best years of my life.

I was from a non-academic home where books were far from prevalent, and I can remember a roll call of forty-four names in my classes at primary school, yet still I was taught by enthusiastic teachers who made much of what we did seem magical and exciting. The Catholic ethos for the working-class children under their care at Holy Family was very much betterment through education. What I learned in that little primary school gave me the foundations on which to base my whole professional life. Much of what I do today is about having a broad general knowledge. So extensive was the general knowledge that I was introduced to that it makes me question the way children are taught today. Right through my own children's lives, for instance, matching age for age, there is no doubt that I knew more about the classics in literature and commanded a wider knowledge and diversity in history than they did. Yet they have more qualifications than I will ever have. Ask them to beat me at Trivial Pursuit or quiz games – well, hard as they try, there is only ever one winner there. I suppose it doesn't make the way youngsters are taught today wrong, it just makes it different. In seven years I had three teachers at primary school – Mrs Devenny for a year, Mrs Cassidy for two years and Mr O'Hanlon for four years. All were excellent, but as I was with Paddy

O'Hanlon for the longest he obviously had the most influence on me. He certainly was distinctive, not only in the way he talked but in the way he looked, with red hair and beard and a penchant for strumming the guitar. He opened up the bigger picture to me, he made science interesting, field trips an adventure, sport enjoyable and books magnetic. He also drove a red Volkswagen Beetle, which forty years later is back in vogue.

He had a lot to deal with in that class of forty-plus boys. Not all of us were from settled backgrounds and some had obvious learning disabilities, which may not have been catered for by the system then. Paddy O'Hanlon wouldn't shirk from using his leather strap to maintain order and discipline in the classroom. Indeed, I felt it myself on a number of occasions usually for talking or being late for class – surprise, surprise – two habits that still afflict me to this day. I never ever doubted that it was a caring discipline, and I'm sure that many of my classmates felt the same, ten or so of whom, like me, against the odds, made it through to grammar school. We witnessed attacks on our teacher in the classroom from a couple of the lads who were bigger than the rest of us, and who obviously needed to be streamed somewhere else that suited their needs and requirements. To be able to be such an influence for good on young minds of such a wide range of ability, Paddy O'Hanlon will always remain one of the most valued people in my life – in fact, a hero. The world outside that classroom was tough. He gave us the belief that if we knuckled down there was a world for us beyond that world.

While the classroom opened up a world of knowledge it wasn't about to open up a world of girls. Holy Family actually had two primary schools but it wasn't until my third year there that I realised this. That's because a giant dividing wall, along with different start, finish and lunch breaks, conspired to hide the fact that alongside Holy Family Boys' School there was also Holy Family Girls' School. It was only in Primary Three, when games took us outside to the playground, that we could hear the voices of girls on the other side of the wall. Outside that I have no other evidence that their school ever existed because I can honestly say that I went through seven happy years without ever seeing a single one of them! Then, having passed my 11-plus, it was off to St Malachy's College, where once again girls were banned. I have to say Mum liked it that way, constantly reminding her sons that she would always be the most important woman in our lives.

Education was to open up a new role for people of my generation, Mum and Dad's roles in life were more clear-cut. In their day school was something they did to pass a few years before the inevitability of going out to work. Each knew what was expected of them. She kept the home, he brought home the bacon – and for them it worked incredibly well. There was no competition between them. I have never once heard Mum bemoaning the fact she had no career. She had a job all right, a bloody tough one – bringing up a family and looking after things on a small budget – which she did second to none. Daddy had a job as well – which he also did second to none. He was a carpet fitter.

He went out, earned the money, and on a Friday would throw his wages into a Waterford crystal bowl that was the centrepiece of our dinner table. Mummy would take what she needed to run the house. There was nothing complicated about it.

They had their ups and downs but they were happy and not only loved each other but were passionate about each other. There was never any question that they wouldn't be together forever.

They met when Mum was just fifteen and Dad was eighteen, catching sight of each other across the street. Mum was head over heels straight away. 'One day I'm going to marry him,' she told her friend. It turned out my dad had the same idea. He adored her. 'My queen, my queen, my Josephine,' he'd often recite. However much he was in the bad books, she would always melt with that line and the way he would deliver it.

Mum is – how do I put this? – a spirited woman and, whether she cares to admit it or not, likes a row. Dad was much more easygoing. Everybody liked him and he liked a laugh, while Mum was the one with more airs and graces and seemingly more ambition. Dad was a much more basic working-class man, who never really saw the need to better himself because he was comfort-able with who he was. Often, Mum had other ideas. Dad had two modes – work and play. When he worked, boy did he work, and when he switched off he switched off. He wasn't a drinker but he did like a drink and, in common with a lot of men on a Friday night, felt he deserved one at the end of the week.

There were two bars close by which my dad would use – McLoughlin's, and Lynch's at the top of the road. In those days, women weren't allowed into pubs, and if ever Mum and Dad fell out, she'd say, 'I know where he'll be – at that top of the road!' It was somewhere he could go, as we say in Northern Ireland, 'to give his head peace'.

Women may have been barred, but amazingly male children were not. If a wife needed to contact her husband urgently, she would send one of her sons in with a note. Now and then Dad would get the Holmes boys into the lounge bar, where cigarette smoke mingled with the smell of stout and the gents' toilets. There were long polished-brass fittings all around the magnificent darkwood counter, and bevelled mirrors that were more yellow than silver due to all the cigarette smoke. Men in flat caps would ask, 'What do you want to drink, son?' Brown lemonade always being the answer because it looked like beer.

The earliest pocket money I remember getting was a 3d bit – that's three pennies in old money and one and a half pence after decimalisation. That became a sixpenny bit, then a shilling, and two shillings by the time I was eleven years of age. But I never reached that magical half crown unless it was a gift from relatives around birthday time. People don't give kids money any more. In my day people always gave you money. You got money for all the usuals – like birthdays and passing exams – but also just for when you visited someone's house where Mum and Dad hadn't been for a while. My mum and dad did a lot of visiting – well, Dad did much more than Mum. We could never go in a straight line from A to B without him knocking on someone's door, and very often not even knocking. It wasn't until I met my future wife in 1976 that I was made aware that you couldn't just walk round the back of someone's house, knock the window and walk straight in unannounced. But people did back then. Well, they certainly did on the New Lodge Road.

The most profitable visits with Dad were on birthdays or after making your first holy communion or being confirmed. First communion and confirmation are two of the great things about being a Catholic; similar ceremonies but different clothes and both incredibly lucrative. First communion at the age of seven involves being dressed in white from head to toe: white shirt, white pullover, white trousers, white ankle or knee socks and white sandals. Finding the white sandals was always the really hard bit. Often they would be some other colour that Mum would cover up with lots of what was called 'whitening' from the shoe shop. I'm sure no one has any reason to use whitening any more. It had a slightly addictive smell and was a sort of pasty, chalky, runny solution that dried rock solid and left lots of tell-tale powder marks whenever you walked on someone's good carpet. In my case the whole white outfit was set off with a red bow tie.

A white prayer book and rosary beads completed the look. The whole white thing was to represent the child's purity and the cleanliness of their soul, having now made their first confession before receiving the blessed sacrament of communion for the first time.

Darn tricky stuff that holy communion. For a whole year we were given lessons in how the wafer was the manifestation of God's body and blood, how so pure was it – and so impure were we – that to let it touch anywhere but your tongue would be a sin. Now for anyone who has ever received a communion wafer you will know that it's a devil for sticking to the roof of your mouth. How many times I must have sinned trying to dislodge it with my fingers and then, worse, let it hit my teeth. I would often have to confess that on a Saturday night in confession and be given a couple of Hail Marys for my indiscretion – but at least it was better than going to hell. Nowadays, not only can you touch the stuff with your hands, you don't even have to be a priest to give it out.

My soul was enriched with the holy sacrament of communion, but so too was my post office savings account. It was the big earnings pay day that all Catholic children awaited and meant that this would be the best year for Easter eggs, summer toys and Christmas.

On leaving the chapel ceremony, a tour of the houses would begin. Off we trooped to basically anybody who remotely knew us, the older the person you visited happened to be, the better. Although old people have less money they are always more generous when it comes to giving it away. So, in we went to Aunt Bridget's house – she was always a good giver because she was particularly religious – Uncle Tommy Brennan's, Aunt Sheila and Uncle Tommy Bell's, Aunt Phyllis and Uncle Gus Hughes's, Uncle Christie and Aunt Rosaleen Holmes's, Aunt May and Uncle Tommy Banks's. And they were just for starters. Real bonus time were friends of Dad's. Dad was particularly good at working this circuit but Mum couldn't really last the pace. The longer the day went on the better, and the more silent the collection. That's when I first remember seeing paper money. Ten shilling notes – that was really big time, but there were quite a lot of pound notes in there as well. A donation would rarely reach a fiver, but a big thrill was at the end of the day putting all the change into piles and running into Katie Hughes's shop and doing a swap – coins for notes. She always appreciated a bit of change for the till.

By the time confirmation came round three years later, religion had to be taken even more seriously. One was older and the stakes were higher. Thankfully they were also higher when it came to the collection round again. The attire for confirmation was much more grown-up: long trousers for the first time, a dark blazer, shirt and tie, shoes that didn't require whitening, and an adult prayer book and beads. At ten years of age this was when I was expected to renounce Satan and all his works, and renounce drink. As long as this didn't involve my new favourite Coca-Cola I was perfectly happy, and since these were the

41

days before alcopops there were no temptations to lead me astray. I'm not sure how long the renouncing drink business was supposed to go on – for some people it's for life; for most of the guys I knew, the next five years was as good as it was going to get.

Confirmation was a scary business. This ceremony would be conducted not by the parish priest but by the big man himself – the bishop. His was the scary picture that adorned every Catholic school in the diocese of Down and Connor and up until then none of us had ever clapped eyes on him. We knew he was important, probably more important than the pope, and we were all warned to be on our best behaviour. Confirmation happened in the evening. It was a real grown-up affair for which you had to have a sponsor – someone who would take the responsibilities of grooming you in the Catholic faith seriously. Since we didn't know anyone like that, I asked my godmother Maureen's husband Ray McGrady to do it and he did it very well. Indeed, Ray, I still have that adult prayer book you signed for me to this day. The scariest bit of all though was having to kiss the bishop's ring. Having completed that task successfully, the money roadshow hit the road again.

Because confirmation was an evening service, there was less time to do the rounds before bedtime, so the hits had to be calculated with precision. For first communion you had all day, probably midday through to nine o'clock in the evening, but now fingers were crossed for a silent collection only – that's when you wanted the people who would drop you a fiver, no messing about. Thinking back on it, I had such a good round-up that night it's put me in the mood to renew my vows and renounce the evils of drink once more!

Money like this and whatever pocket money I got went into a Christmas club fund in a news-agent's on the nearby Duncairn Gardens. I could have lived in that shop. All my needs were there: my weekly TV comic with its stories from *Captain Scarlet*, *Star Trek* and *Catweazle*, but most of all the glass cabinets that contained my cowboys and Indians, and every Airfix kit you could imagine. Although the savings club was designed specifically for Christmas gifts, it was operated all year round. The more we saved, the more we could add to our toy collections, and the easiest way of making money was to collect lemonade bottles.

In those days all big lemonade bottles were returnable to the shop. When you bought a full bottle there was a surcharge of sixpence built into the price, which was refundable when you brought an empty one back. The thing was, very few people could be arsed to do so, which was great news for me and my brother Brian. We became particularly industrious on this front, offering to take empties away for people and always on the lookout in and around people's bins in the back entries for bottles that had been thrown away. Talk about money for old Coke! The newsagent was so sick of seeing us turn up with empty bottles he started asking us to prove they were bought from him in the first place. We overcame that little problem by returning them to lots of different shops, or getting some of our easily influenced mates to do the job for us for a small slice of the action. The result was we built up a very healthy toy collection.

As I got older the action figures got bigger. The daddy of them all was Action Man. I had eight different Action Men with costumes ranging from space suits to wetsuits and vehicles ranging from tanks to space capsules.

To this day I remain fond of toys, partly because my father always showed a great interest in what we had bought. It's a lesson most women would do well to remember when it comes to men. Whatever age we are, most of us at heart are still big kids who like toys. Leonard, Brian and me shared a toy box, an old linen basket sprayed silver, which was our treasure chest. Leonard in particular had some amazing ones, including a bulldozer that had come from America and worked on batteries.

Leonard was a great one for collecting Superman and Batman comics, again from the States, which he stored immaculately under his bed. Under pain of death, no one else was allowed near them, although, never one to follow orders, I would sneak them out and have a read when he wasn't around. When he caught me there was hell to pay! Often there was a news-hound in the stories, a figure in a trench coat and trilby hat. For instance Superman's alter ego, Clark Kent, was a reporter on the *Daily Planet*. The world of news – even in comics version – fascinated me as a child.

44

I was also into Airfix soldiers and models – war planes and battleships – and I collected a brand of figurines called Timpo Toys. My largest collection was of cowboys and Indians, many beautifully mounted on horses, and all with interchangeable weapons, hats and feather headdresses.

Not surprisingly, we all liked Christmas. The tree would go up in the parlour and on Christmas morning that's where our presents would be, arranged in individual piles – one for Leonard, one for me, one for Brian.

Life was very happy for us but our house was small – too small, since Mum and Dad obviously still dreamt of a bigger family.

I must have been about seven years old when I overheard them talking about whether he should give up his job working for the Carpet Selection Centre in North Street and set up business on his own as a fitter. In a house that size it wasn't easy to keep secrets. You were aware of everything that went on. I was anyway. Perhaps I was just nosier than my brothers. It must have been a huge step, giving up a regular wage, but he was convinced it was worth taking a chance. Being his own boss meant more freedom, more flexibility. It might also have meant working harder and doing longer hours, but at least there was a chance to boost his earnings. My dad believed that if your salary was fixed, your options when you hit trouble were too – and I believe he was absolutely right.

FOUR

Gun for Hire

I didn't inherit any of my dad's practical working skills. I have no interest in DIY whatsoever and I strongly believe wherever possible you should do what you do well in life and pay somebody else to do what you can't do well and they can. I did, however, inherit his imagination and his love of the movies, particularly Westerns. Often, the theme is 'gun for hire', as in The Magnificent Seven. *If you can't sort your own problem out, as in the case of the downtrodden Mexican villagers, call in someone who can sort it for you. My life as a freelance TV presenter can sometimes be like that. A lot of the pride you get from the job is from taking on a responsibility that, fortunately, producers deem few other presenters can handle. I do it on live TV. My dad did it as a carpet fitter.*

Taking the plunge and setting up on his own was the best thing Dad could ever have done. That's when things began to change for us.

The bad news in all of this was that he had to hand back his beloved van to the firm. This was no ordinary van. It was called the Magic Carpet and emblazoned along the side of the van was a genie riding through the sky on a rug. Inside were three seats in the front and none in the back.

46

What was in the back was usually me, my brothers and a lot of my cousins, with not a seatbelt between the lot of us. We went everywhere in the back of that Morris van, any bumps being cushioned by big soft rolls of felt.

The good news about my dad going it alone was we got our first car, a Vanguard estate, which he had repainted in two-tone coffee and cream by my mum's brother, Jackie. Dad was thrilled with it. 'It's a beautiful wagon,' he purred, the day he brought it home. Bloody thing would never start, and leaked oil as well, but never mind.

A lot of the cars we had were estates, capable of carrying rolls of carpets and boxes of tools for Dad's work, and doubling up as a family car the rest of the time. The year was 1967 and so few people we knew even had a car. Now you get two or three per household but then probably only one family in five around Belfast had one.

We also got a phone, a state of the art two-tone blue Trimphone with a distinctive high-pitched warble. It was very sleek and high-tech and is a collector's item today. Dad's party trick was to mimic the ring tone so well somebody would rush out to the hall to answer it. Up until then one of the few places to have a phone on the New Lodge Road was one of the pubs. As word got round we had one, such was the novelty that people would turn up on the doorstep to ask if they could use it, leaving a few coins to cover the cost of the call – and sometimes not.

Dad becoming a self-employed businessman made it a real family affair to the extent that I began to dread the long school summer holidays.

Time off should have meant time doing nothing, but the Holmes boys began to be expected to lend their dad a hand. To say Dad was a carpet fitter doesn't really do him justice. He was Belfast's finest, the best there was. If there was a complicated job to be done – an awkward-shaped room, a tricky pattern, a particularly expensive carpet to cut – you sent for Leonard Holmes, the Carpet Man.

Dad was an incredibly hard worker and took huge pride in what he did, but I knew, even as a child, I wasn't going to do him justice as a fitter. I used to dread the days when I had to go with him on jobs. I wasn't just bad, I was useless. I couldn't do it, couldn't get the hang of it, in the same way that some people, no matter how hard they try, will never be able to dance. I had no coordination. If I'm honest, I didn't want to do it. My elder brother, Leonard, managed all right, even looked forward to it, and Brian, although a year younger than me, picked up the basics no trouble at all. They were better men than me. Brian was so good that the business eventually became Leonard Holmes and Son – with Brian being the son. Even though Dad is now dead, Brian still runs the business under that title, happy that Dad's name and standards live on with him and my brother Colm. Right from the start I knew there were easier ways to earn a living.

For one thing, the smell of the felt underlay and the fumes from the thick white Copydex glue used to make me gag. There was always dust, everywhere dust, from the carpet, the felt, the floorboards, the furniture. Dad suffered badly from psoriasis and the work he did made it worse. Just thinking about some of the places we ended up in – cinemas, clubs and pubs – is enough to make my skin start itching now. It was heavy, punishing work, superhuman at times in what was expected of him. It damaged his joints and gave him problems with his knees and shoulders, even made his knuckles swell from constantly having to knead inflexible carpet into the right corners and joins. But however hard the job, however tricky it might have been, he never seemed to charge very much. That made an impression on me as well. There was no way that sort of exertion equalled the sort of return he was getting. Having said that, no amount of money would have been enough for me to do what he did. Among his favourite sayings was, 'A fair day's pay for a fair day's work.' He also believed, 'If a job's worth doing, it's worth doing well.' I'm very much my father's son in that respect.

One thing more than anything I have to thank my father for was making my childhood magical – transporting me from the ordinary to the extraordinary. Psychologists nowadays say that children should always be given the facts and told the truth. One of the reasons I can look back so fondly at my childhood is that Daddy constantly embellished the facts and often hid the truth. He was the sort of dad who knew how to make our world of stories, comics, cartoons and films come to life in the bleak, industrial oh-so-definitely-not-glamorous surroundings of sixties Belfast.

The city nestles round the mouth of a lough and is surrounded on all sides by hills, the best known of which is the Cavehill. How Dad would spin us tales of what went on in those 'mountains', as he called them. Gorse fires were a common sight in the summer months but Dad would tell us, 'Look, there's the Indians making smoke signals.' Of course, at six or seven years of age we accepted that as fact. Where else were all those Westerns we would watch with him made, other than up on the Cavehill? Likewise when he took us walking on Sunday afternoons to give Mum a bit of a break, the story would change to: 'This is where Robin Hood lives.' And we would see the evidence there for ourselves – the river crossing at which the Prince of Thieves was challenged by Little John. Then me or one of my brothers would find what surely had to be Little John's staff or the perfect piece of branch for the perfect longbow, which Dad would take home and by the next day have made up for us complete with arrows, much to Mum's despair. He would constantly regale us with tales of how our treks reminded him of when he was in the army during the Second World War, just the way we had seen it in films like Errol Flynn's *Objective Burma!* or John Wayne's *The Sands of Iwo Jima*. We would troop behind him hacking away the undergrowth and never doubting a single word or working out that during the Second World War he wouldn't have hit puberty yet.

There was also a rich harvest to be had in the shrubbery of the Cavehill – raspberries, black-berries, conkers galore and fresh cold water from

50

running streams, the like of which I have never since tasted in any fancy bottle. Dad may have been a carpet fitter by trade, but he was a storyteller and practical joker by instinct. There was no harm in any of the tales he weaved. If we ever did contradict him with the truth he'd always own up, laugh and get involved in some sort of tickling match or bear hug with us. He was a tactile man who not only made it a point to touch and hold his sons, even kiss us on the cheek or head until we were well into our teens, but he also touched our hearts, our humanity, our sense of decency and our minds. How could I ever repay a debt like that? I couldn't. I just have to be thankful that it came my way and hope that I can in turn pass on something similar to my own youngsters. When he died he had no money to leave us, but why would we have needed it when he made us so rich as people?

FIVE

The Troubles Take Hold

Being a presenter is a bit like being a footballer. Often if you change sides you change where you live. I don't like moving house, not that you would think it looking at my career over the years. I moved to England in 1986 and it was only nineteen years later that I was able to feel I had found a house I could call home, one I wouldn't have to move from again no matter where the job was. During the Troubles in Belfast, people often had to move house for very different reasons...

The New Lodge was all I knew and I was happy living there but the political climate was a-changing, unbeknown to us. We were brought up as Catholics in what would soon become a Republican stronghold and the changes that would sweep through Belfast would happen at a frightening pace. The demographic shift involving Catholics moving to Catholic areas and Protestants moving to Protestant areas was just around the corner. Ironically, we swam totally against the tide – a Catholic family that would move to a Protestant area.

The political and religious aspects weren't the consideration for my folks. They were the kind of people who could bring others together, not wedge them apart. Although the Troubles began in earnest in 1969, the year after we left the New Lodge Road, there was no sense of getting out before things took a turn for the worse. Leaving was simply about a better life in a better environment and a better council house.

Just before we left the most amazing thing happened. Well, amazing in today's context. There was to be a royal visit, and Catholics from our neighbourhood went en masse to the top of the road to stand and wave miniature union jacks at the Queen and Prince Philip as their car gently glided by along the Antrim Road.

How people and things were to change only a year later.

Change for us came in 1968 when I was eight

and we moved into a house up the Cliftonville Road. It was only two miles from the New Lodge, but in reality it was a world away. It wasn't a new property, probably around twenty-five years old by then, a semi-detached with pebble-dashed walls – just what you'd expect of a typical council house. There was a bathroom and an extra bedroom. What wasn't typical about it, and best of all, was that there was a large front garden and a massive back garden, some sixty feet long.

That garden gave us so much space to play in it was amazing. It seemed to go on forever – a bit like our family. Me, Leonard and Brian were about to be joined by a new baby brother, Colm. No wonder Mum and Dad wanted to move to a bigger house with built-in play facilities. There were apple trees, pear trees, blackberry bushes: our own little bit of countryside in the city. Which was all very nice, but where were we to play football? Some of those bushes and trees had to go. That garden became the centre of the world for me and my brothers. We put up tents and camped out. We built bonfires. We made fish-ponds, and pens for our occasional pet rabbits or tortoises. And when it came to sport, if it happened on telly it happened in our back garden. It was our Wembley, our Wimbledon and our Aintree, except we were the horses and the fences were made out of the bamboo poles that ran through the middle of Dad's rolls of carpet. I don't know if those poles were used for carrying the carpets, keeping them from bending or displaying them in the shop, but doing the job he did Dad was never short of them, and they came in very handy for us. Mum used one to prop up the middle of the washing line and in doing so inadvertently created the most beautiful set of goalposts for us. Pity the living-room windows were just behind them – boy did the local glaziers make a fortune from us.

The Troubles were beginning, and the following year, in 1969, they got much worse. There was a growing sense of unease. Families were being attacked and having their homes stoned and petrol-bombed simply because of their religion. We had moved from a very disadvantaged working-class area to a better-off working-class area. I suppose what I'm saying is fewer folk on the New Lodge had jobs compared to those in the new neighbourhood. Here lived mostly blue-collar people, people who had jobs in factories and the odd one on the clerical side. Here it was leafier, more prosperous, more people had cars and practically everybody had fewer children. They were the same type of people, but with a different religion and different opportunities. Often, as the Troubles escalated and fears grew, relatives would come to stay at our new house because it was seen to be in a safe area. The women would sit smoking, calming their nerves, talking about how bad things were. And they were. This was the start of a war.

Very shortly soldiers would be on the streets. Outside, smoke was constantly in the air, as building after building and vehicle after vehicle was set alight. Noise would constantly invade day-to-day life. Not normal noise, but the noise of bells, sirens and horns. The noise of chanting, bin lids banging on the street. The noise of protest and then, worst of all, the noise of bullets and bombs. Me and my brothers would often overhear bits of conversations from the adults about what had gone on the night before in their areas, their neighbours attacked, families intimidated and forced out of their homes. It affected everyone in some way, no matter what your religion. My story is no different from anybody else's who grew up at the time but, thankfully, it's a lot better than many as well.

The first time I remember it getting really scary was 15 August 1969, a Friday. A group of us were on our way back home after a game of football in the grounds of the nearby Girls' Model School. It was a beautiful sunny evening and we hadn't a care in the world. Then before us appeared a sight so unreal the only thing I could compare it to was the scene in the movie *Gone With The Wind* when all around Atlanta was being torched. From our vantage point we looked across at a hill only a mile away where roof after roof of terraced houses were blazing. We didn't know it then but it was Farringdon Gardens in an area of Belfast known as Ardoyne.

I stood with my mates, my most prized possession, my Bobby Moore football, tucked under my arm, watching as people lost possessions much more prized, as their houses were being consumed with flames and collapsing. An entire street was on fire, the blaze spreading unchecked, the cracking of the tiles on the rooftops hurting my ears. Farringdon Gardens was being razed to the ground and it was incredibly frightening to watch. Panic was spreading as fast as the flames. You could see it, you could hear it, you could feel it. There was no order, there were no police, there was nobody in charge. We didn't know then why it was happening. It was just so close, and if it was happening there could it happen on our street as well? The tensions between neighbouring Catholic and Protestant areas had erupted into this. It was a terrible example of what people were going through. Everyone was scared, and in those sorts of circumstances it's not surprising that people look to their own side for protection.

It was people like us, in the middle, who were often to be the most vulnerable throughout the violence.

Around me, there was lots of hurrying about and shouting. I watched as men ran to the petrol station opposite, grabbing the pumps, filling bottles and stuffing rags into them. I thought the rags were to plug the bottles, but in fact it was my first sight of Molotov cocktails – petrol bombs, to give them their less fancy name. There were crates and crates of the things.

It didn't feel safe to stay in the neighbourhood but where else could anybody go? My parents were frantic. These were the days before mobile phones. There was no easy way for them to check their children were safe. My dad jumped in the car and came looking. When he found me and Brian, we were still watching Ardoyne burn. Meanwhile, at home, Mum was packing. You could feel that anarchy wasn't far away. Barricades were starting to go up and the police were completely overstretched. In case it got nastier, Mum and Dad decided to get out of the city while we could. We weren't the only ones. Nearly two thousand families fled that night as things worsened. As darkness fell we looked back on a city glowing orange against the night sky. It was a fifty-mile drive to Cushendall in the Glens of Antrim, where Dad decided it would be safe. He checked us into a bed and breakfast and we stayed until his money ran out ten days later. Ten days in which the city was being ripped to bits. We were like evacuees. The rioting and siege mentality it brought about resulted in milk, bread and petrol shortages. Although we were in the sort of place you would go to on your holidays, nobody was in a holiday mood.

If it was bad for us, it was worse for others. Relatives of ours, living much closer to the trouble spots, took refuge in our empty house. Every bed was occupied. For the next few days, aunts, uncles and cousins slept where they could, in chairs or on the floor if need be, rather than risk the anarchy that was taking over their own neighbourhoods.

Nobody went to work, nobody went to school, and nobody knew what was going to happen. What we did know was that nothing was going to be the same again. The problem was much too serious; there was too much bad feeling.

For a while, rumours were rife that the Americans would come to the rescue. There were serious debates about the US making us the 92nd state, or the United Nations sending in a peacekeeping force. Much more inflammatory were the suggestions, or fear of, troops from the Republic of Ireland crossing the border to restore order. In the event, it was British troops who arrived, sent by Prime Minister Harold Wilson to take over law and order duties from the Royal Ulster Constabulary. Everybody seemed to welcome them, especially folk in the Catholic areas who up until then had felt particularly vulnerable, governed, as they saw it, by a Unionist government in a Unionist state and by a Unionist police force.

People would come out of their houses with cups of tea for the passing patrols and the soldiers, in turn, would give us youngsters cap badges. But the honeymoon was short-lived.

It was against this backdrop that I passed the 11-plus and won a place at St Malachy's College on the Antrim Road.

I'm sure my parents had mixed feelings about this. They were pleased I'd done well, but grammar school was costly. My older brother, Leonard, was already at the College, so now it would be two uniforms, two huge sets of books and two sports kits to pay for instead of one. There would also be two fees of £99 to be found at the start of each academic year. It doesn't sound much now but I remember how much extra Dad had to work to come up with that money. I knew it was a struggle but Mum and Dad always made sure we had whatever we needed to have.

Right away, I loved St Malachy's, an all-boys school with a sense of history and tradition. It was a special place, an oasis of calm in a city of rage. While bombs went off all around its walls, there was always a sense of leaving that hate-fuelled world behind as I went through the college gates and up its tree-lined avenue each morning.

St Malachy's was a world of polish. You smelt the stuff as soon as you went in, and everything gleamed, from the wooden floors to the brass door knobs and handles. Credit for that went to the nuns from an adjoining convent. In charge of polishing our education was the college president, the Very Reverend Patrick Walsh, later to become Bishop Patrick Walsh. He was an incredibly learned man with not one but two MScs in mathematics – one from Cambridge, the other from Queen's University. The teachers were also learned and, almost exclusively, men. Many were classical scholars and all wore gowns. Since it was a diocesan college, we were also taught by priests. Educated and cultured, they were the elite of Northern Ireland's Catholic Church. There was an expectation that a certain number of us boys would follow them into the priesthood, and at times the idea appealed to me. I couldn't have done that parish priest thing though – all those christenings, marriages and funerals; too much routine. A bit of study in Rome and a title like 'Monsignor' would have been more up my street. Black robes trimmed in purple or scarlet always had more appeal to me than just the ordinary black ones.

Outside the classroom, the priests inhabited their own world. A set of swing doors separated the main school from the clergy's wing, which housed the president's office and the priests' refectory (that's a fancy word for their canteen). In the same block, a flight of stairs led to the college chapel, where a relic of the man himself – a piece of St Malachy's skull – sits in a glass case. It was always a beautiful retreat in times of stress, usually brought on by exams or a lack of studying. It's funny how many candles I lit in place of learning Shakespeare. But I can't knock it. Something got me through seven years there and it certainly wasn't all down to me.

The school prized academic excellence, yet ours was by no means an academic household. We had few books, the Bible, a couple of pictorial tributes to American President JFK and the fairytales of Hans Christian Andersen among the more prominent ones. Books, in fact, with a lot in common, now I come to think about it. Our house though was about to begin to resemble a library, such were the amount of textbooks I was required to have. If that was a shock, a bigger one was the sheer volume of homework I suddenly had to undertake. Boy, was that tough. To this day I resent kids getting homework. If it can't be done in the classroom then it shouldn't be done at all. Better I think to extend the school day than to saddle children and parents with another burden on family life.

We had nine classes a day and we'd get homework from each one every night. I used to pray for a double period because that meant one less homework. It was a complete culture shock, and if I was stuck with something like Latin, well, I could hardly turn to Mum and Dad for help.

One subject that completely defeated me was mathematics. I had been fine with arithmetic at primary school but I glazed over at the mention of algebra or logarithms. It was another language, a language I didn't speak, and didn't particularly want to. When was I ever going to need it?

Although the work was hard, the school was wonderful and I always felt a real sense of belonging. While I might not have been the most academic pupil, I still managed to do all right. I could get by on whatever natural intelligence I had and I was good at thinking on my feet. Sport was also a big part of life at the college.

One of the things I could do quite well was run – which at that time in Belfast was a good skill to have because there were plenty of things to run from. And it was a skill that came in very handy indeed the night I made my first television appearance.

It was February 1972, I was twelve years old, and the college choir was invited to take part with a number of schools in an interdenominational service for *Songs of Praise* at the YMCA in the centre of Belfast. Embarrassingly, even then I was transfixed by the red light on the front of the television cameras during the recording. If there's a tape of that show in existence, it will show me staring straight at the camera rather than head down concentrating on the words on my hymn sheet. So it must have been meant to be! Little could I dream that I would go on to regularly present that very programme thirty years later.

We recorded on a cold, gloomy, winter night.

Belfast was often more gloomy than the weather, depending on how angry the natives were. I had to catch the ten o'clock bus home, which in those days was the last bus of the evening. It was a scary prospect, having to worry about who would be on it, or get on it. I still remember the more middle-class kids being collected by their parents, all heading in my direction, but no one thinking to ask how I was getting home. My father would have given anyone a lift in his car any time to anywhere. To this day I can't understand how any parent would drive off and leave a child to catch the bus on their own, especially bearing in mind what was going on in Belfast. Worse, I was still in my school uniform, which meant the chances of being picked on increased. All in all, I had a bad feeling about that night.

Nearly half an hour later I reached my stop and my worst fears were realised. I ran smack bang into one of the infamous tartan gangs that hung around street corners. Tartans had that Bay City Rollers look – half-mast jeans trimmed with tartan, Doc Marten boots and hair that stood on end in sharp spikes. They were looking for someone to beat to a pulp and they had just got lucky.

It was fright or flight. No wonder I was to pick up so many medals at school for running, although to call it 'running' actually does me a disservice. This was warp speed. My legs were rotating so fast I must have looked like Road-runner. While I didn't have time to do a head count, ten or fifteen pairs of Doc Marten's on a concrete road make a spine-chilling sound and, as they got closer that noise grew. It was so loud there could have been a hundred of them. Then another school skill came into play – hurdling. The only way I was going to lose these guys was to jump garden hedges. I did, they didn't, and let's just say with the amount of fallers it was better than a scene from Becher's Brook at the Grand National. It bought me the time I needed. I managed to get to my front door and hit the bell over and over again, desperate. No answer. I ducked round into the back garden and hid in the shadows behind a bush, my heart thudding. When I thought the boyos had retreated and it was safe to come out, I went to our kitchen window and tapped on the glass. Nothing. I banged on it. Eventually, very disgruntled, my older brother Leonard came to see what the commotion was. I was breathless and shaking but he was more bothered about missing *Colditz*, which was the big Monday-night must-see drama on BBC 1 at that time.

Being chased on your way home from school was something not just me but a whole generation in Belfast, boys and girls, Catholics and Protestants, had to learn to live with.

There was a way around it, though. If I joined every single society in school I wouldn't get home until after six, by which time most of the bully boys had all got hungry and gone home for their tea. That meant chess club on a Monday, drama society on a Tuesday, choir practice on a Wednesday, cross-country running on a Thursday and football on a Friday. It was work on top of work and, looking back, it may have created my ability to work long days on top of presenting breakfast TV, but it definitely helped keep me safe from a hiding or two. It also created my deep aversion to bullying. Years of being innocent prey to louts for no other reason but the school badge you wear is a feeling not forgotten easily. It has stayed with me. I dealt with it then by being more cunning than them, including having that school badge attached to my blazer with Velcro so that it could conveniently disappear. But inevitably, as a last resort, I also had to use my fists on the odd occasion. I was never a natural street-fighter but I never lost a confrontation. The odds facing me always meant that failure wasn't an option. You didn't have to go looking for trouble in Belfast for it to find you, and you don't forget what a pounding heart and a dry mouth feel like wondering who was waiting at the next bus stop or round the next corner.

Throughout my teenage years my fight or flight responses were tested to the full, and that extra training on the athletics track never went to waste. The most effective way of dealing with the situation was simply to avoid confrontation. Joining all those various clubs in school was one way. Living the life of a hermit was the other. That meant no discos, no youth clubs, no hanging around street corners and no to pretty much anything else other teenagers in the seventies were doing, including chasing girls.

SIX

Making the News

There's not a day goes by without someone saying to me, how did you get into TV? The truth is, I suppose, TV got into me. I was sitting watching Iraq on the news. The top story was about British soldiers beating up young Iraqi rioters. Expert after expert was giving their analysis. Then the question was raised about the effect these pictures could have once they were seen on Iraqi TV. How that question brought me back in time. As stories from 'children of the Troubles' go, mine could have been a lot worse. Many men my age were influenced enough to enlist with the security forces, the paramilitaries or political parties. I joined up with the media.

Belfast was being bombed and burned to bits. Whatever the IRA wasn't closing down with its war on economic life, the God-fearing Unionist councils were – on a Sunday at any rate. The policy of Lord's Day observation meant no council properties were allowed to be used. No swimming baths, no football pitches, even the very swings in playgrounds were chained up. In addition, that meant no licences for High Street Sunday trading or drinking. Sunday in Northern Ireland was the most boring day of the week. I don't care how boring you think it was for you, compared to us you would have been living in the equivalent of Sodom and Gomorrah. And come to think of it, the Sodom bit was banned as well.

We had little enough in terms of facilities. Practically every cinema had been incendiary-bombed and those that were left couldn't open for business on the Sabbath. Discos, bars and youth clubs were rarely mixed, and that didn't mean boy and girl – that meant Catholic and Protestant. So going to one made you an easy target for the other side to attack. Streetlights were either sabotaged by the paramilitaries to make their areas 'no-go', or by the army so as not to show soldiers up as targets. Add to that the last bus to anywhere was at ten o'clock, making the streets easy prey for murder gangs like the notorious Shankill Butchers to roam and select their victims with impunity. Taking all that into account, a night at home in front of the telly took on a whole new excitement. Well, it was better than the alternative.

TV not only became my escape, it became my world, and most of the news bulletins were reporting my world. We were the story and there were cameras and reporters everywhere. If I looked out the bus window and saw them filming that day, then come that night I would watch all the news programmes to catch that one location just to see how the report came to life. I quickly understood what they were doing. I knew from looking at the reporters which channel or programme they were working for, and I could even spot the ones who were filming docu-mentaries as opposed to news for that day.

Belfast wasn't just a centre for British media, the world's media were on our doorstep too. Vietnam had just finished and we were the next big thing in news terms.

Since 1968, when the Troubles began, more than 3,700 people in Northern Ireland have lost their lives, but if one year stands out as worse than any other in terms of sheer numbers, it's 1972, when almost five hundred people died. To put that in context, that's one in every three thousand people who lived there. We have a population of only one and a half million, in those days about two-thirds Protestant and one-third Catholic. Five hundred thousand of those folk lived in the Greater Belfast area, so most people knew someone who had been murdered, maimed or suffered as a result of violence.

It was nothing out of the ordinary to hear explosions and gunfire. Me and my brothers could even identify different weapons that were being used. We knew when it was the IRA shooting or when it was the army, when the shots came from one of the bordering Loyalist or Republican areas, if it was a pistol or something bigger. You'd wake in the morning to the smell of burning and the news that buses and cars had been hijacked and set on fire during the night. Roadblocks were the norm all over the city – equally operated by the security forces and the paramilitaries. On the news the politicians in London would send out the message that there were no such things as 'no-go' areas. It was a defiant message to the Great British Public to show that the government was in control. In fact, it was gross exaggeration bordering on a lie, since 'no-go' areas were all the go. We, though, lived in the sort of area where the troops could openly operate.

To keep out of trouble, we tended to play in the back garden – as it turned out, even that wasn't always safe. One Friday night about half seven in the evening, when I was about fourteen, me and my brother Brian and a few mates were hanging round, not doing much, lighting a few matches, burning a few twigs in the darkness, when half a dozen soldiers, rifles in hand, leapt over the hedge and swooped on us.

'Hands up! Hands up!'

We couldn't believe it. This was like a scene from a movie. To add to the drama, their faces were blacked out. Terrified, we did as we were told.

'Get in a line!'

Like prisoners of war we shuffled compliantly into a line, hands in the air. Bear in mind, this was happening in the pitch black in our own back garden while, inside our cosy lit-up house, my mum and dad were watching Bruce Forsyth's *Play Your Cards Right*. Can you imagine that happening to you and your kids? This wasn't a riot zone we lived in. This was a respectable street full of aspiring middle-class people. We were children being held at gunpoint. And for what? We had no idea what we were supposed to have done.

I assume the squaddies were after someone, but I never found out. Once they were satisfied we were just a bunch of youngsters up to nothing, they took off again, over the opposite hedge into next-door's garden. Shaken, we went in and told Mum and Dad what had happened, but what could they do? The foot-patrol raid had been and gone. That was Belfast. That was the risk of sometimes believing things were normal at an abnormal time. We also knew that was nothing compared to the situations other people were in. By and large we welcomed the troops being there because they were the people we would turn to if things got bad – not everybody could say the same.

Nineteen seventy-two got off to the most shocking and depressing start with a day which was to go down in infamy as Bloody Sunday. On 30 January, thirteen people were killed when paratroopers opened fire during a civil rights march in Derry. About ten thousand marchers had gathered to protest at the policy of intern-ment without trial, introduced the year before.

Since parades of that nature had been banned, it was deemed an illegal gathering and the authorities had put up barricades to stop the protestors in their tracks. Inevitably, there was trouble. Missiles were hurled at the soldiers, who responded with rubber bullets, water cannon and CS gas. The response was seen as too heavy-handed. What happened next will always be the subject of much debate but things got really ugly. The army say they came under fire from snipers, the marchers say they came under fire first, from soldiers on the ground and around the city walls. Just twenty-five minutes later, though, those thirteen people were dead.

I was with my dad that day, visiting people in our old neighbourhood, the New Lodge Road, when the news started to come through on the radio. With every bulletin, the number of deaths rose. This was no 'normal' riot, even by Northern Ireland's standards. This was serious, serious stuff. As the news became more and more bleak, the atmosphere became more and more tense. I could feel how the New Lodge was different, that what was once just a close-knit community comprising people of different religions had now become one single unit under siege. This was now a Republican stronghold. We were told to get ourselves home, that there would be trouble that night, and there was. Rioting flared all around the New Lodge and every other Nationalist area throughout the country.

These were the days before 24-hour news, before video cameras and pictures being beamed by satellite. Events took an awful long time to be reported. At home, I listened to the radio, wanting to know what was going on and what had triggered such a tragic and chaotic situation. Eventually, when the television news got pictures they were shocking. There is one enduring image from that day that symbolises Bloody Sunday for many people: a priest, Father Daly, waving a bloodstained handkerchief, protecting the body of a young lad who'd been shot and who died before help could reach him.

I wasn't there. Like so many I was only watching on television, but those images never leave you. They affect different folk in different ways. Some they led to murderous retaliation. What we found out was that every action has a reaction. There were always consequences to violence.

Just a few weeks later, on 4 March 1972, the IRA planted a bomb in the centre of Belfast on a busy Saturday afternoon when it was crowded with shoppers.

My dad had gone into town to McAllister's, a menswear shop in Ann Street, to be measured up for a new suit, and Mum was due to meet him there later. As she strolled from shop to shop, she stopped next to the Abercorn Bar, just off Cornmarket, to look at shirts in a window, thinking she might spot something to go with Dad's new suit. Seconds later, there was a huge explosion and, just yards from where she was standing, people flew into the air, blown off their feet.

The bomb had been left under a seat in the Abercorn by two girls who'd come in for a drink. A woman at another table noticed they'd left something behind and was about to go after them but, before she could, the bomb went off. There was utter carnage. Two women in the bar were killed and seventy others, mostly young people, horribly injured. Many had limbs blown off. Even though she was so close, miraculously Mum survived without so much as a scratch. She still doesn't know how she was spared. Around her it was a scene from hell, people covered in blood, many numbed by shock.

Naturally, all she could think about was where was Dad. He, thankfully, was also safe but distraught, thinking the same about her. They were separated by just a couple of hundred yards but at the time they didn't know that. A stranger

71

who saw the state Mum was in helped her find a way through the chaos and debris into nearby Arthur Street and back onto Ann Street. She hurried towards McAllister's, smoke all around her and ambulance and fire bells ringing. There was Dad, looking above the heads of the crowd, staring for her face, anybody that resembled Mum. He ran to her, took her in his arms and held her, both of them glad to be alive.

If we'd been in any doubt, the Abercorn bomb confirmed just how bad things were and that the Troubles affected everyone, whether you were political or not, whether you were religious or not. Belfast at that time was not a nice place to be and it got worse.

In July that same year I was kicking a ball on the Street with my mates. These lads were a different religion to me but we were all friends. Little divided us and the things that united us usually involved a ball. Other kids in seventies Britain would have their play interrupted as their mum called them for tea or the news that their favourite TV programme was about to start. Our only concern should have been whether we were going to miss *Scooby Doo* or the *Banana Splits*, but our teenage years weren't that innocent. Our play was interrupted that day as one explosion after another sent smokey clouds billowing into the sky. Boom! Boom! Boom! Nine people were killed in those blasts on what became known as Bloody Friday. And from the vantage point on our street, which was on a hill, we watched them go off one by one.

Mummy was beside herself, again worried sick

about Dad who was out on a job somewhere. She paced the floor, frantic. All of us waited – fearful that Dad might be close to one of those twenty bombsites. When he turned up safe later that evening, it was a close call between whether Mum was going to beat him to death for not phoning or hug him to death because he was alive. Anyway, I remember he got a particularly sumptuous dinner served up.

It's hard to imagine that normal life went on in the midst of all this, but somehow we had to get on with it. Increasingly, I appreciated my school, St Malachy's, as a place of safety, a place where it was possible to escape whatever was happening beyond the college gates. Often in class we'd hear gunfire or the sound of an explosion. It became part and parcel of everyday life.

The more war raged around me, the more fascinated I became by the TV coverage. News – both what was happening on my doorstep and elsewhere in the world – was my addiction. I knew I wanted to be a reporter, although I wondered whether it might be beyond my grasp, and I did consider other options, like studying to be a chemist or a lawyer, but to be honest I don't think I had the dedication for anything else. I'd sneak a radio into school and, when no one was looking, plug in an earpiece and listen to Radio 1's Newsbeat in class. No wonder I was so bad at maths. I remember sitting in a biology lesson listening to the news of President Nixon's impending impeachment in 1974 when I should have been concentrating on the life cycle of the amoeba.

73

For my third-year project, while everyone else was covering topics like the Easter Rising in Dublin in 1916 or the influence of the Normans in Ireland, I chose the assassination of JFK. I researched at Belfast Central Library and ordered books from the United States.

I put in a huge amount of effort, treating it like an investigative report, cutting out pictures from magazines, making photocopies, spending ages printing everything neatly so that it looked as close to a typewritten document as possible. It was a real dossier and I was very proud of it. It earned me top marks, the first time I'd come top in anything. With that I knew I had it in me to research a subject and compile a report. I thought: I can do this, I can be a reporter, and I want to be a reporter!

I also wanted to understand why there was a war going on in Belfast, why people were rioting and burning cars and killing each other. I thought: what is it about this place? Why can't people just get on with each other? That's where the role of reporters and presenters is so important. So many top-class news anchors on television in Northern Ireland influenced me; people who brought the news into our homes each evening from Ulster Television and BBC Northern Ireland. Men like Gordon Burns, David Dunseith, Barry Cowan, Larry Mc-Coubrey. This was TV coverage that reached out and touched us. It was local television at its best, forming a link of explanation, trust and debate between the public and the broadcaster. I could see what a powerful medium it was for good and for evil. The footage and opinions voiced by politicians and activists each night were capable of swaying people's moods one way or the other. A lot of people have a lot to answer for over the years in Northern Ireland because of the misery their outbursts and rantings of hate resulted in.

Nineteen seventy-six was the hottest summer on record for many, many years. It was also the year I would meet my first girlfriend and future wife, and would sit my O levels. Not only that but at forty-eight years of age my mum was pregnant – again! With shame I remember the embarrassment this caused me. What if anyone found out that my mum and dad were still 'doing it' at their age? These days I don't find forty-eight that old any more – funny that, isn't it? The result was baby brother Conor who joined me, Leonard, Brian and Colm to become the fifth Holmes boy and complete the family line-up. Still no sign of the daughter that Mum yearned for, and I suspect her and Dad practised getting that little bambina for a good few years after that.

I did well in my O levels, passing eight subjects, including Latin and chemistry. I managed an A in English language and literature.

Predictably, I failed maths.

Not only did I fail it, I got a grade that was called 'unclassified'. This is practically impossible to get – it means that you must have scored under 15 out of 100. Today I'm sure you get that just for writing your name at the top of the paper! I wouldn't have cared except St Malachy's wouldn't allow progression to the sixth form without it. I was summoned to see the president, the Very Reverend Patrick Walsh. You could tell he was Very Reverend because he wore more layers of black than any of the other Fathers. In fact, with the pallor of his skin contrasting with what seemed like a vampire's cape, this really felt more like a visit to Dracula's parlour in Transylvania. You'll remember Father Walsh, I mentioned him earlier. He was incredibly tall, authoritarian and, most of all, intelligent. This wouldn't have been so intimidating had he just been intelligent in the arts but his specialist form of intelligence lay in maths. And not just one degree, remember, but MScs from Cambridge and Queen's Universities. Oh dear.

I stepped into his office with its familiar smell of fresh polish and sat down facing him across his vast imposing desk.

He continued to write, never lifting his head, eventually uttering the steely words: 'Who told you to sit down, Holmes?'

'No one, Father.'

'Stand up then.'

I got to my feet.

About thirty seconds went by. 'Now,' he said, 'you may sit.'

He was not impressed by my poor show of manners or maths. By his standards, I had disgraced myself. Why, he wanted to know, should he let me move up into the sixth form?

'Well, Father,' I began, 'the reason my maths has suffered is because I want to be a journalist and I've dedicated myself to English and arts subjects. Unfortunately, I've worked so hard at getting good grades in those, my maths has suffered.'

All of which was true – sort of. I had worked hard at English, but however much effort I put into maths the outcome would have been the same. I was totally useless at it. 'Is it wise to put all your eggs in the one basket in terms of career, Mr Holmes?' responded Father Walsh.

'Well I think it is, Father, because just as the priesthood was your vocation, this is mine.' There was silence for what seemed like an eternity. He could now dismiss me from the college and prevent me from studying A levels, or he could buy what I said.

'I will admit you to the sixth form if you re-sit your mathematics.'

So I did and he did. My dream of a career in journalism was still on course.

By way of celebration I went to the cinema with my newly acquired girlfriend – in fact, my first girlfriend, Gabrielle Doherty, the first girl I kissed, and the girl I was to marry. Our date was to take place at the New Vic cinema, but the movie and Gabrielle weren't the only things worth looking at. With great enthusiasm and pride I drew her attention to the new sound-dampening techniques the cinema had employed, dampening being the right word since the roof leaked. The New Vic had come up with the idea of fitting maroon carpets not only on the floor but up the walls as well. And who was the man that did it for them? None other than my dad, of course.

I think I paid Gabrielle much less attention than she was expecting that night because up on the big screen were Dustin Hoffman and Robert

Redford in that year's big picture, *All The President's Men* – the story of the Watergate scandal. They played *Washington Post* investigative reporters Carl Bernstein and Bob Woodward, whose brand of journalism seemed incredibly bold and sexy. This was my sort of film, made better as my dream of being a reporter was back on track. Redford and Hoffman were movie stars, another galaxy away from downtrodden and blitzed Belfast – untouchable, only relevant in my dreams.

But, spookily, almost thirty years later I would get to meet one of them and tell him about this very day.

SEVEN

A Proper Job

One of the great secrets of life is to be happy in what you do. I often preach to my youngsters, 'If you don't like animals, don't be a vet or a zookeeper. If figures give you difficulty, don't be an accountant. If you have a bad back, don't stack shelves.' In short, find out what comes easy to you, what your passions are. Do what you want to do as opposed to doing what you have to do. I am in a position where I can preach from experience. In what I do today of course I work long hours – but most of the time it's not like work at all. Not when you have something to compare it to. Not when you've done real jobs in your life and found yourself wanting. Ah well, you've got to kiss a lot of frogs and all that...

When I left grammar school in 1978 it was with A levels in English, geography and modern history under my belt. I had also passed Use of English – not quite an A level, but more than an O level – with a grade A. Somehow I had managed to get away without O level maths, having failed it a second time. I couldn't see that was ever going to matter. Words interested me, not numbers.

I had wanted to be a TV journalist for as long as I could remember but I wasn't sure how I was going to manage it. I was aware that you didn't see people like me on television. Whether it was on ITN or the BBC, it was all posh blokes who'd been to Oxford or Cambridge, not that that made them bad people. The ones that got to the top of the tree, people like Ludovic Kennedy and Robin Day, were knowledgeable and entertaining, but let's face it I had absolutely nothing in common with them. No wonder my parents – and everyone else who knew me, for that matter – couldn't quite see where I was coming from. I might as well have said I intended to be an astronaut. Actually, that would probably have seemed more likely.

With Dad having to financially support such a big family, not surprisingly there was a fair bit of pressure to find a job and start bringing some money into the house. With the demands of us lot – five boys under one roof at the time – it wasn't easy for him making ends meet. At twenty-two, my eldest brother, Leonard, was working in the Civil Service. My younger brother Brian, who was seventeen, was working with my Dad, learning to be a carpet fitter. Ten-year-old Colm was at primary school, and Conor was just two. My mum wanted to see me in a steady job – 'a good government job,' as she called it – bringing home a pay packet, any pay packet, as long as it helped the family. It was a point she repeatedly made, and it was a pressure I felt. But, however far-fetched it seemed, I had to give journalism a go, so I applied for a place on a course at Belfast's College of Business Studies, which in further education terms wasn't a bad option. It was only a one-year commitment. Twelve months, I reckoned, and I'd be bringing home that pay packet.

I'm not sure what I expected from further education. I suppose what I wanted was something along the lines of the hallowed halls of St Malachy's, where I had felt a real sense of belonging for seven years. St Malachy's was a college in every sense of the word. The College of Business Studies couldn't have been more different. No tree-lined avenue, no sense of history, no priests walking the corridors reading prayer books in Latin. Instead, a bleak, grey, sixties utilitarian tower block, which was also smack bang in the middle of where most of the bangs were going off – Belfast city centre.

On the plus side, there were girls.

Fourteen years of education, and I had never sat in a classroom with a girl before! Even that wasn't enough to make me think that I wanted to spend the next year here.

Typical of me, I was in a hurry, impatient to get going. Why did I need a course? I knew what I wanted to do. Just let me get on and do it. So, I concluded, what I needed wasn't a year's theory, it was a year's practice. The course in journalism I had applied for was, we were told, the most desired course at the 'College of Knowledge'. Three hundred applicants and only ten places.

My interview must have been better than I thought because one of those places became mine. But a few classes in I realised I didn't want to learn about journalism, I wanted to do it. So I turned down my place and started firing off letters to every newspaper in Northern Ireland, which didn't turn out exactly as I'd planned. The replies that came back all said the same thing: thanks, but no thanks. No one was interested.

I soon realised that when it came to jobs in journalism, it wasn't what you knew, it was who you knew, and I knew nobody. My dad, to his credit, realised my dilemma and my embarrassment and did his best to help. He'd call in after work at bars like McGlade's and the Blackthorn, well-known drinking holes for reporters from the *Belfast Telegraph*, the *Irish News* and the *Newsletter*. There were lots of encouraging words, but no offers.

That's one of the reasons I admired my dad so much. He did what fathers should do and looked after his youngsters. Mixing with journalists wasn't his natural habitat. He had nothing in common with their working world, or they with his, but he did that for me, and did his best to find an opening.

He would have seen nothing wrong with asking for their help because he found it so natural to help others, and he taught all of us to do the same. 'Why do somebody a bad turn if you can do them a good one?' he used to say. Dad judged everybody by his own standards but, just because he would always offer a helping hand, didn't mean everyone else would be as willing, as I was finding out.

I had really messed things up. Not only was there now no place at journalism college, there was no prospect of a job in journalism. No job, no sign of one, and no money.

Then came Plan B. I had to find a proper job.

I managed to get that 'good government job' as a clerk in the Central Benefits Branch of the Civil Service at Stormont. I hadn't got what I wanted but my mother had, so at least one of us was happy. What I had to do was deal with claims for sickness and invalidity benefit – or 'infidelity benefit', as the good folk of Belfast more often than not referred to it. 'What are you going to do about my infidelity?' they'd say. What I was going to do about it was give it up as soon as I could. It was a job without beginning or end.

Every day, a stack of files would appear and the task of the clerks was to plough through them, gradually reducing the pile. No sooner had you cleared one lot than another would land with a thump on the desk. The harder you worked, the harder you were expected to work. Pretty soon I worked out that meant there was absolutely no incentive to work! There were no prizes for being keen, no bonuses for doing more than anyone else. The smart people in the department were in no hurry to get through their in-tray and the only hurry I was now in was to get out. The thought of being stuck in Central Benefits Branch forever frightened the life out of me. I lasted six weeks.

Then an advert in the job section of Thursday's *Belfast Telegraph* caught my eye. Primark, then the cheapest, tackiest store on the High Street, were looking for trainee managers and the money was good. From £1,800 a year in the Civil Service, I could jump to £2,300. There was just one problem. The successful applicant had to have O level maths. Oh, how I knew this would come back to haunt me. I agonised for at least two minutes then came up with a solution. I could let the job go, or I could – lie! It was only a small white lie, adding maths to my list of GCE passes, though putting down a grade B might have been pushing it a bit. This taught me another great lesson in life, that very few people do their job very well, particularly when it comes to checking application forms. As a result, I got the job.

Part of the illusion of doing your job well, of course, is to look the part and I wanted to do just that, so I went out and bought three formal suits – one grey, one black and a navy pin-stripe, all with waistcoats. Waistcoats were very 'in' back in 1978. The retail image in many people's minds was Grace Brothers in the BBC comedy, *Are You Being Served?* My idea was to model myself on ITV's *Crossroads* motel manager, David Hunter, a picture of style and sartorial elegance, who wore two-tone shirts with a coloured body and white collar and cuffs.

Once on the shop floor I soon realised that despite being dressed to kill the job title was much grander than the job itself. There was more trainee than manager. I'd imagined walking the floor, hands behind my back, keeping an eye on things, making big decisions, a bit like being a prefect at school again. A supervisory role. An important role, a regal role, as befits the title of 'manager'. As it turned out, the title of 'navvy' might have been more appropriate, such was the amount of manual labour involved and the hours spent heaving crates of stock off the back of never-ending delivery lorries. Primark was a low-cost, high-turnover operation. Low-cost meant using me for ten different roles. High-turnover meant more and more ruddy delivery vans to empty – all in my three-piece suits and two-tone David Hunter shirts!

Covered in sweat and dust, I'd hear the tannoy: 'Mr Holmes to refunds', where I would have to be judge and jury over whether someone got their money back or not. A shop assistant was always there in this courtroom-like scenario, acting like a lawyer relaying the complainant's story to me.

'Mr Holmes, this lady says she bought these undergarments here two weeks ago. She's lost her receipt and she just wants to change them to a different size.'

Clear-cut case, I would think, saying to my shop assistant, 'Yeah, that's fine. She can change them for a new pair, no problem.'

To which the shop assistant would reply, 'Well,

there *is* a problem, Mr Holmes – she says she hasn't worn them.'

'And?' I would interrupt, knowing another two delivery vans had pulled into the loading bay and were awaiting my urgent attention.

'Well, she has,' the assistant would insist.

'No I haven't,' the irate customer would respond.

'What's this then?' the assistant would counter-act, holding up for inspection what could only be described as irrefutable evidence of soiling on the gusset.

Nothing in the manual had trained me for this situation and countless like it where customers, time after time, were trying to pull a fast one and the streetwise shop girls knew it.

They knew that Primark, in Donegall Place, Belfast, was basically one big thieves' paradise. Many of the city's light-fingered practitioners would descend on our two floors and leave with whatever they could, including other customers' discarded receipts so that they could return and get a full refund on goods they hadn't bought, or an exchange for goods without proof of purchase.

In the beginning I took a very dim view of these dishonest practices, but the harder Primark worked me and the longer the hours became, the more I began to realise that life was too short to have a stand-up argument and make a per-manent enemy of a member of the public who, often in our verbal exchanges, intimated they had very close family connections with members of Belfast's burgeoning paramilitary organisations.

As a result, since the most expensive item in a Primark shop probably cost about £2.99 in 1978, I more often than not decided sod it, give them a refund!

Although initially I was brought in to keep the girls on the shop floor in line and make them work harder, I became closer to them than I did to the management. Most were good people and very good at their jobs, but there were a few bad pennies in there.

One day there was a fight over a missing purse in the staff room, and who was called to sort it out? Me, eighteen years of age, armed only with a three-piece suit and expected to drag apart two madwomen literally tearing each other's hair out. I can remember watching, helpless, as two female assistants in their aqua blue nylon Primark pinnies slugged it out. This was way out of my league. It was never like this in *Are You Being Served?* But while we were not as snooty as Grace Brothers, there was a definite hierarchy. Everyone was Miss This and Mr That. No such thing as first-name terms.

'She f**kin' stole my purse, Mr Holmes!'

'I f**kin' didn't!'

All I could offer in terms of mediation was, 'Now, now, Miss So-And-So ... there's no need to rip her blouse off. Calm down, now ... now, biting is well out of order.'

My decisive tones brought an immediate response. Indeed, I remember well the words being screamed at me in a very broad Belfast accent – 'Away and f**k yerself!' And, with that, the rest of the girls cheered and applauded as the fur well and truly flew.

I eventually found out why that maths O level was required. There was a lot of stocktaking and till balancing – and I wasn't very good at either. There was also a scary ritual at close of business when all the sales figures from every other Primark store would come in. It was the highlight of the day for the managers. They would salivate at the prospect of seeing where their shop ranked in the store league table. It was a bit like the Eurovision results, on a daily basis.

But while the more senior guys were totting up the figures, I was looking for bombs. Being more expendable than the rest of the management, that was my nightly chore. Incendiary devices were the big worry for shops throughout Northern Ireland at the time. A favourite trick for the bombers was to smuggle them in concealed in handbags or cigarette packets, and slip them under a jumper on the counter or into the pocket of a coat where, if undetected, they would go off after the shop had closed. It was explained to me in detailed terms how to look for them, but no one actually said what to do if I ever found one. I must admit running away would have been fairly high up my list of options. Fortunately, I never did find one.

My working experience was beginning to reveal to me that I was more into union rights than management rights. I hated the early starts and I wasn't good at getting in on time. Well, I was, only my time and their time didn't tally. I didn't see why I had to turn up at 8.15 a.m. sharp when I was only being paid from nine o'clock. So even if I was ten minutes late, in my book I was still early. Why should I be in trouble for arriving before I was meant to start?

My argument fell on deaf ears and earned me a black mark on my personnel file for poor time-keeping. Funny how they didn't take into account all the extra hours worked after the store closed looking for bloody bombs!

Lateness in the morning had followed me around for years and now was beginning to count against me. Somewhat ironic, given my role later in life as the official alarm clock of the nation. It was easy to be late in Belfast. Various bomb scares and bus hijackings would often see to that. If the public transport system was risky, accepting a lift from my dad in the morning was even worse. These were the days when cars regularly didn't start. When people put blankets or newspaper over the engines to keep the frost off them at night. Our car always pointed downhill so that Dad could jumpstart it. Jump-starting was an exact science that required the right balance of choke and clutch engaging at a precise point during the 50-metre descent of our street. There was only one chance to get it right before the hill levelled out. Failure would mean us boys baling out of the back, grabbing whatever neighbours were out walking their dogs and all pushing together along the flat.

Needless to say, when accepting a lift from Dad, I was often late for school. The penalty was arriving to find the Dean of Discipline, Father Michael Murray, stern-faced at the top of the school driveway. 'Holmes,' he'd say, giving me detention, 'if you're late for school, you'll be late for everything in your life.'

Yeah, yeah, thought I, not taking much notice of these words, but as I was to find out Father Murray was prophetic. Ever since, it's been a duel to the death between me and the alarm clock, the alarm clock usually, but not always, winning.

As Christmas 1978 approached I was working incredibly hard at Primark, doing long days and getting home late most nights. This was a complete culture shock after the cosseted life I'd experienced at school, and I wasn't taking it too well. Rock bottom was Christmas Eve. Once the store closed, we had to get things ready for the sale, which was starting on Boxing Day. I finally got home around 11 p.m., just in time for midnight mass. To me, so much of Christmas is about enjoying the build-up. Working in Primark made this particular Christmas the pits. At school, you got two weeks off to enjoy the festive season. Sitting in mass that night, I knew Christmas Day would be my only day off. Which brings me to question why anyone would want to go shopping on Boxing Day. Fair enough, if you need a pint of milk or a loaf of bread, but clothes … on Boxing Day? Some of you may, but I certainly don't. Boy, this retail business was tough.

The more I worked in it, the more miserable I was. Anyone who's ever experienced aching limbs and a sore back after a few hours' shopping in a department store, spare a thought for the people who have to walk those floors for a living. But I realised the good it was doing me: it made me realise what I didn't want. I didn't want to pore over the sales figures every night. I didn't want to know that we'd sold more ladies' cardigans in Belfast than in Glengormley. I didn't care.

I had been working in retail but had still been thinking as a journalist. Every lunch break was spent on a bar stool in some pub or other, not drinking, but watching Peter Sissons, Michael Nicholson or Sandy Gall on ITN's *News At One*. It was a world that was now further away from me than ever but it was a world I was going to get into.

That's if I could get onto the College of Business Studies' Journalism course once again.

I got another interview and once again faced the head of the course, Joan Fitzpatrick. This was only the second time I had set eyes on her but already I knew she was not the kind of woman to be messed about. She was a gritty, chain-smoking former hack who had become a lecturer.

'Why do you want to study journalism?' she said.

Relief. She hadn't remembered me from the year before. 'Well–' I began.

Before I could launch into the speech I'd prepared, she stopped me. 'Just a minute,' she said, consulting a file. 'You were awarded a place last year.' She frowned and gave me a severe look. 'Not only were you offered a place, you turned it down. Do you know how many people apply for places on this course and how few we're able to take?'

I knew exactly: three hundred applicants for ten places.

She said, 'There are people falling over themselves to get on this course. Why should I be wasting my time with you?'

I'm not good at many things in life, but I am very good at thinking on my feet. Faced with the endless hell of dealing with 'infidelity' benefit claims or unloading Primark lorries, I thought, a lie got me into shop management, so maybe one could get me out of it. Drawing on every reserve of my acting skills from St Malachy's drama society, I put on my saddest face and delivered a soliloquy worthy of a Greek tragedy.

'Because, Mrs Fitzpatrick, I wasted a year of my life supporting my mother, brothers and father. Yes, Mrs Fitzpatrick, there is nothing more I would have wanted to do than to accept the place I won against the odds on this course last year. But I had to put my dream on hold because of the nightmare unfolding for my family.'

Already her defiant look was beginning to thaw and I could see the curiosity of the reporter coming out in her.

'You see, Mrs Fitzpatrick, illness struck my father, and with him confined to his sick bed and seven mouths to feed, my mother had no other means of financial support. Sadly, it meant that until Dad recovered I had to be the man of the household and forgo my training as a wordsmith to work in a shop. Doing so may affect my life for the worse in years to come, but at least I can look into my mother and father's eyes and know that for one year I affected their lives for the better.'

The silence was palpable. I lowered my eyes from Mrs Fitzpatrick's gaze and looked at the floor, biting my lip and praying. God forgive me – but, God, it will be worth it if it works. Still she said nothing, but opened the cigarette packet that was by her left hand and lit up. After the first puff, she said the words that sent my heart sinking. 'Don't believe a word of it. But anybody that can put together a story like that has got to have a future in writing.'

When I told her I could have kissed her, I could see for the first time what I was to appreciate thereafter: that behind the hard hack exterior was a woman with a sense of humour and a heart of gold. With a huge guffaw and blushing face, she refused my advances, but I was in. For the second time in my working career, a fib had done the trick.

Everyone on my course wanted to work in newspapers – broadsheet newspapers, at that. They dreamed of a job on the *Irish Times* or the *Guardian*. That didn't appeal to me. I knew I wanted to work in television, although that seemed to be regarded as inferior somehow, not quite serious journalism. That didn't worry me.

There was always a big drinking culture around reporters and the same went for our course. A lot of them went to the pub a lot of the time. I did too, but not to drink. Since I was sixteen I'd had a job pulling pints at the Christian Brothers Past Pupils Union. Most nights, I was working behind the bar. It wasn't a chore. In fact, I enjoyed it so much I kept it on even after I found a day job.

I also had a grant of around £1,000 to help see me through the twelve-month course. I spent just over half of it, £550, on a car, a mushroom-coloured Fiat 124. It was a sporty wee thing and I jazzed it up with rally lamps, go-faster stripes and a green sun visor on the windscreen. In the seventies, everyone was influenced by Starsky and Hutch and their Ford Torino jacked up at the back, and I did the same with my little Fiat. It was a great car and it took me to college and well beyond. The only problem was that the windows leaked and let in the rain. I tried everything to sort it out but nothing worked. There were always sheets of newspaper in the foot wells to mop up the water that collected there. In the end, it was easier to drill holes through the floor so the rain could just drain out.

In all honesty, I didn't think much of college. It was a means to an end. Still, I worked hard at it, wanting to do well. I got my chance to shine at the end of the year, when we all competed for the Esso Prize. We had to produce a news story, a piece on the Esso refinery in Belfast and a feature-length profile piece. The subject for my profile was my uncle Tommy, who was married to my aunt Sheila. At that stage, Uncle Tommy was the most famous member of the family. He was a war hero and had spent much of the Second World War defusing limpet mines.

When I won the prize it was like a shot in the arm and I began to believe I might actually make a decent reporter. The cheque for £100 came in handy too.

Esso Prize or not, it wasn't easy to get a job. No

one would take you on unless you had a National Union of Journalists card. The only way to get your NUJ card was ... to have a job. Catch 22. In the end, I was taken on by a construction magazine, the *Ulster Building Report*, in Dublin. It wasn't what I would have chosen as my entry into journalism but it got me that all-important union membership. I spent six months in Dublin, driving down in the waterlogged Fiat every Sunday, spending the week lodging with my aunt May and uncle Tommy, and returning to Belfast at the weekend. My job on the *Ulster Building Report* was deathly dull. There wasn't any reporting or writing to be done as such. It was more a case of collating information. There would be building projects – a new school or whatever – and we would list all the requirements so that firms could tender for the work. I must have been good at it, because I'd barely been there six months when they offered me a job in Belfast. The magazine was about to launch a Northern Ireland edition. I got the editor's job, which sounds a lot grander than it actually was.

I'd only been doing it six weeks when fortunately something much more interesting came along.

EIGHT

Cue Eamonn!

Presenters like me don't have staff jobs but we do have agents. That means every time somebody well known pops up on telly it has involved contract negotiations. However tough these negotiations are, they will at some time involve a lunch at a very nice London restaurant like the Ivy or the Wolseley. I used to think a restaurant was all about what was on the menu. In media land it's more about who else is dining there. TV executives like to be seen with well-known names and well-known names just like to be seen. But getting the detail to suit both sides is a bit of an art form. Nowadays I have some idea of what I'm doing – but it wasn't always that way.

I had been working as a journalist for just a few months when Joan Fitzpatrick, my old tutor at the College of Business Studies, tipped me off about a job going at Ulster Television. Her husband, Rory, who produced the station's farming programme, was looking for a reporter.

'But, Mrs Fitzpatrick, I don't know anything about farming,' I said.

'Rule One of journalism, Eamonn – find out,' she said. Never were wiser words spoken because, as I was to find out in the future, I knew nothing about horseracing, darts, certain authors and many soap stars, but it never stopped me presenting the programmes or doing the interviews. Not a working day goes past without Mrs Fitzpatrick's words ringing in my ears.

I was called in for a screen test and found myself up against some of Northern Ireland's most experienced agricultural journalists, but luckily knowing a subject didn't necessarily make them on-screen performers. Even better the screen test we all had to undergo had nothing to do with farming at all. It was an interview with a police officer in the UTV car park about why driving during the autumn months was particularly treacherous. It was all to do with changing weather conditions, the hazards of wet leaves, observing safe braking distances, that kind of thing, and because it had nothing to do with farming, that turned out a big advantage for me.

There were about eight of us up for the job and we all had the same brief: a short piece to camera setting it all up, and three minutes for the interview. Everything was on film in those days, which meant someone with a clapperboard shouting, *'Farming Ulster*. Audition – Eamonn Holmes. Take One.' CLAP! And thankfully one take was all it took.

A few days later the call came summoning me to producer Rory Fitzpatrick's office. I slipped away from my desk at the *Ulster Building Report* during my lunch break and went round to UTV two streets away.

Rory Fitzpatrick was a great bear of a man. Six feet five inches tall, broad shoulders, a mop of red hair, eyebrows to rival Denis Healey's and massive hands, the right one usually holding a cigar. He could use his physical presence protectively or as a threat. To me, he was always protective, and under the big, bushy eyebrows on this day were two smiling eyes.

'Right,' he said, 'we're in a position to offer you a couple of days' work a week on *Farming Ulster* at the current NUJ rate.'

Fantastic. I had got the job. I was in telly!

He pressed a button on a speaker on his desk and spoke to his secretary in the outer office. 'Ruth, what's the NUJ rate?'

'£44.44, Mr Fitzpatrick,' she replied.

He was smiling but suddenly I wasn't. I may have been keen to get into TV but not at any price. In my head I started to do some calculations. Since, as you now know, maths was never my strong point, I tried to keep it simple. £40 a week ... that's £80 a fortnight ... £160 a month ... that's £1,600 for ten months, plus a bit more – let's round it up to £2,000 a year. Hang on, I thought – that's less than I'm getting now. At the *Ulster Building Report* I was on £2,300.

I might have been young and eager but I wasn't stupid.

'Well, Mr Fitzpatrick, I don't know. I just don't think the money's right.'

A bushy eyebrow shot up in astonishment. It was obvious no one had ever turned Rory down for a job in TV before. Most people would probably have been happy to work for nothing just to get a foot in the door; pay for the privilege, if need be. And there was me saying hold on a minute.

97

He was a bit taken aback but, to his credit, he tried again. 'Right,' he said, 'you're interested in sport, aren't you?'

I nodded.

'We'll see what we can do.' He picked up the phone and spoke to Terry Smyth, the sports editor. 'Terry, I've a young lad here, he's very good. Big sports fan. Could you use him?' The answer was yes. 'You can work in sport as well. Three days a week.'

I had pushed my luck but it had worked. Things were definitely looking up.

'And how much would that be, Mr Fitzpatrick?'

'Same rate. £44.44.'

What? OK, I might be a youngster, and I desperately wanted to get into telly, but what sort of a fool was he taking me for? Did he really expect me to do another three days a week for the same dough? I wasn't falling for that.

I took a deep breath and sighed. 'Well, Mr Fitzpatrick, I don't think so. I have a very responsible job. I'm Editor of the *Ulster Building Report* and my money's much better than that, so I really do think I have to say thanks, but no thanks.'

He stared at me in utter disbelief. The cigar dropped from his hand into the ashtray. 'What?' He frowned. The big, cuddly Rory bear was becoming more of a roaring bear. 'I'll tell you this. I think you better think very long and hard about what you're being offered here. Agriculture is the biggest employer in Northern Ireland and you are being offered a chance not only on the

98

farming programme but also the nightly sports desk. At nineteen years of age, do you feel you want to turn that down?'

Put like that, it did seem an odd decision. The *Ulster Building Report* was hardly going to make my name. But Gabrielle and I had been dating for four years now and we were thinking of getting engaged. Money was an important consideration. I wasn't about to give up what was a better salary.

'I think you better go away and examine what you want to do in journalism,' he concluded.

Meekly I said, 'I will.'

'Ruth!' bellowed Mr Fitzpatrick. 'Show this young lad out.'

I left his office thinking about what might have been. His secretary could see how disgruntled I was.

'What went wrong?' she said.

'Well, Ruth, I may be a youngster, but I'm not dense. £44.44? They want me working there for that when I'm already getting £60 a week just now – and even that's rubbish money.'

She stopped in her tracks. 'But that's not £44.44 a week – that's per day!'

I went pale. Even with my poor maths, I could gather I had just turned down money beyond my wildest dreams. Quickly, I began to assess the damage. £40 x 5, that's £200 a week. That's £800 a month. So in a year, that's ... hang on. Ohmygod, ohmygod! I've just turned down a pay rise of more than seven grand!

I had made the odd mistake in my life, but nothing so far compared to this.

It would have been easier to get out of jail than it was to quickly exit from UTV at the time. Because of the fear of terrorists taking over the building, every door had double bolts and locks, bells and buzzers, and the foyer was guarded by four security men. As the front door clunked shut behind me, I knew it would be easier for the IRA to get back in there than it would be for me. OK, OK, big deep breath. How do I turn this around? Don't panic.

I sprinted to the nearest phone box. Out of order. I was now getting frantic. Found another phone box – no coins. I went to the Post Office and came out with a fiver's worth of 10-pence pieces. 'Can you put me through to Mr Fitzpatrick's office, please?' A wait. More coins swallowed up – but I had plenty in reserve. 'Ruth? It's Eamonn Holmes again. Can I speak to the boss?'

'He's just having his lunch,' she said, 'but it's only a sandwich so I'll put you through.'

A disgruntled Rory came on the line. 'Yes?'

I prepared to grovel. 'Mr Fitzpatrick, Eamonn Holmes here. I'm really sorry about this morning. It's just I really felt I had an affinity with the construction industry and that's where my passion lay.' I winced. 'Now I realise, after meeting you, Mr Fitzpatrick, you have convinced me that farming is the future for me. And I know now that's really what I want to do–'

'Hmm...'

'–and it was only that I was intimidated because I'm a city boy born and bred and I know so little about agriculture...' My words tailed off. A moment of dead air hung between us. I held my breath and bit my lip.

'Right. When can you get out of your other job?'

'Now – if you want me to. But out of decency I might need a bit longer.'

'You have two weeks but you can start filming straight away with us at weekends.'

'Thank you, Mr Fitzpatrick.'

What I really meant was, thank you, God.

Often today I hear Terry Wogan on his Radio 2 show calling me 'Barratt' – as in Barratt Homes, the house builders. I have to say, it makes me smile thinking what a great company surname I would have had if the *Ulster Building Report* experience had led me into construction instead of broadcasting. Not sure that the kids would have been happy with names like Wimpey, Persimmon and Octagon though.

So there it was. I was working out my notice on the magazine and filming for TV at the same time. At last I really was in the communications business.

My two years spent working for Rory Fitzpatrick and the farming programme were two of the happiest in my entire career. Every day new people, new places, new smells – boy, were there new smells but that's the country life for you. The farming community was welcoming and hospitable, always preparing meals and hospitality for the visiting TV crew.

And, although I was hired as an outside reporter, my studio career was about to sprout faster than watercress in a greenhouse.

The studio links for *Farming Ulster* were recorded on a Saturday for transmission the following afternoon. As the new boy, keen to see how things were done, I found a quiet corner of the studio floor and watched from a distance. Studios are make-believe places where set designers and lighting technicians can create any world they want. They have a different atmosphere from the real world outside. This was television and I was part of it, and that part was just about to become bigger as the rehearsal was interrupted by the presenter, Eugene Moloney – funnily enough, an old boy of St Malachy's, who'd been a couple of years above me. The resident expert on the show, Peter Morrow, a farmer, had done an item on something or other and was in the script as 'our reporter'. Eugene objected. He drew the line at calling a farmer a reporter. As the rights and wrongs of this were debated, Rory Fitzpatrick burst through the heavy soundproofed doors onto the studio floor. 'Is there a problem?' he said, trademark cigar in hand.

'I'm not calling him a reporter,' said Eugene.

'You'll call him whatever it says in the script.'

'I will not.'

The exchange rapidly took a turn for the worse. 'If you're not going to call him a reporter, then you can eff off,' said Mr F.

And that's exactly what he did.

'Holmes,' boomed Mr Fitzpatrick, 'have you got a jacket with you?'

'Yes, Mr Fitzpatrick.' I quaked.

'Well go and get it. You're going to present this programme.'

My heart started to beat a bit faster. What did he just say? I had been two weeks in the job – the junior – now about to become the senior. But nothing's ever simple, is it? Someone else's loss was going to be my gain. Worse, being a fully paid-up member of the NUJ, I tended to agree with Eugene. Peter Morrow was not a reporter. This was my big chance, but as my mouth opened I knew I might be about to blow it. 'But, Mr Fitzpatrick,' I said, my voice sounding small, 'I don't think I can call Peter a reporter either...' I waited for him to thump me. Or, worse, sack me.

Instead, he gave a casual, unconcerned shrug. 'Well, we'll not call him a reporter then. Call him whatever you like.'

'Now,' he said, matter of fact, 'get your jacket and get in there.'

So, two dabs of a powder puff later, there I was in the studio presenting my first programme. I couldn't believe it. I was in the presenter's chair, and although my mouth was dry and my hands were shaking, it felt very comfortable indeed. The scariest thing was listening to the floor manager shouting out the serial number of the programme and setting off a big old-fashioned clock that ticked down to the opening titles. This was for real. My dream was now for real as well and as the opening credits rolled there was no going back. I had talked the talk but could I walk the walk?

'Cue Eamonn!'

'Hello and good afternoon. Welcome to *Farming Ulster*.' My voice sounded odd, not like mine at all. It had suddenly got a lot higher. I only found that out when I watched the programme the next day, because at that moment, with my heart beating so hard against my chest and my ears pounding, I swear I couldn't actually hear a word I was saying. How the microphone didn't pick those heartbeats up, I don't know, but by and large I was OK. I looked OK, I sounded OK, I could do the interviews OK and what really seemed to impress them was the autocue – the bit that tripped most people up – I could do that OK as well.

But actually, whether I was or I wasn't OK, a golden rule of television is, in truth, you really don't have to be. You just have to have somebody in authority who thinks you're OK and can give you a job. In my case, that somebody was Rory Fitzpatrick and I will be forever grateful.

NINE

Saying the Same Thing Only Differently

My partner, Ruth, always tells me she knows when I'm talking to my mother, my brothers or any of my children on the phone. 'How do you know?' I ask her. 'Because you screw up your face and go all be-Jaysus, be-gorrah.' What she means is I stop using my TV voice, which I suppose I've also got to use in day-to-day life in England. The words are the same, only different – they're Ulsterisms. Northern Irish chat has

104

a vocabulary all of its own. So complicated is it, that sometimes we don't even understand each other.

Although I was now the studio presenter on *Farming Ulster*, I continued with the outside filming as well.

One day I went to do a report on the mushroom industry in South Armagh. It was to be a serious piece and I was confident I'd done my homework. The interviewee was a genial man by the name of Seamus, a farmer whose family was one of the big mushroom producers.

Being shot on film, the sound was recorded separately from the pictures – just like a movie. The production assistant brought out the clapperboard. '*Farming Ulster*, South Armagh. Mushrooms. Take One.' Clap.

'So, Seamus,' I began, 'this is a very impressive operation you have here. What sort of yield have you had this year?'

'Well, Eamonn,' he said, 'it's been a good year but I'll tell you this, and I'll tell you no more, without the fairies we are nothing. You don't realise how much you rely on them.'

Very humorous line, I thought, bringing the fairies in – fairies, mushrooms, toadstools ... very good.

'Being a less favoured area,' I continued, 'what sort of help are you getting from the Common Agricultural Policy?'

'Well, Eamonn, the bureaucrats in Brussels can do all they want. They can sing to the high heavens for all I care, but if the fairies don't do their work there's nothing I can do.'

'Cut!' I said. 'Seamus, that's great. We've got the line about the fairies and we're happy with that, so we'll move on now and talk about other things.'

He nodded. 'Fine, fine.'

'*Farming Ulster*, South Armagh. Mushrooms. Take Two,' announced the PA.

'Seamus, how has industrialisation changed the mushroom business?'

'Well,' he said, 'I've been here a long while, and my father before me, and my father's father before him, all growing mushrooms in Armagh. And it's been a real struggle, but I'll tell you again we are nothing without the fairies.'

'Cut!' By now, the joke was wearing thin. 'Seamus, all that stuff about the fairies is great, but can we just talk about more important things now?'

'*Farming Ulster*, South Armagh. Mushrooms. Take Three!'

'What is your profitability per hectare?'

'Well, Eamonn, as you can see, we have these big heated domes, but profitability counts for nothing without the fairies—'

'Cut! Cut!' Now, film was very expensive, and not only were we running short of stock, I was running short of patience. 'Seamus, for the last time, we've got the fairy bit. I understand the joke – fairies, mushrooms, toadstools, little people ... all very good, very funny. But please will you drop it and talk about the whole economic situation?'

He gave me a most peculiar look. 'What are you on about, man?' he said. 'I'm talking about the

106

ferries between Holyhead and Dun Laoghaire. They're on strike and I've got six container loads rotting at the docks. That's what I'm trying to tell you.'

The lesson from that was always listen out for the accent. Many of you may think I've got a strong Northern Irish accent and find it hard to understand but, believe me, you ain't heard nothing.

One particular misunderstanding passed into legend at UTV. During the Troubles, a news reporter was sent to a house in the Duncairn Gardens in north Belfast where there had been a sectarian attack. As a family watched television, a hail of bullets shattered their front window. When the reporter got there, the police were still on the scene, and the woman whose early evening viewing had ended in real-life drama came out to talk to him.

'Madam, can I ask you what happened?'

Still in a state of shock and deeply distressed, she said, 'It's *terrable*, *shackin*'. Bullets flyin' everywhere, flyin' through the windee. *Shackin*'. We're just minding our own business watching *Carnation* Street and all hell broke loose. It was awful.'

'Was anyone hit?' asked the reporter.

'They hit the cat,' she said. 'About six shots went into the cat. It was terrable. Me nerves are shattered.'

'They hit the cat?' asked the reporter. 'And is the cat dead?'

She gave him an odd look. 'Dead?' she said. 'I'm talking about the cat the baby sleeps in!'

Perhaps I should explain that in the Belfast vernacular, cot is pronounced 'cat'.

A few years down the line I encountered another language barrier – with hugely embarrassing consequences – and this time it had nothing to do with the Belfast accent.

My good friend Bill McFarlan and I found ourselves hosting the opening of the Monarchs Course at Gleneagles. As the schedule of events wound down on the first day we ended up in the clay-pigeon shooting area talking to the last two celebrities to shoot: the golfer Colin Montgomerie, and His Royal Highness Prince Andrew, the Duke of York. The evening reception was by now only an hour away and Bill and I had to get back to the hotel, shower and change into our dinner suits. Bill was extremely taken with the Duke of York and after chatting for twenty minutes or so felt that he and Prince Andrew were the best of friends. I was a bit more cynical and not entirely convinced that Bill's plan to introduce his wife to HRH later in the evening would go without a hitch.

Sixty minutes later, there we were, milling about prior to the evening meal, champagne flutes in our hands, when in walked Andy. Bill stepped forward. 'Your Royal Highness, this is my–' he started to say. The word 'wife' didn't even depart from his lips as Prince Andrew duly blanked him, walked past and spoke to someone else more important. This story is worth telling because, having witnessed this episode, I felt Bill's embarrassment, and that affected how I felt about the prince the next day on the tee.

It was my duty to introduce each of the celebrity foursomes onto the tee box. The problem was my microphone was playing up. Anyone who ever remembers the act of comedian Norman Collier will get the idea – sort of one word on, two words off type of thing. Prince Andrew found this hilarious. Royal he may be, but I gave as good as I got, warning people that his golf swing was about as reliable as my microphone lead.

Fast forward to later that evening. Golf over, dinner suit donned again for the prize-giving, I emerged from my room to find Prince Andrew in the corridor talking to his sister, Princess Anne. My wife, Gabrielle, and I dropped our heads, not so much out of deference, but in that 'we are not worthy because we are Belfast council-house working-class and shouldn't really be here' way. Anne went back into her room as we passed. At that point Andrew bellowed, 'You, man – sound?'

'Is he talking to me?' I murmured to Gabrielle.

Another bellow. 'You, man – sound?'

At this stage, I realised he was indeed talking to me, but now that he'd got my back up on two occasions, I reacted somewhat wrongly.

What does he mean – sound? I could only think he was referring to my microphone breaking up earlier in the day.

'No, I was not sound – I was the host,' I said, indignantly.

'I beg your pardon?' he said. 'Sound?'

'Look,' I said, getting pent up, 'how many times do I have to tell you – I wasn't working on sound, I was the host holding the microphone that was broken!'

There's no way, thought I, he's going to make light of me again or ignore me and my wife the way he'd ignored Bill and Caroline the night before.

'What are you talking about, man? I'm asking you if you are sound – you're walking with a limp, and I was just wondering if you were all right.'

Ah. He was absolutely spot on – I was! I then entered into a grovelling, 'Oh, no, your Royal Highness, it's an old football injury I have, but thank you for asking.' And with that, red face and all, I limped down to dinner.

It's funny how two people can speak the same language and yet mean something completely different. But who in real life uses the word 'sound'? It's the way you would speak about a horse, isn't it?

I suppose that says it all.

TEN

The Showbiz Branch of the NUJ

As part of the BBC's Children In Need I got to sit in the famous Mastermind chair. The questions in the quiz weren't as difficult as one of the ones John Humphrys began with. 'Name?' 'Eamonn Holmes.' So far, so good. 'Occupation?' For a moment I had to think. I am trained as a journalist but I'm sure that's not how people see me. I stumbled, searching for an answer, recalling how my middle son Niall was once asked in primary school what his dad did for a living. 'He just talks to people.' Out of the mouths of babes ... John Humphrys was waiting for an answer. 'I talk to people,' I said.

Now that I was on the box and people were beginning to recognise me, there was no reason to hang on to that leaky old Fiat car of mine. I traded it in for another Fiat, a sporty Strada. I got a good deal too, partly because it was a demonstrator and partly, I suspect, because I was one of the few people willing to drive around in a car that was the same colour as Kermit the frog. Even so, suddenly I had a car that cost more than I'd have earned in a year at the *Ulster Building Report.* Things were definitely looking up.

Progress in the farming department was great. It was a bit more difficult on the sports desk, where I worked the rest of the week. Well, I was supposed to work, but I was more like a spare part most of the time. UTV's sports anchor, Jackie Fullerton, was the equivalent of the then ITV god of sport, Dickie Davies. Jackie was also a bit of a god. I remember that, because he told me.

Three days a week I'd turn up to work in the sports department, sit at my desk and be given precisely nothing to do. Everyone else was busy and no one showed the slightest interest in getting me to write anything or send me on a story. I sat immediately opposite Jackie, face to face. He was always busy, writing, phoning or on location. I'd spend hours trying to look as if I was doing something, reading the back pages, coming up with stories, but all to no avail. I was getting the message. No one here was going to go out of their way to help me fit in. Most of my day was spent talking to the sports secretary, Mary Anderson, whose theory was that Jackie, Leslie Dawes, the other reporter, and the sports editor Terry Smyth, himself a former reporter, felt a bit threatened by new blood and weren't going to give me a chance to progress up the ladder.

Through Mary I knew that they all simply referred to me as 'the boy'. If they weren't going to allow me to work, I was going to watch and learn. Fullerton was the best. He had a way about him – talented, slightly cheeky on screen, knowledgeable, and he knew how to com-municate. I had huge admiration for him. Amazingly, despite his pin-up status, I remember regarding him as a bit of an old codger. I laugh looking back at this now, as he would only have been a mere thirty-five in 1980, and in his prime.

Jackie liked writing out his scripts – I never saw him type anything – and every now and then, without looking up, he'd snap his fingers in my general direction. I soon learned that this meant he wanted me to fetch him a cup of tea. If his phone rang, he'd go click click, which meant answer it. God, did that piss me off. I hadn't gone to journalism college to be a tea boy. Didn't he know I'd won the Esso Prize?!

So one day I thought, enough is enough. Jackie's phone rang and he, as usual, ignored it. Without looking up, he double clicked and I saw red.

'Why have I to answer your phone?' I said, defiantly. 'I'm not here to make your tea and lift your phone.'

He put down his pen. 'Young man, let me ask you something. Do you think if someone rings up ITV Sport and asks to speak to Dickie Davies they'll get through to him?'

Stopped in my tracks by the question and somewhat stunned, I replied, 'Well, no.'

'So, why should people be able to ring here and get through to me?'

Must admit, he had me there. I picked up the phone.

But that was a watershed for me and Jackie. If he had been setting me some sort of test, he now decided it was time to stop. From then on, he took me under his wing. I have learned a lot from watching others present TV over the years but Jackie Fullerton, to this day, has been the only person to sit me down and actually teach me anything. He was a master at work, and I was getting one-to-one tuition in his master class. Jackie taught me to make my writing more conversational. 'Write as you speak,' he said, which may seem obvious in a medium which relies on the spoken word as much as pictures, but most people write as if their words are going to be read off the page. The best broadcasters never make you think there is a page in sight.

He taught me how to look, how to dress, how to be more animated on screen, and at the same time gave me tips on how to avoid that blank, hypnotic look that many presenters and reporters have when the video they link to doesn't appear.

'If the film isn't there, look off to a monitor – it'll buy you two seconds, which is an eternity on screen,' he said.

'But what if there is no monitor?' I asked.

'Then pretend. The viewers don't know it's not there,' he said.

Thanks to Jackie, I learned how to keep my head when things fell apart. I made light of disasters and bluffed my way through technical failures. As the years went on, all these things became my strengths. Live TV was my thing, and my aim was to do it better than anybody else.

Then, in 1982, came the chance to put all of Jackie's teachings into practice. The good fortunes of the Northern Ireland football team getting into the World Cup finals in Spain was to be my good fortune as well because the entire UTV sports department went with them leaving me behind. Being stuck in Belfast while all the action was going on in sunny Spain might have seemed like the raw end of the deal, but it turned out to be the best thing that could have happened.

With everyone else away, it was left to me to present the nightly sports slot. Although I'd been doing the Sunday farming show, that had nowhere near the profile of the teatime news, which attracted the lion's share of the audience in Northern Ireland. Something like 70 per cent of viewers tuned in to *Good Evening Ulster*. Suddenly, I was on every night, exchanging banter with the star of the station, Gloria Hunniford. It was a fantastic opportunity and Gloria was good to me. Although I was the new boy, and way down in the pecking order, she was in favour of giving me a chance. While I may not have been the most polished presenter, she thought I had a spark, which would be good for the programme.

She had a wonderful, relaxed style in studio. I'd be at the sports desk waiting for her to hand over to me and, you could guarantee, it was never a boring handover. I would watch her in awe.

Gloria was without doubt a star. She looked like a star, she acted like a star. She dazzled. She had huge energy and charisma. While other ITV regions were more conventional in their nightly output, Gloria was pushing the boundaries. She was having phone-ins when other programmes were still reading out viewers' letters. I watched, keen to learn from someone who was a dynamo and knew how to make ideas come alive on screen. So many presenters are spoon-fed, happy to read other people's words, work from a list of questions someone else has written for them. Not Gloria. Although she had never trained as a journalist, she was as sharp as anyone. She had her own questions. In many cases, she had the answers too. She was Queen of the Castle, the kind of presenter who can also produce, and that's exactly what she did.

You could see that Gloria put a huge amount of effort into everything, and it paid off because she just radiated energy. Energy that made people watch.

One of the things I learned from watching her was that you get out of life what you put in.

Ironically, her success also brought her problems. She was almost too popular, which ruffled a few feathers. Gloria *was* UTV, certainly as far as the viewers were concerned. That didn't go down well with some of the people running the station. TV stations like their presenters to be popular, but only up to a point.

At UTV, Gloria managed her career alongside being a mum and, as with everything she did, made it appear effortless. Her children, Michael, Paul and Caron, would often come to the building to wait for her to come off air. My first memory of Caron Keating is of her in her school uniform outside Mum's office doing her home-work. I'd nod and say hello in passing, little imagining that a few years later Caron would be a successful presenter in her own right, and that a few years after that she and I would host BBC Daytime's magazine show, *Garden Party*. It was little wonder Caron made the grade, bearing in mind who she was learning from. As for me, I didn't just learn from what Gloria did on the screen.

I remember one rainy lunchtime walking from the studios on Ormeau Road into town with her. It was about a mile into the city centre and it was amazing how she had a word for anyone who spoke to her along the way. Soon we passed the BBC on nearby Ormeau Avenue, where Gloria had been a radio presenter. She knew everybody, or if she didn't, she appeared to. What's more, she was very good at remembering names. Gloria has the knack of making people feel special. She had started out as a cabaret singer and knew all about engaging with an audience.

The more I watched her the more I realised

that within the NUJ there was an unofficial showbiz branch, of which Gloria was Queen and Jackie Fullerton King. In the space of a few weeks, I gleaned a huge amount from her. Just in the nick of time, too, because she wasn't to be around at UTV for much longer. That summer she left to join Radio 2 in London.

Just before she went she left me with some wise words, which have always stayed with me. She was on her way into make-up. As always, she had a huge pile of papers and scripts under one arm, and a bag stuffed with yet more paperwork over her shoulder.

'Gloria,' I said, 'would you have any advice you could give me about the business?'

She settled into the make-up chair. 'See this?' she said, indicating her bundle of papers. 'Always be prepared. Have something to say if it goes wrong.'

From that I picked up another golden rule – presenters aren't paid for when it goes right, they're paid for when it goes wrong. For getting the programme out of a hole. With good ones you should rarely ever realise a problem has occurred. That's the way I see my job.

Those teatime stints on the sports desk meant I got my face known. That's where local TV is so much more a litmus test than national TV. The feedback is immediate, as soon as you walk out the door.

Just as I was settling into UTV, out of the blue BBC Northern Ireland tried to poach me.

Their weekly current-affairs programme *Spotlight* was well regarded and what you might call highbrow in comparison to what I'd been doing. They wanted me on the team as a reporter, which seemed like a good move. It was a serious, respected programme, and a chance to do the kind of investigative journalism I'd always had in mind but never quite got round to. This I thought could be the next stage, the next challenge. I decided to take the job. That, as it turned out, brought a flurry of activity from my present employers.

One evening I got a phone call from Derek Murray, head of programmes at UTV, who had tracked me down to my mum's house. He told me Brian Waddell, who ran the station, wanted to see me. Brian Waddell was a bit too high up for me to have had any dealings with before, so I was rather nervous at the prospect of meeting him. He must have been really hacked off at me planning to go to the BBC, I thought. As it turned out, he was perfectly charming.

He smiled at me across the desk. 'Well done for all your work over the summer,' he said. Good start. Then his expression turned serious. 'Now, what's all this about the BBC?'

I said, 'Well, Mr Waddell, they've offered me a job in current affairs.' I talked about the gritty news stories they wanted me to do, the investigative reports, the in-depth features.

He nodded. 'And is that what you *want* to be doing?'

Good question. Was it what I wanted to be doing? Certainly, it's what I thought I got into journalism to do, but my two years to date had demonstrated to me that journalism has many facets, as does presenting. Current affairs at the BBC seemed like a step up the ladder. Then again, I was having a good time at UTV. It had introduced me to friendly, accessible television, the sort of television you just know people want to watch. I began to have doubts. 'I don't really know,' I responded.

'So, what would make you stay?'

Jokingly, and with a smile on my face, quick as a flash, I said, 'Gloria's job.'

Hardly had the words come out of my mouth than he nodded. 'Right, it's yours.'

I was hearing things, surely. I could have sworn I'd just asked the station boss – a man I'd done no more than nod at in the corridor from time to time – for Gloria's job, and he had just agreed. That couldn't be right. Clearly, I was having some kind of out-of-body experience. Any minute now I'd wake up and he'd be shaking my hand and wishing me well at the Beeb.

I pulled myself together. 'Gloria's job?'

'That's right.' He looked more pleased than me, stood up, slapped me on the back and said he'd be in touch re a new contract. 'I'm delighted you're staying, Eamonn – you'll not regret it.'

Staying? Was I staying? The BBC think I'm going. How will I break the news to them?

I stumbled out of his office in a bit of a daze. Just four years after leaving grammar school, three years after working in ladies underwear and two years after being stuck on the most boring publication in the history of the world, I was going to succeed Gloria Hunniford and become Mr Teatime in Northern Ireland.

At twenty-two years of age I was the youngest news anchor on the ITV network.

We set to work on a new-look programme. There would be new music, new opening titles, fancy new camera angles, a chance for me to make my mark. In the past, there had been a standard 'hello and welcome to the programme' greeting to kick things off, but this was a new start and we needed a new opening. The programme was called *Good Evening Ulster.* Why not start with, 'It's six o'clock. Good evening, Ulster – the headlines tonight...'? Just to make it a bit different, we could run a pre-titles sequence highlighting the main stories. It sounds simple enough now, but that's not how things were done then.

It was a never-to-be repeated opportunity to be able at such a young age to put my stamp on UTV's flagship show. What I wanted to do was to bring network ideas to local programming. Once again I just couldn't believe I had landed such a terrific job. This was the biggest programme in Northern Ireland. And Northern Ireland was the most important and sensitive news region in Britain. For their sins, Brian Waddell and Derek Murray had given me the keys to the shop. I can only hope that TV history judges them as men of vision. Personally, I think they must have been drinking that day. When I look back, I wonder what it was that led them to take a chance on me, to give such a responsible job to someone so young and relatively inexperienced.

From the outset, I loved the energy and un-predictability of live broadcasting, and still do.

You can go into studio with your running order and your script, and it can all change on air. Frequently it does. Recently, I tried to recall moments when things had gone wrong but I couldn't think of anything specific. That's because it happens all the time, and finding ways to cover when a telecine machine goes down and a film doesn't appear, or a guest isn't there when they should be is just part of the job.

There's nothing like live TV. The fact there's no going back, that you have to get it right first time – or at least make it work if it goes wrong – is the buzz for me. I'm not so keen on recording shows, doing things again and again. I'd much rather just get on with it. I anchored *Good Evening Ulster* for four years and, in the process, learned how to handle just about anything thrown at me.

Being in the studio came easily. I felt at home in front of the camera. I understood the mechanics of television and made it my business to know not just my job but everybody else's around me, which didn't always go down well. But that was the way I had to do it to be able to predict what was going to go wrong, and to know how to get out of trouble when it happened.

It felt natural to be talking to camera and at the same time listening to the director or producer in my earpiece. I'm often accused in my day-to-day life of not paying attention because of my tendency to do two things at once – have a conversation and read a newspaper, for instance. I'm not being rude – it's just one of the few useful things I've learned from working in telly.

On the subject of two things at once, my very

uncomplicated love life was just about to become very complicated. A new makeup artist had just joined the station and increasingly I found myself wanting to sit in her chair to be made up. This had nothing to do with the ability of the other two make-up artists, Connie and Sheila, more to do with the fact that they were matronly ladies in their fifties while the new girl was a stunning, doe-eyed, strawberry-blonde. Well, that's how she described it – I thought she was a redhead. Her name was Claire Smyth and I had begun to fall head over heels for her. The complication was she was engaged, I was engaged, and from here on in I was to learn that with my increasing profile my business was everybody's business.

Besides Claire's obvious attractions and lovely nature, she was working in this new, exciting industry. There was the feeling that she would understand what was happening to me more. Whether that was true or whether it wasn't, it highlighted weaknesses in my relationship with Gabrielle. If I needed an excuse to break our engagement off, this was it. Ending the engagement was one thing, but I was to find out over the next year or so that I couldn't end many of my feelings for Gabrielle. I was constantly plagued by guilt and continuously worried about her without me around. What should have been a very carefree time in my, Claire's and Gabrielle's life was too often filled with tears and angst. Added to that, Claire was from the other side of the tracks in more ways than one. Her family were affluent middle class to my not-so-affluent working class, and we were of different religions.

Not so much of a problem today but this was eighties' Belfast. What we had in common though was a mutual attraction and working in the same industry.

It was a period of my life that I didn't handle well. I knew what to do to be the perfect broadcaster; I had less of a clue what to do to be the perfect boyfriend. But we were all young and had a lot of living to do and mistakes to make before we grew up. This was the first time I experienced everyone having an opinion on my life to the degree that I felt my life was not my own. Family pressures were particularly strong. In the end, and after a long while, Gabrielle and I got back together, although I don't think she ever truly forgave my confusion. If so, that probably explains a lot of what happened to us further down the line. I just wish we had realised the obvious ramifications way back then. Today, I'm glad to say that Claire and I are still friendly and, by a strange quirk of fate because of the school her children went to, one of her best friends is none other than Gabrielle's sister, Kathleen. It's funny how what seems so life and death at certain parts of our existence just turns out to be – well, life!

ELEVEN

Don't Shoot – I'm a Reporter!

I've just been speaking to my friend and fellow presenter Dale Winton on the phone about ties. Dale is always an immaculate dresser and is a good man to take advice from. We are often in the market for the same type of entertainment shows and what we wear is regularly the subject of intense debate. Dale can wear anything; these days I'm just delighted anything fits me. Helping us in the task is our shared wardrobe designer Lynda Wood, who also puts together clothing ensembles for the likes of Michael Parkinson, Terry Wogan and Natasha Kaplinsky. And there was me thinking when I started out that the only decision I had to make regarding clothes would be whether my flak jacket would be black or khaki! Isn't it funny how things turn out?

Although it was never my plan to be a presenter, I have to say it came very naturally indeed. When I was growing up, it was the reporters – the likes of the BBC's Brian Barron and ITN's Desmond Hamill – dodging bricks and bullets on the front line, who were the ones I wanted to emulate. The reporters were the ones getting to the heart of the stories behind the headlines, explaining why Northern Ireland was the war zone it was. I had always seen myself doing that job but, increasingly, I was finding myself in the fictitious entertainment branch of the NUJ. Not wishing to become a fully paid-up member, I still pushed the news editor to send me out on stories. One such outing, though, did much to convince me that maybe the studio was a better place to be.

It was August 1985, and I was sent to cover the funeral of an IRA volunteer in Derry. At twenty-one, Charles English had died when the home-made grenade launcher he was aiming at a police Land Rover exploded. The night before the funeral, masked paramilitaries had fired shots over the coffin and the police and army had been pelted with petrol bombs and bricks.

The chances of trouble at the funeral were high, especially because it was rumoured that Martin Galvin, leader of Noraid – the organisation raising funds in the United States for the IRA – was due to turn up. There was an exclusion order on Galvin, which meant he was banned from entering the UK, which, of course, Northern Ireland is part of. The year before, all hell let loose when he showed up at a Republican anti-internment rally and police tried to arrest him. In the violence that followed then, a demonstrator was shot and killed by a police plastic bullet. The whole thing was captured on film and shown around the world.

I had a fair idea as I set off with the camera crew for the Bogside that there would be trouble. What I didn't expect was that I'd almost get myself killed that day. Twice.

There were several hundred mourners, a hefty police and army presence, and an air of unease.

125

Word had gone out that Martin Galvin must not score a propaganda victory. The situation had all the hallmarks of a riot waiting to happen. From our vantage point looking down on it all it seemed clear it wouldn't take much for things to kick off. Suddenly, word spread that Galvin had appeared, and my crew set off like greyhounds out of a trap to get the pictures. At this point, the pictures were everything. Getting him on film was all that counted. Any report from me could be added later. To that end, my role became driver as the cameraman shouted at me to jump in the crew car and follow them with the video-tapes.

I got into their big gold Ford Granada and realised it was an automatic. Now, I'd never driven an automatic before but I knew roughly what to do. I slipped it into D for Drive, put my foot on the accelerator and off it went. Simple. Everybody was heading in the same direction – camera crews, policemen armed with batons and shields, and a dozen or so soldiers clattering along in two columns, one on each pavement either side of the car. Their attention was now on said gold Ford Granada advancing at speed. I could see them looking at me, which I think made me forget I was driving an automatic. As I reached 30mph or so, instinct took over, and as I pressed my foot down to change gear the clutch felt odd. That's because it wasn't the clutch – it was the brake. The car skidded to a halt, tyres screeching, in precisely the kind of scary manoeuvre guaranteed to spark panic at a para-military funeral that was fast turning into a riot.

The soldiers freaked. Straight away at least six rifles were trained on me, and the soldiers were now screeching louder than my tyres had.

'Get out of the car! Out of the f**king car!'

The door flew open and someone dragged me into the road. 'On the ground! On the ground!'

I lay face down in my smart reporter's white raincoat. 'I'm news crew!' I shouted into the tarmac. 'Press! UTV!' I hoped no one was looking. Worse than death would have been that the rest of the press corps were watching. How undignified.

'Stupid f**ker! Stupid f**king c**t!' yelled one of the soldiers.

'Just f**king leave him,' barked his superior, which I thought was really good advice.

As I got to my feet they were already off, sprinting towards the action. I climbed back into the car. By rights, I should have been scared stiff, but I was just soooo embarrassed. Now – P for Park. Mirror Signal Manoeuvre. D for Drive. There would be no mistakes this time.

But, if that was bad, worse was to come.

I left the car and made my way on foot to join the camera crew. There were reporters from the BBC, ITN, CNN. If you were claustrophobic, this was no place to be. Cable Street, two rows of terraced houses, was blocked at either end with scores of RUC Land Rovers. All police vehicles were painted grey and looked like Daleks. It resembled a scene from *Dr Who*. The bigger armoured vehicles were called pigs – often a word used for the police in various parts of the world but not in the Bogside, where much stronger terms were readily on offer. Wherever you looked there were soldiers and police with batons and shields. This was it then, the front line. I started to think the studio might actually be a better bet after all.

Then Galvin appeared in a cap and dark glasses, as if that would stop us recognising him. He didn't fool me. Men in black hoods came from nowhere to form a paramilitary guard of honour either side of the coffin. That was enough for the security forces. The police came forward from both ends of the street, which created a concertina effect. People screamed in panic, running in all directions, but there was no way out – unless you were Martin Galvin. It was beginning to dawn on me that I was in the middle of what was known in the trade as a full-scale civil disturbance, with stones raining down, batons flailing, punching, kicking and screaming all around.

A brick landed at my feet, much too close for my liking. Sometimes, though, it can be an advantage to appear on TV and this was one of those times. A voice behind me piped up. 'How are you doing, Eamonn?'

I turned to see a couple of young lads sitting on a doorstep, calm as anything, like they'd seen it all before. Which, no doubt, they had.

'How do you think?' I said, dodging another brick.

'Do you want out of here, Eamonn?'

'Too right I do,' I said.

'It'll cost you...' They scrambled to their feet. 'Come on, we'll show you.'

I couldn't believe my luck. 'That's great, lads.'

They wanted £10, which seemed a small price to pay for my life.

I gave them £20 and they led me, cool as cucumbers, in through the front door of their house, along the hallway, through the kitchen and out into the back garden to safety. As I passed the front room, a couple sitting at the table with a cup of tea gave me a nod. Galvin had probably passed by a couple of minutes earlier.

Outside, ambulances screamed towards Cable Street, sirens wailing.

That twenty quid was without doubt the best I've ever spent.

But the risk of getting killed wasn't just an occupational hazard. At twenty-four years old and by then the veteran anchor of *Good Evening Ulster*, it was my job to relay the news, not just the daily bombings and shootings, but also the happier side of life, to the people of Northern Ireland. Usually the show ended with something light, in the hope of distracting the audience from what was mostly going on outside their front doors.

Although I was on screen five nights a week, and a face everybody knew, I learned that being recognised didn't buy me immunity from the violence that was affecting the audience I was broadcasting to. No one was safe and, just by being in the wrong place at the wrong time, I was as likely as anyone in Belfast to end up a target.

That's exactly what happened in 1984 when I had a gun put to the back of my head.

It was late, almost one in the morning, as I left

my fiancée Gabrielle's house and set off for home. Although we lived just a short distance from each other – 300 yards or so – walking was never the wisest option. It was too dangerous. Belfast in the small hours was a spooky, scary place, poorly lit, much of the street lighting disabled by the paramilitaries or the security forces, both of whom could operate more effectively under cover of darkness. It didn't take much to imagine figures lurking in the shadows, since they almost certainly were. It paid to be streetwise and to look over your shoulder.

This was one of those times when a wave of sectarian killings was under way – murder squads on the loose, prowling the streets for victims. Being caught was not an option. Suffice to say, abduction meant torture, murder. Still fresh in many minds were the exploits of the Shankill Butchers, a gang of Loyalist paramilitaries who operated in the seventies, picking off Catholics, torturing and mutilating them with knives and cleavers, before eventually killing them. All it took was to be in the wrong place at the wrong time and, just by crossing a road, you could suddenly find yourself in that 'wrong place'. People would be bundled off the street and into a car, only to turn up days later a battered, bloody corpse. Often these were youngsters, sixteen and seventeen years of age, lads who hadn't had a chance to live their lives. Unless you lived through it, it's hard to understand the sort of terrible fear that hung like a cloud over the place.

Although I lived just two streets away from

Gabrielle, her family was on the edge of what was regarded as safe territory. Nearby Oldpark Road marked the boundary between two different communities. That night, in 1984, I got into my car, drove down the hill and less than a minute later pulled up behind my father's car. I was just about to switch off the engine when a blue Ford Cortina drew level. Immediately, I knew I was in trouble.

Inside were four thickset men. They stared at me, stocky heavies, all with thick sideburns as black as their zip-up padded jackets. I'm dead, I thought. These guys weren't looking for directions or about to ask for a light; they were on the lookout for someone and I just knew that someone was me. My mouth went dry and my heart was beating so fast my ears pounded. A tense few seconds went by. I turned off my lights as they drove off up the street. Then, with them about thirty yards away, just what I didn't want to see: the red glow of brake lights as they stopped again. I had switched off the ignition, but I knew I couldn't get up the garden path and get my key into the front door without being caught and that, even if I did, the door would be like a piece of balsawood to them. They'd be in behind me in no time and I'd be putting my father and my two brothers, asleep inside, at risk.

I saw the brake lights go off and the white reversing lights come on. Sweet Jesus, they were coming back. All I could think was, I'm done for if I don't get out of here fast. I couldn't go forward so, as they reversed towards me, I turned the key in the ignition, started the engine and

131

backed away at speed, swinging the car into a side road, tyres screeching. The Cortina came after me, engine screaming, as the driver floored it in reverse. It was the scariest thing that had happened to me yet. As I slammed my car into forward drive – rubber burning, smoke coming from the back wheels – I couldn't help thinking it was like something out of *Starsky and Hutch*. Except it wasn't.

The streets were deserted, not a soul about, every house in darkness, everyone tucked up in bed for the night. There was not the slightest chance anyone would help me. A few minutes ago I had kissed my fiancée goodnight and now I was heading back towards her front door, chased by what had to be a murder squad, and she hadn't a clue. I took a right turn at the top of the road. They were still coming after me. What was I to do? Head for the police station, now only a mile away? The only problem was that Belfast's police stations at that time weren't exactly the sort of places you could just turn up at to report a missing cat in the middle of the night. They were heavily protected, ringed by fortifications and sentry posts. Oldpark Road station, which was the one closest to me, had an unmanned barrier blocking the road, which meant I'd have to halt fifty yards away from its front door. If the gang didn't get me, the squaddie with a night sight there to protect the building – thinking I was a car bomber – would.

I reached Cliftonville Circus roundabout, which bought me some time. Round and round I went, feeling like I was on some kind of death-defying carousel, tyres screeching, smoke billowing from the back of the car. The Cortina stuck with me. At one point I looked across the traffic island to see the guys inside watching me for a few short, surreal seconds. This had to be a terrible nightmare, but there was nobody to wake me up. What was I going to do? I then decided getting to the police station wasn't going to work.

A mile and a half away was the Nationalist New Lodge Road, the area I grew up in and knew well. To the gang on my tail it was surely enemy territory, and I banked on the hunch they'd never follow me in there. It was my only chance. I came off the roundabout and spun the car onto the Cliftonville Road. All I had to do was drive in a straight line for a mile or so and I'd be safe.

I tried to accelerate away but, however good a driver I thought I was, these boys were better. Whoever they were, they had clearly done this before. Giving them a long, straight road had been the wrong decision. All I'd done was make it easy for them. I had barely driven a quarter of a mile when they drew alongside, forcing me off the road. I slammed into the kerb, stopping outside a church, the front end of my car slewed across the pavement. In front of me, the Cortina came to a stop, the four heavies piling out, running at me, all brandishing handguns. Oh Christ, this is it. This is where it ends.

I fell back in my seat, certain I was about to die.

Within seconds, one yanked open my door, grabbing me by the scruff of the neck. As he dragged me out, I pleaded with him. 'Don't shoot, don't shoot, don't shoot!' He pushed my head face down on the bonnet, and then I felt the cold metal on my neck as he prodded a gun into the back of my head.

'Who the f**k are you?' he demanded to know.

My words tumbled out, tripping over each other, not really making sense. I kept pathetically yabbering, 'I'm on the telly, I'm on the telly!' Somehow hoping that would save me.

'What the f**k were you up to?' another voice demanded. 'What were you f**king doing outside that police officer's house?'

I had no idea what they were on about. 'What police officer? I live there.'

A moment's silence followed. I couldn't work out why he was bothering to ask questions, why he hadn't just shot me. There was another thing: these weren't Ulster accents. The barrel of the gun pressed harder against the back of my head. God, it hurt. The same question again. What had I been doing hanging around outside the home of a police officer?

Even in my fear and confusion I knew something didn't add up. These guys definitely had English accents. Amazingly, the journalist in me started to take over. I was in no position to ask questions, but I did anyway. 'Who are you?' I said.

'Never mind that. We want to know who you are.'

'I've got ID, honest I have,' and rummaged in my pockets, hands shaking, spilling coins onto the road, trying to find my press pass. One of them took it off me and passed it round.

All the time I was asking myself, who are these

guys? And, if they are going to shoot me, why do they want to see ID? I began to dare to hope that my prospects for survival were improving.

Again they barked: 'You were outside a police officer's house – why?'

'There is no police officer there,' I said.

The longer it went on the more I believed I might actually get out alive. Pushing my luck, I tried again. 'Who are you guys?'

'Security. Covert,' came the reply. I could have kissed his feet. Praise the Lord, this was an undercover unit of soldiers.

Then I heard a crackle from the radio. 'It checks out.' My press pass was tossed back at me and the man who moments earlier had held a gun to my head said, 'Be very careful.' He slipped the gun out of sight under his jacket and, with a nod to the others, ran back to their car. Four doors slammed shut, the engine started up and they were off, leaving me at the side of the road. My body felt like jelly, my legs about to give way underneath me. As I got back into the car and slumped over the steering wheel, shaking from head to toe, my heart was beating much too fast. I felt utterly drained. Several minutes passed before I felt able to drive.

The next morning, in shock, I told my folks what had happened. They were scared, astounded and relieved, but also as puzzled as me over the reference to a police officer living beside us. I went next door, rang the doorbell and discovered that our neighbours' son – who was a joiner – had recently enlisted in the police and completed his academy training for the RUC. They had kept it quiet, they said, for safety reasons.

I'm not sure what difference it would have made, if any, had I known that the night before. I would still have been coming home late, still acting suspiciously as far as the soldiers doing their rounds were concerned. The truth was I had come close to losing my life because my neighbour had changed jobs, which I suppose neatly sums up the madness that was Belfast at the time.

TWELVE

Fame and (Mis)fortune

There I was sitting between takes with the pop group Girls Aloud. 'Are you from Derry, Nadine?' I said to the Irish girl in the group. 'No, just a few miles away, in Muff,' she replied to uproarious laughter and giggles from her bandmates. It had taken me a few years to realise it but even I knew what they were guffawing about. 'Better than that,' interjected blonde beauty Sarah, 'I used to work in directory enquiries and there's a Muff Diving Club!' The Girls Aloud laughed louder and I went redder remembering how Muff became a regular Saturday night appointment for me in my early days at Ulster Television.

As the presenter of Good Evening Ulster, I became a familiar face around Northern Ireland. To my astonishment, I even got fan mail. Not only that

– people were willing to pay me for personal appearances. Although I learned to play the part when I had to, I could never take any of it entirely seriously. Me, famous? I tried to act it, even tried to look it, but I was always uncomfortable about people thinking I was it. Each day, when I arrived at UTV, I honestly expected the security man to stop me and demand to see my pass. 'Excuse me, sir, you can't go in there,' sort of thing, and if he had, I would have said, 'It's a fair cop.'

The expectation of that tap on the shoulder has never left me.

Derek Murray, UTV's Head of Programmes, was always at pains to make sure I kept my feet firmly on the ground. Success had come very quickly to me, and he was always cautionary. 'Don't let all the show business stuff go to your head,' he would drawl in his slow, down to earth Ulster accent. 'Always remember, you're a word-smith. That's how you'll survive.' I hadn't heard that term before – wordsmith. It wasn't only old fashioned it was strangely medieval, like black-smith. It had a no-frills practicality associated with it – a bit like Derek himself. He was a rock solid journalist who had come from newspapers into television. He rose to become Ulster Tele-vision's top political correspondent during the seventies and now found himself in management, where editorial responsibility for the station was his.

So the effect of having his mantra of 'Remem-ber you're a wordsmith' constantly drummed into me was to make me treat being on screen as a job, pure and simple. He stopped me from falling into that trap of just wanting to be there to be famous and all things that go with it. That side of it more or less passed me by. So, no revelations about steamy affairs with glamour models or secret love children. I took it all very seriously, perhaps, looking back, too seriously, always aware that survival on the box would depend on my skills as a presenter, not on being part of the celebrity circuit. I was a willing pupil. I had so much to learn from so many people around me. Going to parties or functions or standing night after night in the pub came much further down my list of things to do. It's not that I wouldn't do those sort of things, I just couldn't understand those that did them at the time.

Although I had become a face people knew well enough to stop in the street, some things didn't change. I was still living at home and still working behind the bar at the Christian Brothers Past Pupils Union on the Antrim Road in Belfast four nights a week. I was very good at it, loved the job, loved the people I met and it now paid me £10 a night plus tips. So I saw no reason to give it up. I'd present *Good Evening Ulster*, come off air, and instead of going out pulling birds would spend the rest of the evening pulling pints. Looking back I must have been mad, but the truth was I was saving up to get married. How silly it seems now to have been so young and so responsible. In the bar the immaculate Hugo Boss television suits were swapped for the more utilitarian uniform of black trousers, white shirt, black bow tie and a Chelsea blue bar coat trimmed with a black collar. I thought I looked the part, but it had now come to a stage where my boss Pat Thompson reluctantly pointed out that the part didn't look good for me.

Pat was the deputy bar manager of the club and the tops at what he did. He looked like a more willowy version of Gerry Adams, the Sinn Fein leader, and indeed his voice sounded quite like his as well. We worked behind a horseshoe-shaped bar, and by watching Pat in action I was to pick up skills that not only could be applied to bar work and life in general, but also TV presentation as well. Pat was a human dynamo. From him I learned how to do three things at once, conversation being the most important. He had a good ear for listening, could strike up a chat and more importantly look interested in anyone. Not only could he talk, he could work at the same time. One hand would be pulling a pint, the other filling a glass under a whiskey optic, while he was in full flow conversing with the customers. It was fascinating to watch and learn from such a master at work. It was also a privilege to be led by him and serve under him. Although we were friendly, there was a line. He was first and foremost my boss and not only did I respect him, I respected the way he carried out his role. He worked in a bar but he didn't drink. When I first got the job he made me aware that trust was everything, and I had to earn it. He pointed out that we were surrounded by alcohol and cash and that both had been the ruination of many a good barman. By doing so he put the ball in my court. But he led by example, which made following orders all the easier. Whether it was Pat's influence or not, to this day I still don't drink alcohol – much.

Pat's second bit of advice came six years later, when I moved from the nightly sports desk to the main anchor chair on *Good Evening Ulster*, vacated by Gloria. Things were going so incredibly well that I just couldn't believe it. I suppose it was for that reason that I held onto my night job. I was now a month into my new elevated role, and I left the Ulster Television studios at 7 p.m. to report for my bar shift at 7.30. As I was putting on my bow tie in the stock room, I could see Pat asking one of the very junior waiting staff to man the counter for ten minutes. It was always quiet at that time of night so although it was an unusual request it was doable for the youngster. At first I thought he wanted to go through some stock accounts with me for future orders but when he closed the door between the back room and the bar I could tell something more ominous was about to happen – and it did.

Pat always had a good way about doing the difficult things. He turned two beer crates on their end for seats and poured us both a drink – orangeade of course. He even did that in style. He taught me that even in the orangeade stakes there were good drinks and bad drinks all made better with just the right amount of ice. As we sat down his first word was 'Cheers' and we clinked our glasses together. Then shaking his head he said, 'It's not right, is it?'

'What's not right?' I responded, thinking that the till hadn't added up from the night before.

'You being on TV and then coming in here.'

I sort of shrugged my shoulders knowing he was right but not really knowing what to do about it.

'I mean, you can't be serving up people the news at half six and then serving them up a Bacardi and coke at half seven – can you?'

Well, not if that was to be my full-time job I couldn't. But what guarantee had I got except a year-long contract that it would be? I told Pat that the only thing I had ever been good at up till now was working in the bar. Kindly he agreed that I was good at what I did and they had plans at one stage at the club to promote me to an under-manager if that's what I had wanted.

'Of course you're a good barman, Eamonn – but you're a better TV presenter. Now don't be stupid. Take your bow tie off and go to where you should be – on the other side of the counter, as a customer!' It was the end of a special era.

We downed our drinks, shook hands and with that I left behind the boss who I suppose I have been looking for in every job since.

Other things changed as well. As the jobs got better so did the cars. But I hadn't given up working in bars totally. Offers started coming in for personal appearances, mainly at discos dotted around Northern Ireland, sometimes south of the border too. That was the good news – the bad news was that they never really got going until midnight. I was always very nervous doing these appearances and with good reason – I was never very good! I'd set off in the middle of the night, filled with dread. What if there's nobody there? What if they don't like me? I read the news, why do they want me hosting the disco? I'd torment myself before every PA I did.

Getting to them wasn't as simple as it would be in England. In the eighties in Northern Ireland we had two motorways, each with only two lanes – the M1 and the M2. Everything else was down an A or B road. A lot of the discos took place at what were called 'roadhouses', which basically meant they were tucked away in the ass end of nowhere. There were always a few obstacles in the way of getting there ... quite a lot of fog, often heavy rain, small windy roads, lack of road signs and plenty of roadblocks – some even belonged to the police and army! My nerves were shot before I even got there. Muff was always an interesting place to go to – only a mile across the Northern Irish border, but a world away. Derry on a Saturday night in the eighties was often a hotspot, and I don't mean as regards the social life. The result was that many young people from there looking for somewhere to bop would have Muff in mind.

The licensing laws in the Irish Republic were more relaxed so the discos went on later, and the rate of exchange between the pound and the punt meant that drink was more affordable. The only thing standing between anyone from the North and a good time was an army security check as you left Derry, and a Gardai one before you were allowed to enter Muff.

I decided it would make life easier if I had someone to help out, so I roped in the trendy young runner from the UTV newsroom, Paul Fitzsimmons. Paul became my roadie, and he was brilliant. We'd work out a playlist of records, come up with some party games, I'd sign pictures, give away a few prizes and that was it. Most people were convinced it was a good act – most people but me. It got to the stage where it didn't even matter if I made money as long as the organisers and the crowd liked me. I'm sure more often than not Paul and I spent more money on prizes we gave away than we were both paid. But this was the eighties: this was big hair, lots of make-up, tanned bodies and bare feet in white shoes – and that was only me and Paul! As for the girls, of course, it was a problem but not in the way I had anticipated. You may not think it to look at me now, but at one of my gigs at the Fairways Hotel in Dundalk the crowds were so big that the crush barriers couldn't contain them when I came on stage, and in the resulting surge forward to touch certain parts of my anatomy one poor girl had her leg broken. Then there were those who waited by the stage doors.

After a particularly good night at the Gaelic football hall in Omagh, I made my escape only to find a girl lying prostrate across the bonnet of my newly acquired silver Toyota Celica. Not a bad problem you may think, but then you didn't see her – all twenty-five stone of her and with more facial hair than Gerry Adams.

'Hello there. If you wouldn't mind getting down, I have to be off now.'

She refused to budge. 'Come on, Eamonn, let's have a kiss,' she said.

I really wasn't in the mood and as far as she was concerned I would never be in the mood. In fact, there would be more of a chance that I would kiss the aforementioned Mr Adams. It was 2 a.m., I was tired, and I had a long drive home in front of me. I asked her again.

'I'm very flattered, but I'm not that sort of boy. So if you could just get off my bonnet that would be lovely.'

But she was going nowhere, and if she sat there much longer the only place I was going to was a bodyshop to get the dent out. Then the cavalry arrived in the form of burly bouncers. I tried again to reason with her but it was pointless. In the end, it took the combined strength of four bouncers and Paul Fitzsimmons to prise her spreadeagled body from my silver dream machine. While they did the lifting work on the outside, I was on the inside revving away, only stopping to pick up Paul as he broke free. Needless to say she was not too pleased, but although I would like to take all the credit for her unbridled lust I do think the devil's buttermilk had a large part to play.

However, if that girl was less than blessed in the looks department, she was a beauty queen compared to one May McFettridge – a woman, bloke, you have to see her to know what I'm talking about – who has played a very big part in my professional life, and me in hers. As anybody from Northern Ireland knows, May is not only our funniest and most famous housewife, she's also not the best looking by far. That is because she is a he, and used to be my motor mechanic. In real life May is my very good friend John Linehan, who is married to my cousin Brenda. I have known John since I was a child and to the Holmes boys he is the sixth brother. John was always the wit of our extended family circle and the life and soul of any party. As to how such a macho bloke became such an ugly old bird is down to me. The disco scene led to me being booked for a two-week stint presenting on local station Downtown Radio. And since I was then new to radio, I asked John to help me out.

At the time Radio 1's Steve Wright and his afternoon crew were setting the tone with some hilarious spoof calls. I thought something similar might work for me. Why didn't John with all his natural banter become a make-believe character? He agreed to give it a go and created May, named after his mother-in-law and my aunt. The reaction from listeners was amazing. May was rude, abusive and full of banter – and they loved it. John was a natural. What had started as a joke between the pair of us soon caught on and, by the time the two weeks at Downtown was up, he had the newspapers knocking on his door wanting to meet the lady herself.

That was the good news. The bad news was that although John had put together a voice, he hadn't put together a look. Aunt May's wardrobe got a rifling and John brought the character to life with a dress, an old cardigan, a wig and a hat that looked like a tea cosy. A couple of blacked-out front teeth completed the picture. If you remember Les Dawson in drag gossiping over the garden fence with Roy Barraclough, you're not far wrong. John never looked back. Appearances on radio and television followed and have never stopped. Primarily through panto May has become, among other things, the most popular performer ever to have trodden the boards in the history of Belfast's Grand Opera House.

The one drawback in all this was that I then had to join the RAC because John became far too grand to lie under cars any more.

As May took off, I saw her as a good way to bolster my insecurity at the discos. She could be a whole new string to my bow and I convinced John to give it a go. The venue for her debut appearance was to be the Four Seasons in Monaghan. John didn't know what he was letting himself in for and neither did I. Around that time, I had been hosting beauty competitions in Northern Ireland with former Page 3 girl Linda Lusardi. Another Page 3 girl, Sam Fox, also happened to be over at the time. That night in Monaghan, I gave May a huge build-up, whipping the audience into a near frenzy. All night I had been teasing them with hints like...

'Tonight I have a special guest with me – a special Page 3 friend.'

The crowd would go wild, whistling and whooping. Eventually, around half past one in the morning, I could tease them no longer. Backstage, May straightened her woolly hat. 'Are you ready to meet this very special lady? I've got to warn you she's a big girl – in every sense of the word...'

The noise was deafening – there was no doubt they were ready for my female friend, or who they thought her to be. Out of sight, May began to feel nervous. Rowdy, drink-fuelled teens and

146

twenty-somethings were to be her first audience – a baptism of fire.

Amidst wild cheering and wolf whistles I announced, 'Let's reveal her. Here she is, all the way from Page 3 – page 3 of the *Monaghan Chronicle*. Please welcome Ms May McFettridge!'

May, in her drab outfit and sensible flat shoes, shuffled into view. For a split second nothing seemed to happen, then there was a sudden surge – just how I always imagined the storming of the Bastille to be. These country boys had worked hard all week and come Friday night they knew what they wanted and this wasn't it. May disappeared into a sea of bodies and like some human threshing machine they ate *her* up and spat you out.

First the slippers, then the hat, the wig, the cardigan, and, yes, even the DD brassiere. All this in less than a minute before bouncers yanked her, him, it, to safety. With her wig angled over one eye and her clothes in tatters, May was hoisted onto my DJ's podium, out of harm's way. Bouncers stood guard below to keep the now more than playful mob at bay. It was the only time I can remember John Linehan stuck for something to say – he was breathless and speechless.

On the way home, John barely spoke – which is often a natural reaction from people who believe their jaw is broken. He spent the journey slumped in the passenger seat, reflecting on his narrow escape and wondering whether he should forget all about May and stick to fixing cars. It probably didn't help that I found the whole thing hilarious,

147

which I'm glad to say he now does today. Besides, it's given him a mountain of material down through the years – everything from how we got the clothes torn from us in Monaghan to going down a treat at the Muff Diving Club.

THIRTEEN

Moving On

Sometimes people say to me, 'You're on everything at the moment.' I respond, 'And what would you do if you were me? Would you turn down anchoring The National Lottery, *your own network radio show, your own page in a national newspaper, or your own prime-time special?' Let me give you an insight into what it takes to survive in broadcasting. Oh, how I would love to open my diary and see the year ahead taken care of with one job, but I learned the hard way that you've got to worry about the year after that as well, and experience has taught me that when it comes to employers in TV Land, love many and trust few if you plan to be around for a few years.*

In October 1986 the BBC launched a full pro-gramme schedule on daytime television for the first time. Up until then the only programme that really featured was *Pebble Mill at One* from Birmingham. Now Manchester was to be the hub for a raft of new shows that would precede *Pebble Mill* from nine o'clock in the morning. I was just

148

twenty-six and king of the castle on television in Northern Ireland. I was four years into presenting the teatime slot and it was going ever so well. Then an approach came from a man called Peter Weil, who had worked at the BBC in Belfast and knew what I did on UTV. He was the supremo of an incredibly exciting concept called *Open Air* – ninety minutes of live daily programming from Manchester. It was to be the jewel in the crown of the new Daytime schedule.

Open Air was massive in its ambitions and resources. Put simply, it was a sort of extended *Points of View*, a chance for folks at home to have their say, good and bad, on the programmes they'd seen the night before, not just on the BBC, but ITV and Channel 4 as well. It was to be interactive television, a concept taken for granted today and made so easy with digital TV, but which in the mid-eighties was truly stretching technicalities to their limit. There would be phone-ins and lots of viewer participation. If you couldn't come to one of our regional studios, then we would quite often come to your house. Today that would involve somebody turning up with a video camera that they could plug into your phone line, but then it really was a sight to behold. A wagon train of articulated lorries which made up the outside broadcast units of the time would have to be in position the night before, generators running, miles of thick, thick cabling trailing across gardens and rooftops, and a satellite dish the size of Jodrell Bank to beam the signal out. Add to that twenty-odd people in attendance to make sure it all worked, who had

149

to be fed and watered too.

This was telly at a different level to what I was experiencing at UTV. It was like being spotted playing for a local Irish League team and being asked to play for Manchester United. How could I say no? Maybe I'd fall flat on my face, but I had to find out, and a programme on TV about TV was right up my street. There was one small problem – I had to do an audition and I was up against someone equally keen, a bright young guy by the name of Peter Bazalgette. The sort of name you're not likely to forget, and in Peter's case – Baz to his friends – not many people in TV have forgotten it since. You see, Peter Bazalgette turned out to be the guy who brought *Big Brother* to Britain. And obviously because of that he has become one of the most influential independent programme-makers in the UK, heading up a company called Endemol. Often when we meet the conversation goes back to that day when his ambitions, like mine, were just to be a humble TV presenter, as opposed to nowadays where his ambition is total TV domination. I may have won the battle for *Open Air*, but looking at how things turned out for multi-millionaire Peter, I think I lost the war. Thankfully the way the cookie crumbled meant that he bore no malice against me and has since cast me a few crumbs from his cookie in terms of work.

Moving to Manchester was a life changing experience. I was hardly worldly-wise and I had reservations about leaving Belfast. I was a big fish in a small pond and in a staff job. I was giving up £25k a year, a pension and meal

150

allowances to relocate across the water on a freelance contract that paid £8k a year less. But in truth there was no decision to make. Home-boy that I was, I knew that I couldn't discover new oceans unless I plucked up the courage to lose sight of the shore.

On my last night in Belfast, friends and family gathered for a farewell party. Although I was excited about the future, I was also nervous about leaving and more than a bit emotional at the thought of saying goodbye. That night, in front of everyone, my dad sang 'Danny Boy' to me.

But come ye back, when summer's in the
    meadow,
Or when the valley's hushed and white with
    snow,
'Tis I'll be there in sunshine or in shadow,
Oh Danny Boy, oh Danny Boy, I love you so.

The words and the memory still choke me up. For so many Irish people who left the Emerald Isle in search of work or betterment, that must be one of the saddest songs ever written. Watching him serenade me, it was all I could do to stop the tears in my eyes welling over. Outside a rendition of 'Happy Birthday' I don't think anyone else has ever sung a song to me before. It was a big moment in terms of all those unspoken things between father and son. All he needed to say he said with that song, and even though he is no longer here I can recall his voice doing that at any time I want and hear him as clear as a bell as if he is once again standing in front of me.

Puffy-eyed and with a sore head the next morning, I loaded my belongings into the car, caught the Liverpool boat like so many Irish emigrants before, and headed off for a new life in, as my mother called it, 'That Pagan Country'. Mum was worried on a number of fronts. 'How will you get enough to eat? Why do you want to give up a good job here?' And, most importantly of all, 'How will you get to Mass – do they have any chapels over there?'

I didn't know England well but if I was going to live anywhere, where better than Manchester, home of United? I'd been to two games at Old Trafford with my dad and brothers and I had also been to a wedding in Rishton in Lancashire where my cousin Sheila lives. Outside that I had no other experience of being in England. It was scary but it was also a huge adventure.

My new colleagues at the BBC made me very welcome and the Manchester people were extremely friendly – just like the way you see them on *Coronation Street*. The BBC was on the Oxford Road and was a fantastic base, a major production centre for a variety of programming, including the sports outside broadcasts for most of the country. The sports production teams in the north-west were responsible for coverage of *Match of the Day*, rugby league, cricket, snooker, darts, and even indoor bowls. Not only that but *A Question of Sport* was made there. There was also a strong light-entertainment department producing *It's A Knockout*, *The Russell Harty Show* and various quiz shows. The city itself had two massive football teams in United and City, and the Granada TV studios were just a mile away, making all the programmes they did including the *Street*. A massive urban regeneration was going on, which included the building of a new tram system, plus bids to host both the Olympic and Commonwealth games. This was the place to be.

It didn't take me long to realise that it would have been naïve to think I didn't have to move at some stage if I wanted to keep working. I had left the top job in Northern Ireland but having held it already for nearly five years, how much longer would UTV have let me go on? Everybody has a shelf life. I had to move to Dublin to get my first job in journalism. I had to leave Belfast to get on in television. Getting on, doing well, was always going to mean chasing round the country after work.

And all that chasing wasn't going to end in Manchester.

With *Open Air* I was like a child let loose in a sweet shop. We had access to all the top shows. I can remember going on the set of *Only Fools And Horses* during rehearsals and getting a rare live interview with David Jason and Nicholas Lyndhurst. If it was in production, we went to its location – *Emmerdale, Last of the Summer Wine, All Creatures Great And Small, Grandstand,* even behind the scenes of the massive operation that brings general election night to your screens. Some nuts were tougher than others to crack. Terry Wogan, who at that time had a thrice-weekly chat show, was very resistant, calling us

Open Wound, but eventually he granted us an audience, took calls from the viewers and was a great guest.

It was a privilege to speak to the people who made these shows – the actors, presenters and producers – and discover how they all came together. I don't think anything was off limits – even the big bosses like Michael Grade who ran the stations. Anything was possible under Peter Weil. If you could think of it, you could do it. I was in my element. It was, without doubt, the most exciting time in my broadcasting career.

There was enormous variety. We'd tackle serious issues, such as how abortion or drugs were handled on popular dramas like *EastEnders* or *Brookside*, or *Panorama*'s coverage of controversial subjects such as filming the IRA taking over a border village in Ireland. Was it staged for their cameras and were they giving the 'provos' Mrs Thatcher's much hated 'oxygen of publicity'? Heavyweight interviews with politicians and political activists sat alongside chats with the stars of popular sitcoms. There was a huge degree of light and shade and changing gears, which, luckily, because of my experience at UTV came easily to me. The Troubles and their consequences may have dominated my programme in Northern Ireland but we also had to serve up more than doom and gloom otherwise none of us would have survived the strife. The ability to interview the Reverend Ian Paisley and link to Rod Stewart 'after the break' is one that, happily, has always stayed with me.

Open Air also gave me access to my broadcasting heroes. It was a television education that no other presenters of my generation could claim. I not only got to interview the men and women who presented the programmes of the day in their own environment, but also to chat with them off camera. All the newsreaders, the reporters, the anchors. Big names like Frank Bough, Des Lynam, David Coleman, John Motson, Ludovic Kennedy, Esther Rantzen, Jeremy Paxman, and also the actors who were just that cut above the rest – John Thaw, Diana Rigg, Robert Hardy, Sir Michael Hordern who, despite his long and distinguished career as a thespian, may be best remembered to so many as the narrator of *Paddington Bear*.

But Daddy of them all to me was David Frost.

We had only been on air a few months and naturally enough I was nervous at the prospect of having to interview the country's top interviewer. Like so many guests, he had to fly from London to make the section of our programme, which began at five past eleven. I waited in the corridor to greet him, running through in my head what I would say. Hello, Mr Frost, my name's Eamonn Holmes, I'm one of the presenters on the programme. In the event my rehearsed words became redundant when he appeared, a waft of cigar smoke three foot in front of him, from which he emerged like one of those contestants from *Stars In Their Eyes*. I didn't get the chance to speak as he got in first. 'Ah,' he boomed from several yards away. 'Eamonn, my boy – love what you do. I'm a big fan.'

I have no idea what else he said because I

155

couldn't quite believe my ears. As we shook hands, I was thinking, wait a minute, does he know who I am? Did he just say he's a fan?

It was quintessential Frost, and whether he actually meant a word of it was of no consequence. The fact was he'd done his homework. He has that ability to make you feel special, and my awe for him only increased as a result. I have always found David Frost's personality off screen very similar to the one he has on screen, and that is something that often separates the best from the rest; Michael Parkinson, Des Lynam, Gloria Hunniford, Terry Wogan, Ant and Dec, Chris Tarrant rank among the better-known examples of the same thing.

Frost was one of the broadcasters I had grown up watching and admiring. He belonged to an Oxbridge clique along with people like Ludovic Kennedy and Robin Day, bright, talented, educated individuals from roughly the same middle-class backgrounds. Although I was now appearing on network television each day, I wasn't a member of that club and never would be. I hadn't even gone to university. In reality, you can only be who you are; trying to be something or somebody you're not has a higher risk of failing.

Besides, times were changing. TV was no longer the preserve of the posh. Suddenly there was room on the network for people who didn't have a degree and spoke with a regional accent, and thank God for it. *Open Air* was a big part of that change. Involving every part of the United Kingdom and giving a voice to every accent was a lot of what we were about. This was a new wave of broadcasting and I was part of it.

Open Air was my first taste of working with co-presenters, an entirely new discipline, which took a bit of getting used to, although veteran Bob Wellings went out of his way to make things easy. I had been a fan of his for a long while, having watched him on *Nationwide,* the BBC's highly regarded evening news magazine programme. In many respects, Bob was the presenter I aspired to be. Incredibly adept and experienced, he was also a lovely man, an absolute gentleman. On and off screen, he had a kind, graceful manner, and it was lovely to work with him.

Patti Caldwell's appeal was more about her plain-speaking, seemingly down-to-earth manner. Patti was a brusque northern lass. Like me, she had a regional accent – but nobody had an accent as strong as hers. Each of us had our own different way of doing things, which seemed to complement and dovetail nicely.

In TV terms at that time *Open Air* was on a different planet – a bit like its editor, Peter Weil. Peter must have been born with an aerial coming out of his head. I was a student of television but his enthusiasm could never have been equalled. Half-Austrian, half-Northern Irish, he would tell stories in his very distinctive accent of how as a child he wouldn't just watch TV programmes the way normal kids did, he would concoct his own television schedules. So how appropriate that he became the man to launch this whole concept of viewers telling the television bosses what they wanted to see on the box. Putting his childhood pastime into practice, Peter leapt on the idea of

157

the audience having its say in determining at least part of the schedule. And all credit to the then head of Daytime, Roger Laughton, for playing ball.

For the first time, the public was able to vote for some of the programmes they wanted to see that afternoon on BBC 1. I suppose it was the earliest incarnation of Sky Plus which, twenty years on, gives you the option to decide exactly what you watch and when.

Many thought Weil a genius – but isn't there a thin line between genius and eccentricity? You see, whereas most TV executives had trusted assistants, Peter Weil had a monkey. I kid you not. He had a tendency to consult a hand puppet called Mr Ching, which he had owned since childhood. Mr Ching had been the only one who had listened to those early scheduling ideas so I suppose I can understand why he didn't want him to miss out on doing the job for real.

Often official meetings would be held with Peter and Mr Ching in the chair. Serious programme items would be discussed among knowledgeable and vibrant people. Then, before deliberating, Weil would often say, 'Let's see what Mr Ching thinks.'

Around the table, the team would wait patiently while Peter, straight-faced, went into a huddle with his hand up a monkey's backside. There would be a bit of nodding and so on before the monkey apparently whispered in Peter's ear and he spoke on its behalf. What's worse, he would ask members of the production team to offer their ideas to the monkey as well.

Now there are two ways of dealing with this sort of thing. Laugh and play along, or think – what bollocks! I was firmly in the 'what bollocks' school, but I never ceased to be amazed at the amount of grown-up people who entered into serious conversations with a fecking monkey.

One infamous day Weil made the mistake – or perhaps it was quite deliberate – of asking me what I would like to say to Mr Ching. Naturally, the words just flowed out. 'What I'd like to say to Mr Ching is – why don't you just f**k off and leave the rest of us to put a programme together?'

Oddly enough, my relationship with Peter Weil, who went on to become a really really important television executive, was never quite the same after that.

My relationship with my fiancée, Gabrielle, would never be quite the same either. This had to be the longest courtship on the planet. We had known each other for an amazing eleven years by now. We had been engaged, unengaged, back together again, and now I had relocated to England. I wanted to know once and for all, was she going to join me or not? I saw it as a chance to wipe the slate clean and start again without the baggage of everyone knowing our business and having an opinion, as they all do in a small town like Belfast. Gabrielle had a very good management job with the Department of Health in the Northern Ireland Civil Service and was really unsure about the move. That vulnerability made me more determined to make everything right for her – to take away the risks. It brought out my protective instinct, something I still feel for her to this day. It wasn't easy for her but in the end she gave up her executive position and came over. We felt as a couple we had messed around with this relationship too much. It was now time to, as the saying goes, 'Pee or get off the pot,' and that meant marriage.

We arranged it very quickly and had a full white wedding, complete with an expensive honeymoon. What we didn't do, though, was get married at home in Belfast, and outside our parents we didn't invite any guests! It seemed the right thing at the time and we had a lovely, romantic and meaningful day. But maybe in hindsight there was something Freudian about not getting married in our home town and the lack of guests. Neither of us wanted to make a big public splash. I certainly felt I was marrying for life, but maybe having taken eleven years before getting around to it had weakened the foundations.

The only folk in attendance were my mum and dad, Gabrielle's mum and dad, Gabrielle's sister, Celia, who was our bridesmaid, and her husband, Frazer, who was my best man. The most sensational thing of all was how to get the parents over to England. Because we wanted to enjoy our day in private, free from press intrusion, particularly from back home, my mum and dad and Mr and Mrs Doherty were only given two days' notice of the ceremony. That was really to save them from themselves because, certainly as regards secrets, my mother and father would have been useless. Naturally, they would have been bursting to tell everyone – and walls have ears.

The only way to get them to the church on time was by plane. Not a problem unless, like my mum and dad, you had never set foot in one before, nor did you ever want to! In the end, to their credit, they overcame their fear and with the help of a few nerve tablets and some rosary beads they did it. Neither of them ever did it again though.

By 1990 *Open Air* was the flagship of the BBC Daytime schedule. I really felt at home with the BBC in Manchester. Although I had initially come in on a freelance contract, they'd given me so much other work and increased my fee for *Open Air* that financially and professionally things were very good. As well as various regional specials, I co-presented a weekly Friday night sports programme on BBC 2 called *Sportsround Northwest*. That was the good bit. The really good bit was that my co-presenter was royalty – Manchester United legend, Denis Law. Me and the Lawman, somebody wake me up please! And it got better. Not only did I work with him, I was his taxi as well, often volunteering to drop him off at home after the show. Well, it was the honour, wasn't it?

While things were very settled at the BBC, ITV had started sniffing around me too. Steve Leahy, who ran a production company called Action Time, approached me about a new game show he was developing from an American format called *Wheel of Fortune*. I was going to the States with *Open Air* anyway and, while I was there, Steve suggested I go to Burbank Studios in Hollywood, where the US version of the show

161

was made. It was quite something rolling up on the lot at Burbank in my hire car and finding they'd given me my own parking space with my name and a star on it.

Wheel of Fortune was a huge hit in the States and had made celebrities of its presenters, Pat Sajak and Vanna White. I think the reason I was in the frame for the UK version was because the producers felt I was in the same mould as Sajak – a former sports presenter with chubby cheeks.

I was so tempted, but it would have meant leaving *Open Air*, which I wasn't keen to do. I loved that show and, after all, the BBC had given me my network break. Loyalty was still a big thing to me at that stage in my career. I'd have been giving up a well-paid and secure – so I thought – job for an eight-part series that might not even take off. I turned it down and, as everyone knows, *Wheel of Fortune* went on to become a massive, long-running hit in the UK. I still think I made the right decision, though. At the time, pursuing programmes that involved journalism and interviewing, be they current affairs or sport, was more what I wanted to do. Basically, I was incredibly happy at the BBC.

Life was good. And that's when it has a habit of turning round and biting your fingers – or, in my case, sticking in your throat. No wonder so many prospective TV presenters never make it. Training doesn't come with the job. That doesn't only mean no one tells you how to look, act or write, it also means no one tells you how to speak.

So many people speak differently on the telly than they do in real life. I'm not sure if I was sounding different but I certainly was projecting differently. Sore throats from either overuse or wrong use were becoming more commonplace for me. Eventually it got to the stage where they just weren't going away. It was darn inconvenient because I was doing more and more work and a lot of it was hurting. After seeing my GP I was referred to a specialist. I was expecting him to say, 'Take these antibiotics.' What he actually said was, 'I'm going to have to operate!' He had found a nodule on my vocal cords. Although I hadn't heard much about them then, they have since become all the rage – Elton John's had one, Rod Stewart's had the operation, so too has Julie Andrews. Maybe broadcasting hadn't done it to me – maybe it was all that singing in the shower.

Obviously, it was a worrying time. I wasn't ready to lose my career but I was even less ready to lose my life if this turned out to be something malignant. The operation took place at the Alexandra Hospital in Didsbury, Manchester. 'All the Coronation Street people come here with their ailments,' the receptionist assured me. The operation itself, thankfully, went well. The coming around after the anaesthetic, less so, with me opening my eyes and then throwing up all over the nurse who was trying to wake me. Well, it's not nice having things stuck down your throat. Recuperation was quick. I learned to speak a bit less harshly, and one of the benefits for those around me is that I've been warned not to shout too much. Touch wood, in the eighteen years since the operation, I've had no recurrence, but it was my first warning that this job of mine could be subject to many different threats. This, as it turned out, would just be one of them.

I wasn't long married, I was earning good money, I had bought a house, our first child had just been born, and with things going so well I had splashed out on a luxury car – a 5.3-litre Jaguar XJS which, at £36,000, was a complete and total extravagance. Talk about getting above your station. This was bling before bling was invented. It was a cabriolet, which meant the roof came off, British racing green in colour, with a hide interior. Instead of looking back at it with fondness, it has made me think ever since not about sunny Sunday afternoons on country roads with the top down, but that no matter what you do in showbusiness you should never bank on it lasting.

New bosses at TV stations mean new programmes and around this time a new boss arrived at the BBC in Manchester. New bosses don't like inheriting previous bosses' programmes. They like to get credit for making their own. That requires money – money that is usually tied up in existing projects. *Open Air* was one of those projects. Its number was up but I didn't see it coming. Certainly, there were no warning signs, no discussions aimed at softening the blow. I never even met the man who fired the bullet. I found out the hard way, in a phone call from my agent, Anita Land.

'Eamonn, I'm afraid it's over,' she said.

'What's over?'

'They're axing *Open Air*.'

It was a bolt from the blue, but I was doing lots

of other work for the BBC. 'At least we've still got that,' I said to Anita.

'No,' she said. 'It's all over.'

Not only did the new boss not want certain programmes, he very definitely didn't want me. From being the network face of BBC North West, my face, chubby cheeks and all, suddenly didn't fit.

I was out of work and I was soon to be out of money. Where was *Wheel of Fortune* when I needed it! After my staff job at Ulster Television, I still hadn't quite got the hang of the freelance business and the fact that income tax was paid two years in arrears. Accountancy makes me glaze over. I had assumed all my taxes were up to date – goodness knows, I'd written enough cheques with HM Inland Revenue on them. What I didn't realise was that they were all for money earned two years previously. This was very definitely not the best time to be paying three years' hire purchase on a £36,000 car. One man's whim had resulted in the bottom falling out of my world.

I was in Manchester but any new work would be elsewhere. That would mean leaving my wife and newborn son while I pursued whatever was going. When you're out of work in TV, beggars can't be choosers. I was lucky in that at least I had more choice than others in a similar position. I had a reputation as a studio presenter and an outside reporter. I could work in most disciplines and I never felt that any job was beneath me.

As I worked on regional shows in Leeds, Newcastle, Birmingham, London, Southampton and Cardiff, sometimes with the fees not covering the ten-miles-to-the-gallon that thirsty Jaguar 5.3 engine devoured, my wife felt increasingly lonely in Manchester with a year-old son and another child on the way. My network profile was kept up with a reporting job on the *Holiday* programme, which as anyone who has ever worked on it will tell you is a much less glamorous gig than it sounds. You're never in the one place long enough to get a suntan, and while many of those places were rich in culture and scenery, the pay packet was only going to send me to the poorhouse. At that time I was getting £250 for up to five days' filming. That £50-a-day fee wasn't going to pay off what I owed the taxman.

My lowest point came in January 1991. The first Gulf War had created a fuel shortage, petrol prices went through the roof, there was snow on the ground in London, and I was driving a soft-top sports car with a massive thirst. The taxman had made a red-letter demand for £11,000 and the only way I could meet the bill was to get rid of the car – for that exact same amount. The car that I had bought only ten months before for £36,000. Paying off a loan is bad enough for anyone, but paying off a loan of £25,000 over the next two years for something you don't even have any more is the pits.

Things were changing big time in my life and lessons were being learned all the time. It was tough paying the bills, it was tough holding on to a career and it was even tougher holding on to my marriage. Gabrielle felt she didn't see enough of me in Manchester and desperately wanted to go back to Northern Ireland. Rather than convince her it would be better for us to move to London, we both agreed that she and any family we were to have could live a better quality of life in Belfast surrounded by her family circle while I commuted and hopefully brought the bread home. I had a lot of face to save.

Ever since that time nothing has made me think that TV is anything other than a job – a job like any other. Anyone who sees it as simply a route to celebrityhood won't last long, and lasting long was what I intended to do.

FOURTEEN

Back to Basics

Even though I had moved away from Northern Ireland, got married and started a family, Northern Ireland hadn't finished with me. Nor has it ever. I have spent nearly twenty years living in various parts of England but always calling Belfast home. In fact, listening to some of my conversations would really confuse you. When people ask me, will I be home this evening? – I often say, 'Not 'til the weekend.' 'What?' comes the incredulous response. Then I realise that what they mean by home and what I mean by home are two different things. I suppose I'm making the distinction between where I live and where I'm from.

I spend so much time travelling between both that it even confuses me. And while there's no denying the attraction of Belfast as home, it's been an attraction that more than once has nearly proved fatal.

Any thoughts I had of settling in Manchester for good had gone. Air links from Belfast could get me to Glasgow, Leeds, Newcastle, Liverpool, Manchester, Birmingham, Bristol, London and Southampton, all main production centres for both BBC and ITV. I could commute back and forwards, depending on what work I managed to find. Well, that was the theory. Flights didn't always fly, and timetables were often ridiculous. Add to that, these were the days before budget airlines. My ideal was to build a nest in my home town – something to look forward to at the end of whatever working week I would have and wherever it would take me. If I could make Gabrielle happy then I could shoulder whatever came my way, I thought.

Soon we found our perfect house in Belfast. Double the size of the house in Manchester. Four bedrooms, two bathrooms, a living room, a sumptuous lounge, a generous hallway, a large staircase, a state-of-the-art kitchen, utility room, double garage, outside storehouse and a big, big garden. Ideal for the big, big family I was hoping to have, and all for £120,000. That was the good news. The bad news was it only existed in a brochure and would take nearly a year to build it and the development it was part of. So, Gabrielle and Declan moved in with her parents and I moved in with my folks who lived a few hundred yards away just across the road.

Things were tough and the future was very unpredictable, but what was certain was that I had resolved that no one was ever again going to control how I worked, where I worked, when I worked, and how much in total I would be paid.

To this day I believe in the 'love many, trust few' business philosophy. I would preach to anyone that your freedom and happiness as a worker is better safeguarded by not working for a single employer. I had my fingers burnt by BBC North West and if I needed my view reinforced I had only to recall a planned family outing on St Patrick's Day when I was a child.

It was my father's tradition that he didn't work on 17 March, the patron saint of Ireland's day. The day wasn't only special to Paddy it was special to Leonard as well. And he in turn made it special for us. We all knew the routine. Best clothes, fresh shamrock pinned to our jumpers or lapels, off to St Patrick's Chapel in Donegall Street for a Mass in Irish and a blessing with St Pat's hand, which was solid gold and contained a relic of the great man. After that, next stop Holywood (pronounced as in the film capital of the world) in County Down, for lunch in a lovely little eaterie, then down to Bangor on the coast.

There'd be a bit of shopping along the seafront stores there, and invariably we always ended up in Woolworth's. I've always loved Woolworth's, always something for everyone. Daddy would head straight for the tools, Mummy would check out the latest Ladybird clothes for us, and me and my brothers would be split between the pick

169

'n' mix counter and the most wonderful displays of toys. Not Christmas toys, but the sort you just needed to get through the week – water pistols, footballs, dumper trucks, fire engines, aeroplanes, kites.

All that sea air in Bangor worked up a healthy appetite and the big treat on the way home, to save Mum slaving over the stove for all of us, was to call into the world's most divine fish and chip parlour – Long's in Belfast's Durham Street. So many brownie points would my dad clock up on this annual excursion that he would then have divine absolution from Mum to what was called 'drown his shamrock' with his mates down at the club. It was the one day of the year he'd get drunk, the only time he would be really visibly worse for wear. That was the tradition. He looked forward to it, she looked forward to it, and we looked forward to it.

This particular year, though, something was wrong. When we came out of Mass and got back into the car, Dad looked sad. Although he'd made arrangements to take the day off as usual, it turned out that his main paymaster was demanding he get into work, and he made his point in no uncertain terms. I remember Daddy telling Mum how much this man had sworn, threatened and shouted at him, telling him if he didn't change his plans for the day he needn't expect any more work.

Daddy was in such a quandary that his voice started to break and his eyes started to fill up. It's not a pretty sight to see a grown man distressed like that. It left me with an inherent hate for

170

people who demoralise others, who take away their dignity. In the intervening years I've always prided myself on being a good man to work for. Getting someone to do something better doesn't have to involve taking away their dignity and I react very badly to people who do it to others. My hero and role model in that was Dad.

'If I don't go in today, I'll never work for them again. I told them I'd be taking today off. It's just one day and they knew about it,' he said.

Mum was furious and her advice was what he needed to make his decision. 'Tell him to stick his job. You are the best they have. It'll be their loss, not yours.'

We were sitting cowered in the back of his Morris Oxford estate car expecting our annual day out to be cut short and to be brought back home. He took one look at us and said, 'Feck him.' Hurrah! Now for those that don't approve of parents swearing in front of their children, let me just say I might have been exposed to curse words, but more importantly here I was exposed to a great lesson for life – one which I went on to implement a few times.

This was a victory for the small man, for right over wrong, for the sanctity of tradition, for family life over the tyranny that work often imposes. He couldn't and wouldn't have made his decision without Mummy's approval. You taught me well, you two. Stand up against oppression and bullying, never be a victim, and with the support of your partner by your side, together as a family, you should achieve what you deserve – thanks!

171

The beginning of the nineties marked the start of a strange half-life for me, chasing after work, being apart from my family, pulling out the stops to clear my debts. With what I was earning, it was going to take a while. It was a worrying time. People often ask me, 'What do you want to do next in TV, Eamonn?' The truth is, it has nothing to do with what I want to do next. Presenters rarely decide what their next project is going to be. There's no point me saying I want my own talk show or documentary series. If the bosses don't want it, it won't happen, so they decide what you do next – not you. Being available at the right time and at the right price also plays a part – and boy was I available on both counts.

One of the programmes I got to work on was a debate show out of Newcastle for Tyne Tees Television. It was called *Late And Live* and it did what it said in the title at 10.35 on a Friday night. These sorts of shows occupied that slot in so many regions around the country, perhaps the most famous being *Central Weekend Live* from Birmingham. Often the debates were colourful, to say the least. One night I was about to orchestrate a big 'gay' debate. As I was addressing the audience before we went on air, I could feel the hostility from the gay rights activists who were in a very mischievous mood. Going live like this is a scary prospect, not helped by the strength of feeling that both sides conjure up over the subject matter.

Just as we were about to go live I dropped my pen and bent down to pick it up, with my back to the audience. As I did so, my trousers split right

172

around my backside. Now, these were in the days when there was no particular pressure on my trousers to split – about four stone ago. Well, as you can imagine, the gay lads loved it and although I asked them to keep it a secret as the opening titles rolled, I knew that was never going to happen. As the programme progressed the various wolf whistles made me aware that I was picking up a few admirers in the audience. But there was no containing them when at a particularly heated moment I asked someone from the anti-gay lobby: 'What are your feelings towards homosexuals on the whole?' Such were the whoops of delight and joy and references to the split in my trousers that the director had no other option but to take us to a very early commercial break, although it wasn't long enough to take the redness from my face.

Of course my agent also played more than her part when it came to finding work. So many presenters grumble about paying their agents' commission. I never have, partly because I have a very good agent, and this was one of those instances where she came up trumps.

Anita Land and I had at this stage been together for three years. Anita was born to be an agent. Part of the Grade family dynasty, she was the daughter of the theatrical agent Leslie, who booked stars like Bob Hope and Danny Kaye, and the niece of impresarios Bernard Delfont and Lew Grade. It was Bernard who brought the *Royal Variety Performance* to our screens, while Lew ran ATV, which made shows like *The Saint*, *Crossroads* and *The Persuaders*. He had a film

173

career too with movies like *On Golden Pond*, *The Pink Panther* and *Raise The Titanic* to his credit. Little wonder that showbiz and deals are in Anita's blood.

That aside, she's not only a bloody good agent, I could see right away that she was honest and straight (sometimes too straight!). It seems a funny thing to observe that an agent is honest, but five years of appearances in dance halls and discos around Ireland working for or through a dozen or so of them did more than raise a few suspicions, and led me to settle with a lovely lady I could trust in the form of Claire Kerley from Monaghan. But British television required a different expertise than Claire's and on the advice of Irish broadcaster and author Frank Delaney I set off from Manchester to London's big smoke to see Anita. She was the first and only agent I went to see. At that stage she represented daytime talk-show king Robert Kilroy-Silk, *Newsnight*'s Jeremy Paxman and the BBC newsreader Martyn Lewis, so would she want me? I'd put together a showreel of what I was doing on *Open Air*, and things that I had done at UTV in Belfast, and sat apprehensively as she watched it. It is so excruciating watching others watching you.

At the end of fifteen minutes in her office in busy Shaftesbury Avenue in the heart of London's theatreland, she was noncommittal. So I gathered up my pieces and said my goodbyes. I crossed the road and went to a phone box to phone Gabrielle, who was eagerly waiting to find out how I had got on. Even though my carefully crafted and dynamic ten-minute video showreel wasn't enough to get Anita to sign me up – that telephone call was. Later she told me how she stood watching me out of her window with her secretary Karen Baker and both agreed that they liked the fact that I hadn't imposed on them by expecting a cup of tea, using their loo or asking to use the phone. Because they felt sorry for me, Anita decided to take me on.

Incidentally, she is also the sister of Michael Grade, who was then controller of BBC 1 and is now chairman of the BBC. To back up her instinct she asked him what he thought of my showreel, to which he replied, 'He'll always work – he'll never be a star – but he'll always work.'

So far, he's been proved right on both points, because part of the reason I believe that I do continue to get work is that I don't exude star quality and that audience and employers alike aren't shackled by the limitations that brings. If in the early days Anita did feel sorry for me, in the intervening years I repaid her gamble. Certainly in the weeks and months after *Open Air* was axed, I was very grateful for her.

Keeping her ear to the ground as all good agents do she heard that some sports shifts for BBC *Breakfast News* were up for grabs. The money wasn't great, but there was a great willingness from the editor *of Breakfast News,* Bob Wheaton, to bring me on board. That compliment in itself helped make up for the lack of cash. Wheaton was a top man in BBC news. So often bosses can't see different qualities in presenters but Bob could see past the pretty-boy-

175

presenter thing and felt that I could handle myself journalistically. Bob Wheaton was the neatest man I had, or have, ever seen. He never had a hair out of place, five o'clock shadow or a single wrinkle in his trousers or jacket. There was never a stain on his tie; he was always impeccable. His attitude towards me, although never overly pally or tactile, was one of belief. I could tell he expected me to earn the respect of the other journalists in the newsroom, who at that time included seniors such as Nicholas Witchell and juniors such as Fiona Bruce. Bob Wheaton breathed self-belief back into me, and I will always be thankful for his quiet but solid support and understanding during personal troubles that were to come my way.

I found myself digs in London during the week. Having no one to go home to and having to make ends meet, I'd do three shifts a day if I could, writing and presenting the early sports bulletins, spending the rest of the day filming, and returning to the cutting room to edit whatever I'd shot for transmission the following morning, which I would then in turn again present. Often by the time I'd finished it wasn't worth going back to my digs, so I'd grab a couple of hours sleep in the Green Room or at my desk, wake up, shave, brush my teeth, put a new shirt on and there I was ready to be back on screen.

London only ever felt like a place to work and, every chance I could, I'd be out of there back on the next plane to Belfast – although it wasn't always the safest of places to be. In 1990 there were still bombs going off and people being

A courting Mum and Dad with Granny Holmes. Note the whitewashed backyard wall.

Looking like a snowball on my first trip to Santa, 1961. It must have been a cold winter that year.

Me and Granny Fitzsimmons outside her front door, 1962. Spookily, the building behind was where I would spend seven happy years at grammar school.

On Dad's knee and celebrating my fourth birthday at 161 New Lodge Road, 1963.

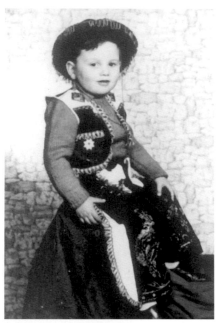

There were a lot of cowboys in Belfast — I was no different.

On holiday in Cushendall, 1965. I'm in the middle with Leonard, left, and Brian, right. We were so proud of our new leopard-skin trunks.

A sickly me on my First Communion day, 1967. Despite a bad reaction to penicillin I still managed to look whiter than white.

Dad with his Magic Carpet van — our family wheels for the first six years of my life.

What every young trainee shop manager aspired to: a hot suit and hot wheels. A Fiat worse than death. . .

In Woolworth's photo booth on my first date with Gabrielle, the hot summer of 1976. A slave to fashion, look at me in my Foster Grants and Adidas T-shirt.

In our kitchen, 1986, at my farewell party. The beers flowed and so did the tears after Dad (second from left, back row) sang 'Danny Boy' to me.

The next day on the Liverpool boat heading to a new life in England.

October 1987. Smile,
please. The wedding
party and guests —
yes, all eight of us.
(Dennis Hylander)

While filming Koo
Stark in 1988 she
turned her camera
on me. She also leant
me this great jacket.
(Koo Stark)

Learning from the masters. *(Anti-clockwise)* Five of the best there have ever been in the business: the king of Irish chat, Gay Byrne; 'Hello, good evening and welcome' to David Frost; enjoying craic with Terry Wogan; Des Lynam, who believes I owe him 10% of all my earnings, and on familiar territory in Belfast with the irrepressible Gloria Hunniford.

Only a mother could love a face like that — and me! Having a sing along with Northern Ireland's favourite housewife, Ms May McFettridge. *(Belfast Grand Opera House)*

1995 and on the town with BBC Breakfast colleague and friend Jill Dando, whose smile I still miss.

Misery — being held hostage by my biggest fan Ma, actress Olivia Nash, in BBC Northern Ireland's sitcom *Give My Head Peace.* *(BBC Northern Ireland)*

At rest in my 'luxury' GMTV dressing room complete with fold-out bed and Manchester United shrine.

In all my years I've found the best time of the day to present breakfast television is Dubai time. I never got the hump while filming there for GMTV.

Being crowned King of Breakfast Telly by the gorgeous Princess Penny Smith.

It was always a rush in the morning for Fiona and me to get into work on time. . .
(Nicky Johnston / Childline)

Lean on me, 1998. Fiona and I were great props for each other. You couldn't rehearse what we had.
(Kuldeep Kaur Channa)

Double trouble: the best chats between me, the Chancellor and the Prime Minister were always off screen and about football, April 2005.

A helping hand: in the twelve and a half years I was at GMTV, it was the interview I was most famous for. This cartoon, immortalising the infamous David Blaine interview, was Fiona's going away present to me, 2005. *(Michaela Blunden, www.michaelablunden.com)*

The long goodbye:
John Stapleton
delivering his farewell
speech to me on my
last day at GMTV,
2005. It was so good
I wish I'd written it
down!

Fiona saying 'Farewell,
partner'. There wasn't
a dry eye in the house.

Adios amigo. No
more 'See you in the
morning'.

Having a ball with Man Utd legend Ryan Giggs, 2000.

With the kids after a kick-about in the garden. You'd never think to look at him but Niall (centre) hates football!

Running onto the pitch with Man Utd against Newcastle, 2001.

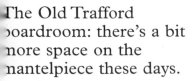

The Old Trafford boardroom: there's a bit more space on the mantelpiece these days.

'Declan, it's really simple — I just need you to keep Thierry Henry quiet for 90 minutes.' Talking tactics to my boy in the Man United dressing room.

'Fergie was here.' The Boss in my kitchen in Belfast 2003. There's now a blue plaque outside the house.

A new player hero of mine: presenting an award to the unstoppable Wayne Rooney, 2004. *(Empics)*

Believe it or not, this is Rod's back garden.

An eye for the birds: winning the Prince's Trust clay pigeon competition.

Prince Charles realising his mistake after asking me, 'Where did you learn to shoot like that?'

Happy times.
On holiday with
the kids —
always laughter.

That's my boy!
Me and mum in
2003.

Whiskers — that's
me. Eight out of
ten times
preferring them
on my days off.

Welcome to the world, baby Jack, February 2002.
With proud Dad and Mum Ruth.

And then there were four! I must find out what's causing this. . .
Declan, Niall, Rebecca and Jack.

Doctor in the house. Receiving my degree from Staffordshire University, July 2004.

'Hello pilgrim.' I never got to meet my great movie hero John Wayne but you can sure see the family resemblance with his son Michael.

No wonder Carol's Smilie — getting the chance to wrap herself around me! *(Pacemaker Press)*

At the 60th VE Day celebrations in Trafalgar Square, 2005. It was vital that I kept Natasha Kaplinsky's chest protected from the cold. Vital.

Good game, good game. Saturday night legend Bruce Forsyth joins me on my own Saturday night show *Jet Set* to push the lottery button, 2005.

I don't know why make-up artist Philippa Hall is looking so concerned — it's only taken three hours to look like this. . . *(Kuldeep Kaur Channa)*

My first pair of glasses. I thought they would stop me getting headaches during the *Jet Set* planning meetings but then I didn't bank on the effect of the producer Suzy Lamb! She knows I love her. *(Kuldeep Kaur Channa)*

Matching words and pictures. Behind the scenes at the BBC, 2005. *(Kuldeep Kaur Channa)*

Congratulations' if you spot it: Cliff's the one on the left. Interviewing the Peter Pan of Pop with my good friend, the stunning Tess Daly. *(ITV)*

All aboard! Having my tickets — and my leg — pulled by Girls Aloud for *Children in Need*, 2005.

Man in black — walking the line as Johnny Cash in *Celebrity Stars In Their Eyes*, 2005. If you think this is bad, you should have heard me sing! *(ITV Granada Manchester)*

Joining the lads who have to clean up Belfast for a 2005 BBC Northern Ireland documentary. Honestly, there's so much rubbish on TV these days. . .

Getting to grips with Ant and Dec's *Gameshow Marathon*, autumn 2005. *(Ken McKay / Rex Features)*

Following in the footsteps of real life couple Richard and Judy: hosting *This Morning* with Ruth, 2006.

Sky's the limit. A new start but at the same time, with my *Sunrise* co-host Lorna Dunkley, 2006. (© *Sky News* / *Justin Downing*)

The best of times, the worst of times. I said goodbye to a legend; George's dad Dickie had to say goodbye to a son, 3 December 2005. *(Empics)*

Brothers in arms. Conor, Colm, me, Leonard and Brian down the pub, Christmas 2005.

Growing up fast. My four kids with Granny Josie, 2005.

Taking the Mickey with Jack and Ruth, Christmas 2005
at Disneyland Paris.

Cheers. A night on the town with Ruth, 2006. *(Edward Lloyd)*

abducted and shot because they were the 'wrong' religion or part of the security forces. Eighty-four people died that year, more than half of them civilians. Paramilitaries controlled various territories throughout the city and policed and patrolled them. Many of their areas were clearly defined, but some less so, including where I lived in north Belfast.

After returning from London one night, I spent the evening with Gabrielle and Declan at her parents' house. My journey home to my folks' house would take only sixty seconds uninterrupted. It was just after midnight when I kissed Gabrielle goodbye on her front doorstep and crossed the main road. As teenagers when we were dating, she always stood and watched me until I disappeared into my street. To let her know that I completed the last fifty yards safely, I would let her phone ring three times. Being married must have made her forget our old routine. She closed the door and headed off up the stairs to bed. That left me alone, unobserved, crossing the main road and down into my dimly lit street; dimly lit, except for a car that swung around the corner and pulled up beside me.

Before it had even stopped, the back doors flew open and two hefty blokes with baseball bats leapt out. They ran at me yelling, lashing out with the bats. I thought I couldn't run as I used to all those years ago but amazingly I could. If I could run like that again, I could jump those hedges again – except I couldn't. There was much more of me hitting the landing pad than there was when I was a schoolboy. I knew straight away that

177

my knee was buggered. Once again it was fight or flight and even with a wrecked knee flight seemed the better option.

They must have decided I was more trouble than I was worth or they recognised me because back they headed towards the car and off it sped. I was nearly dead and Gabrielle had unwittingly gone to bed. In those thirty seconds, like so many other unfortunate souls, I could have been gone and she wouldn't have been any the wiser until morning. That's the way these Troubles claimed lives. It was a scary, scary experience. Trembling and in acute pain with my knee I phoned Gabrielle when I got home, questioning why we had ever come back to 'this place'. That was always the great contradiction of Northern Ireland – loving it and hating things about it all at the same time.

By morning, my knee had swollen up and I was in agony. I'd torn the ligaments. The knee eventually healed. My memory of that night never did.

If I thought that was bad, things were about to get much worse.

FIFTEEN

Losing My Father

I was sitting at Gatwick airport waiting for our flight to Spain for the Easter holidays. Doing what dads do, I was holding everyone's tickets. Noticing that the contact details needed updating on the back pages of the kids' passports, I started to fill in the next of kin addresses and phone numbers. I stared at those little photo-booth pictures looking out at me and there it was in print. I was officially responsible for them.

Doing what I did – anchoring a teatime news programme at twenty-two years old, providing for a young family – I had to become responsible at quite an early age. But when do you become a grown-up? After puberty? At eighteen? When you have children? I would suggest you become a grown-up when you have to. And most of us have to when a parent dies.

In 1991, I'd spent Easter at home, and returned to London after the long weekend to continue my duties with the breakfast sport bulletins. It was always tough heading to that airport, especially hard since Gabrielle was six months pregnant with Rebecca, our second child, but at least the new house was nearly ready and my dad had been round to measure it up for carpets. London was looking nicer as well, spring was on the way, and my new digs with a lovely lady

179

called Prue Geary in Fulham were pristine, clean and homely. Cherry blossom covered the trees that lined her street and I had begun to know some of the neighbours around the area, like Jill Dando and Catherine Zeta-Jones – maybe London had its plus points after all.

I was in for the evening, looking forward to watching a documentary on Gazza, then an early night, ready for that 4 a.m. alarm call the next morning.

My parents had spent the Easter break in their caravan at Ballycastle, a lovely, unspoiled spot on the north Antrim coast. My youngest brother, Conor, who was fourteen, was with them. The caravan site was a real home from home, full of Belfast people my dad was either related to or knew, and believe me if he didn't know them he knew somebody belonging to them. Among those who had a mobile home there was my good friend John Linehan, who you may remember used to be my motor mechanic and ended up becoming Northern Ireland's top entertainer as comedienne fishwife May McFettridge. John was married to my cousin Brenda and it was good to see things going so well for them.

I knew Mummy and Daddy were planning to come home that day, 3 April, the Wednesday after Easter, and I called to make sure all was well. It was teatime and there was no answer, which was strange. I knew they should have been home by then, so I tried again half an hour later – still no answer.

At just after seven o'clock my brother Colm called me. Colm and I loved football and I inter-

180

rupted to remind him that the Gazza programme would be on shortly if he wanted to see it. That, though, was the furthest thing from his mind. Quietly and sadly he told me that Daddy had collapsed and died of a heart attack on the road home from Ballycastle.

If the news of the death of a loved one is bad, the feeling of not being able to get home to them is worse. I needed to be there, I needed to see Dad and to hold Mum, I needed a flight to Belfast and I couldn't get one – they were all fully booked. But I couldn't wait until the morning. One of the other lodgers in the house drove me to Heathrow and, thankfully, there was a no-show for the last flight. I've flown to Australia before but this was the longest journey of my life. It was the early days of mobile phones, different brothers had heard different messages, and then a cousin phoned me to say that she had heard that Daddy had been brought to hospital in Coleraine. Did that mean he wasn't dead? Could there have been an awful mistake? I wouldn't know until I touched down on the other side. I prayed that I would get off at the other end and it would all be a misunderstanding.

Sadly, it wasn't.

When Mum and Dad had set off for home everything seemed to be fine, although Dad was driving at a snail's pace, which wasn't like him. Mum said to him, 'Leonard, what's wrong with you? We want to get home tonight, not tomorrow.'

He shook his head. 'I feel awful sick,' he told her.

181

'Well then stop,' she said. 'Pull in if you feel bad.'

When he stopped the car, it was clear something was seriously wrong. He opened the driver's door but didn't get out. He couldn't move. Behind him, traffic began to back up. My little brother sat helpless on the back seat as Mum did her best to comfort Dad. On a country road, in the middle of nowhere and with no mobile phone, there was little she could do.

Meanwhile, John Linehan and his family had stayed on in Ballycastle, intending to spend another night. Within minutes of my parents going, though, something made John decide that they would also head home. To this day, he doesn't know why he suddenly decided to pack up and go. He just had a feeling they should make tracks. A few minutes down the road he found out why. Three miles out of Ballycastle, on the Armoy Road, there was a tailback, which was unusual. John went to see what was going on. Up ahead, he saw Daddy's car – a Renault estate. They always had to be estates, Dad's cars. Mum, who couldn't drive, didn't want to ride around in a workers' van so estate cars were the only things big enough to carry the carpets on the roof.

When John got to the car, Daddy was still in the driver's seat. Mum had already flagged someone down who telephoned for help. Conor, loyal to the end, took on the role of an adult and was still on the back seat, leaning over holding on to his dad. He grew up a lot that night. Realising his distress, John steered him away from what was going on. He then knelt beside Dad.

182

'I just can't breathe – it's my chest,' my father told him.

As they waited for an ambulance, John kept talking to him until he became unconscious. He tried to resuscitate him but by the time the ambulance crew got there it was too late.

At sixty-five years old, before he could retire from work and spend many more days with Mum, a heart attack had taken my dad away from us.

As I arrived at Aldergrove Airport on the outskirts of Belfast, my friend Ronan Kelly came to pick me up and console me. Ronan had already lost his dad just a couple of years before. While my other brothers were running here, there and everywhere in the aftermath of the news, Ronan looked after me and brought me back to Mum's house, leaving us to our grief. To see my mother and youngest brother return home that night is not something I would want to see again. Her sense of loss, not only at losing Dad but from then on being lost in life, is something she never got over.

The next day, I gathered with my four brothers, Leonard, Brian, Colm and Conor, to do what we had to do. Although we were torn apart emotionally, not for many a year had we been so together. Our first duty was to head the sixty miles to the mortuary at Coleraine to identify Daddy's body. Being the eldest, Leonard took control and drove. Certainly, he had the right car for the job, a black Renault 25 saloon. And even in the midst of our grief it wasn't long before we kept each other going with Mafia jokes about how we all looked dressed in black in his black car.

Mortuaries are cold, clinical places. It was a terrible thing to see Dad lying there, incredibly painful for all of us.

I had last seen Daddy the week before Easter and he had seemed to be his usual self, although his health had been causing him some concern. His blood pressure was high and it seems likely he had already suffered a minor heart attack, which he had kept to himself. My brother Brian, who worked with him, remembers him taking a bit of a turn one day. The irony was he'd been to the hospital for various tests, none of which had detected anything wrong, but he was due back for one more. He didn't live long enough to make the appointment.

I suspect Daddy knew that all was not well, although he kept it from us. I remember a life-long friend of his, Frank Roberts, died the week before he did and I remember Dad being very badly affected by it. After Frank's wake he came into my room that night to talk about it. Normally after funerals he was quite upbeat with a few drinks in him but that night he had one of those talks with me about how everybody he knew was dying off. On the plus side he did give us a good pointer towards his own funeral, telling us what a great send-off Frank had had and how he would want 'a harpist like Frank's' playing him out. You got your wish, Dad. I'm just sorry it was so soon. I was also glad that I was living with him and Mum at that stage while my house was being built. That was the last week I was due to stay with him and it turned out to be the last week I ever would stay with him.

His body was brought from the mortuary to home, which is the done thing in Catholic Northern Ireland. To say Dad was a popular man was an understatement and for the next three days the house was full at all hours of the day and night as a steady stream of people turned up to pay their respects and reminisce. There were prayers and tears but laughter too and, inevitably, a few glasses. I don't think we were alone for a moment. In retrospect, that's always the most comforting time, when you have your family and friends around you. It's once the funeral is over and you're left to try and get back on with life that the sense of loss becomes even more acute. The funeral isn't the end of the grieving process, it's the beginning, and it takes a long, long time to come to terms with the fact someone you love is no longer there. It's not about getting back to normal, more about coping.

Before the funeral, we placed photographs in the coffin and said our goodbyes. Dad had always been very loving, always one to kiss his children, even as we got older. I still remember the familiar feel of the bristles on his cheek as I bent over to kiss him for the last time.

The funeral took place at St Patrick's Chapel on Donegall Street, at 9 a.m. on Saturday, 6 April, Grand National Day, which happened to be Dad's favourite sporting event. That morning, it was pouring with rain, absolutely pouring, but that didn't stop more than a thousand people of every religious and political persuasion and

185

background packing into the church, many of them having to stand.

On the coffin lay an arrangement of red roses and tiny white gypsophila – a copy of the bouquet Mum had held on her wedding day more than forty years earlier – but as the Mass began the priest, Father Martin Kelly – an old teacher of mine from St Malachy's – signalled to one of the altar boys to remove them. Why, I have no idea. When Mum saw her flowers being taken away, she gripped my arm in distress.

'Where are they taking them?' she said.

I gave her a squeeze. 'It's all right.'

I wasn't about to see her upset any more than she already was. As far as I was concerned, whatever she wanted that day, she could have. I got up, retrieved the bouquet and placed it back on the coffin. As the altar boy went to take it again, Father Kelly, seeing the look on my face, stopped him.

I felt the onus was on me to say a few words during the service, although there's no provision for that in the Catholic Mass. Usually, there are readings, nothing more, but when I looked round at the packed church I felt it was appropriate to break with tradition. All those people were there for my dad, which was a remarkable tribute to him, and although I was pretty choked up I did manage a few words.

We left the church, me and my brothers carrying his coffin. It was a gloomy day and the rain was so heavy that within minutes we were soaked through. The cortege moved slowly up Donegall Street, bringing the city centre morning

186

traffic to a halt. Up ahead, as the lights changed to red, we heard John Linehan's voice behind us. 'Typical Leonard – never did stop for a red light!' That was Belfast humour, that's what we appreciated as much as all the other lovely prayers and tributes, because most of all we knew that Daddy would have laughed. For a few seconds our six sets of shoulders – the Holmes boys plus John Linehan – shook up and down. We were carrying our dad's coffin and we were laughing – only in Belfast, only in Belfast.

The graveyard was five miles out of town. Needless to say, we didn't walk the whole way. Five years earlier when my uncle Gus died, Dad remarked on what a wonderful plot Gus had in the graveyard. Gus was married to my mother's sister, Phyllis, and both our families have always been very close. 'Look at the great view he's got,' Dad would say whenever he visited the grave – surrounded as it is by the Cavehill on one side and looking out to the vista of Belfast Lough.

So my brother Leonard and I bought the plot next to where Uncle Gus lay. That meant Dad knew where he was going to end up. It may seem slightly morbid, but Dad was happy knowing that when his time came he'd end up next to his good friend, and I have to say it was very comforting for all of us to know that he knew where he was going.

As we got to the graveside the rain continued to pour and Father Kelly passed round a small trowel holding soil so that each of us could toss a handful onto the coffin as it was lowered into the ground but that wasn't enough for us. We wanted to do something else too, something more personal, to mark the fact that Dad was the best carpet fitter in Northern Ireland. So my brothers and I threw not just a handful of soil but also a handful of carpet tacks down onto the coffin. Every day of his working life, Dad would have used tacks. As we threw them into the grave they clattered against the wood and the priest looked up in surprise. I'm sure people must have wondered what was going on. Now you know.

Afterwards, there was a reception at the Christian Brothers Club, where Dad went for his pint and a game of snooker on Thursday and Saturday nights, and where I had worked behind the bar. His memory lives on there because now they have an annual tournament for the Leonard Holmes Snooker Trophy.

After that day life of course went on, but it takes time to come to terms with losing someone you love. It was hard for all of us, particularly Conor who saw Daddy dying and lived in the same house as him, and Brian, who partnered him every day of his working life. The carpet business was called Leonard Holmes and Son and Brian has never changed that. People often ask me what I'm most proud of, and it's my brothers – how they've made their way in life, and how we each know that we would be there for one another if needed. If the chips were down they're the men I would want around me. Most of all I am proud of them because they have never betrayed the legacy of decency handed down to us from my mother and father.

There's not a single day that I or I'm sure any

of my brothers don't think about Dad or miss him but I suppose the best tribute he could have is that he lives on through all of us. I don't think I was anything like him in my twenties but, like the rest of my brothers, the older I get the more I can feel myself becoming like him, doing the things he did in the way that he did them. Some of us are even beginning to look more and more like he did.

Whatever our pain, his loss had to be hardest for Mum. We all had family or careers to get on with. She was totally lost without him. Everything that followed was, for her, a pale imitation of what had gone before. A part of her died with him. Despite the happy times they'd shared at Ballycastle, she never wanted to go back there again and to this day Easter is still a sad time for all of us. Those first signs of spring, the trees coming into blossom, should signal regeneration, a starting over again, but instead they just bring me back to the night I heard the bad news.

When it came to the headstone for his grave, we wanted something personal, and got the stone-mason to incorporate the illustration from Dad's business card. The card had, appropriately enough, been designed by Uncle Gus, a printer, and featured several rolls of carpets. Mummy then added her own message, using a code she and Daddy had devised years earlier when they first started going out together. I think my dad would have approved.

Some of you mightn't understand this, but all her sons know that to keep Mum happy, while a bunch of flowers, a box of chocolates or a meal out won't necessarily be guaranteed to do the trick, a visit to Dad's grave brings an instant smile to her face.

One problem remained. For several weeks after the funeral, Dad's car, that Renault 18 estate, sat outside the house. When it was there it was normally a good sign because we knew he and Mum were at home. Now every time any of us pulled up in our cars it just reinforced the pain. But the prospect of getting rid of it was also painful. This wasn't just a car; it was where he had died. No one wanted to face up to doing anything about it, but it couldn't stay there forever. In the end, I grasped the nettle and took it away.

I felt less like going to London than ever once Dad had died. I wanted to be around Mummy, give her some support as she tried to get on with life. All kinds of things were new and unfamiliar to her: paying bills, dealing with the Inland Revenue. Anything official-looking that came through the letterbox was a cause for concern. Dad had always handled all of that.

I had to get back to work, but I never felt the same about being away from home. The thought of travelling made me anxious, and claustrophobic when it came to flying. I associated being away with bad things happening, but on top of everything there were problems at home too.

SIXTEEN

Wilderness Years

If you're anything like me there's no room in your day-to-day life for things going wrong. Like me, I'm sure you haven't got time to lose your mobile phone and then have to reprogram a new one. Like me, you could do without one of the kids telling you they need their sports kit clean and ready, the problem being it's still in their kit bag, damp from last week. As I was lying on a wet road changing a tyre and cursing the white van men honking at my discomfort, I realised that people often think that if they become well known their problems will disappear. Sometimes being well known can create more than its fair share of problems and make recovering from them harder because you can't do it in private. Like most people, I've learned that life has a habit of knocking you down. That's not so much the problem. The problem is being able to get back up again... One of my great heroes, Muhammad Ali, put it like this: 'Inside of a ring or out, ain't nothing wrong with going down. It's staying down that's wrong.'

In the aftermath of losing my dad I became aware that my marriage wasn't all that it should be. Gabrielle was increasingly indifferent and I didn't know why. I needed her close, I needed her to reach me and ease my pain, but she had

191

concerns of her own, principal of which was an impending birth.

It was a desperate time and I was lonely and miserable racing around the country chasing whatever work there was. I pushed myself to the limit to keep busy, keep earning, keep a roof over my family's heads and keep mine above water. A job at, say, Yorkshire TV in Leeds would get me that all-important flight from Belfast where there was then no work for me, to England where there was. Whatever I earned – maybe a couple of hundred pounds – I'd spend on hiring a car to get down to London for shifts at *Breakfast News*, or to one of the ITV stations – in Newcastle, Cardiff or wherever. I did everything I could to make each precious job count, each one leading to the next, but it was incredibly tough and I was very much on my own. It was like being in a pressure cooker; inevitably, the lid would have to come off.

I'm not a good traveller and hated being away from home on *Holiday*. In contrast, some of the crew absolutely loved it, which never ceased to amaze me. They were separated from their loved ones too but most didn't seem to mind. They were stronger people than me. I would rather have been with my wife and kids. Maybe other people were better at coping with estrangement than me.

In Israel, we had been filming after dark on the waterfront at Tel Aviv when suddenly I started to feel unwell. I couldn't get my breath and the more I gasped for air the faster my heart raced. It seemed to have come from nowhere. All I could think was that I was suffering some kind of allergic reaction. A few minutes earlier someone had offered me some crispy snacks and, as I ate them, I'd noticed how spicy they were and how the flavouring had left a dusty residue on my tongue and the roof of my mouth. Perhaps that was it.

As I tried to get my breath, I started to panic. 'I can't breathe, I can't breathe,' I said.

The director and crew gathered round me, sat me down and gradually I calmed down and my breathing returned to normal, but it was a bit of a fright and I kept waiting for it to happen again.

A couple of days later it did.

We were in Galilee and this time it was the middle of the night. I woke up feeling dis-orientated in my hotel room, which was so dark I couldn't make out anything around me. The atmosphere was oppressive, airless, and my heart started pumping so hard I panicked. Again, I couldn't get my breath. As the room started to spin I managed to pick up the phone and call for help before passing out. When I came to, I was on a stretcher being lifted into the back of an ambulance. A paramedic was taking my pulse and wiring me up to a heart monitor. An oxygen mask was clamped to my face as I drifted in and out of consciousness, vaguely aware of the ambulance hurtling along, siren wailing. I was convinced what had happened to my dad was happening to me. I must be having a heart attack.

The paramedics thought the same since once in the hospital emergency room the state of my heart seemed to be of most concern. By then, I wasn't aware in any detail of what was happening. I think I may have been given some kind of sedative. I just remember drifting into the most wonderful, relaxed state, feeling utterly weak and wiped out, as if all my strength had deserted me.

I slept for what remained of the night and the following day the doctor arrived to check that everything was as it should be. It turned out that my heart was fine. I had not suffered a heart attack; I had suffered a panic attack.

In the cold light of day I was horribly embarrassed to have caused so much fuss. I went round apologising to everyone before going to the airport and getting a flight home. Being rushed into hospital semi-conscious had left me feeling anxious and fearful. Although there was nothing wrong with me, my symptoms had been real enough. I couldn't put my finger on precisely what had triggered the attack in Israel, but I suspected it was the culmination of a few horrible things in a very short space of time: losing my job at *Open Air*, being in debt, being without a home for so long, being set upon by men in masks with baseball bats, the increasingly distant attitude of my wife, and my father dying. After that lot it was hardly surprising I'd had a panic attack. I hoped it was a one-off but in the back of my mind I feared it could happen again, and that left me feeling incredibly vulnerable and nervous.

I also worried that ill-health would stop me doing the job I loved. Once home, I went for a check-up and was given the all-clear. I carried on working at an intense pace, commuting back and

194

forth from Belfast to wherever the work was. With my own talk shows in Newcastle with Tyne Tees Television and then later with HTV in Cardiff, what was I to do? Say to them maybe I shouldn't take this incredibly good job in case I have a panic attack? I would have been dropped as a bad risk. In TV land work follows work. You will either have too much or too little. That's the way it is – there's no in between.

Work was getting better, but I was not, as I was to find out a few months later on *Breakfast News*. It was the same old 4 a.m. start and I'd gone into BBC TV Centre in Wood Lane without having had any breakfast as usual. When I got there I drank a small bottle of Lucozade, which perhaps in retrospect wasn't the wisest thing to do on an empty stomach first thing in the morning.

I felt fine when I went on air at 7.20 a.m. Half an hour later, back in the studio with a sports update, out of the blue, midway through the bulletin, I felt my heart rate quicken and my breath shortening. I knew the feeling – 'Oh Christ, here it comes again.' Like a demon from the past back to haunt me and wreak havoc, it was in control and I was not. I had to leave the studio before the end of the bulletin. I simply linked to a film report and staggered off gasping for any breath I could snatch. I made it to the Green Room, hoping that if I could just lie down for a minute the feeling would pass and I'd be all right. Wrong. I passed out and had to be taken to Hammersmith Hospital by ambulance.

Anita, my agent, was the closest I had to next of kin in London and when I woke up in a cubicle in the accident and emergency department it was she who was there by my side. Again, I was embarrassed; again I felt unhappy and alone and just did not know how to sort out the pressure that was building up on my shoulders. If the papers had found out I passed out on air and had been carted off to A & E that would have been the end of my career. How they didn't I will never know, but I'm grateful that all the folk I worked with at BBC *Breakfast News* at that time kept it to themselves. Again, I went home, slept, and, later that day, caught a flight to Belfast.

Fortunately, my editor Bob Wheaton wasn't ready to write me off. Since I was freelance, he was under no obligation to offer me anything, and although I was obviously a liability to him he made it clear that, as far as he was concerned, I did a good job and he was prepared to keep the door open for me.

'Whatever you're going through, your job's still going to be here,' he said – which was incredibly decent of him.

Meanwhile, he arranged to bring someone in to cover while I took a couple of weeks off. My replacement was Bill McFarlan, a sports presenter with the BBC in Glasgow, who saw an opportunity to make his mark on the network. Bill was ambitious and didn't hide it. As far as he was concerned, he was there to take my job. That may have turned out to be the best bit of medicine I could have got. As I phoned Bill to thank him for standing in I was of course sizing him up at the same time, and we immediately hit it off. We were the same age, from the same

196

backgrounds, had followed the same career paths, almost identically, and both understood the pressures and responsibilities of being family men with youngsters. Spookily enough, we were each also married to our childhood sweethearts. Boy, did me and Bill have a lot to talk about.

From that moment on I never regarded him as a rival or felt threatened by him and, far from trying to see him off, I accommodated him, even found him a bed in the house where I was staying. We not only shared the same room in the same house, we shared the same ambitions and the same outlooks on life. Bill had that competitive sporting edge that I'd had instilled into me at St Malachy's, and what's more for the first time in all my time in TV I'd come across someone else who saw it as a business rather than a way to celebrityhood. As I got my strength back, Bill had made a good enough impression on Bob Wheaton to alternate the sports presenting with me while I went off and did other things. It turned out to be a very good arrangement for all concerned.

We were very often in London on different nights, so although we shared the room at Prue's we split the rent, which began to make living in the capital a less expensive option.

Bill was good company. Having him around meant there was someone to have a bite to eat with, play tennis or golf, or see a film with without a whiff of scandal. We worked hard but we enjoyed ourselves as well. London was becoming less alien to me because I had a regular mate to knock around with, and we still knock around with each other to this day. I am proud to call Bill one of my closest friends.

In the background was that fear of another panic attack, which was now making me nervous about flying. And flying was something I did a lot of, not only because of my commute, but also because of the *Holiday* programme. What if something happened in the sky? No escape, no doctors, no injections to calm me down. It was Anita, my agent, who suggested hypnotherapy. I'm extremely open to complementary medicine and, to be honest, I would have tried anything. Anita found me a doctor whose practice was in the attic of an elegant Georgian house. For a good few months, I saw him a couple of times a week. To my surprise I began to love those sessions under hypnosis, mainly because they were an oasis of peace in an otherwise frenetic life.

I was never sure if he did actually hypnotise me or because of the starts on *Breakfast News* and the schedule that followed I was so knackered I just drifted off. I'm also not sure exactly what he did to help me, since I was out of it whenever I was with him, but whatever it was it worked. By the time he'd finished I had my confidence back and no longer had a fear of flying. Today, to my immense relief those debilitating attacks that had twice landed me in hospital are a thing of the past.

Even though I was on the road to recovery, this hobo life I was leading wasn't compensated for by being on the telly. I poured my heart out to Gabrielle, saying that as a family I thought we

198

could get more out of life if I came home and got some sort of full-time job in Belfast. I thought she would be overjoyed but the look on her face told me otherwise. My whole motivation had always been my family; they were the reason to work so hard. I desperately needed her love and support. I lived for that flight home every Friday and got depressed at the thought of going back on Sunday nights. But I could see I was in a world that she was frightened of. We had developed two separate lives and I needed to find a way of making us one family again. Naïvely I believed the right job could do it – the right big job. It would enable me to buy a house in England to which Gabrielle and the kids could relocate. And, most important of all, the right job on the longest contract possible.

Little did I know that the job that could offer me all that was just around the corner.

SEVENTEEN

GMTV is Born

It's strange how people use words like 'star' and 'famous'. It's even stranger still who they apply them to and who believes the label. I'm neither famous nor a star. I'm just well known for being well known. To get to that position you've got to be on the telly almost every day for at least five years. A certain amount of skill can get you into that position but it's more likely

199

to be a very large dollop of luck. You don't even have to be a good presenter; you just have to have somebody in authority who thinks you're good and gives you the gig. That's how thin the dividing line is between people who make it on the telly and people who don't.

'A new day, a new year, a new television station – welcome to GMTV.' Those were the words written and spoken by my good self and which launched GMTV on January 1993.

I was the first voice but I wasn't the main anchor. Not that I minded.

I had regular work again and a twelve-month contract worth a whopping salary – which was exactly what I needed to get back on my feet. I talked things over with Gabrielle and she persuaded me not to move back to England from Belfast immediately but to wait and see how it went and whether I could eventually get a longer contract than the year I had been offered. After all, there were lessons from history here.

GMTV was replacing TV-am, which it had controversially outbid on its franchise, and although TV-am ended up being much loved by viewers, it had got off to a terrible start despite its 'famous five' presenters of Michael Parkinson, Angela Rippon, Anna Ford, David Frost and Robert Kee.

And history was about to repeat itself. As it turned out, not getting the main gig was a huge stroke of luck in my career.

With Anne Davis, I was the other half of GMTV's Friday and Sunday team, with Monday through Thursday the domain of Michael Wilson and Fiona Armstrong. Saturdays were devoted to children's programmes. Gone were TV-am favourites Anne Diamond, Nick Owen, Mike Morris, Cathy Taylor, Lisa Aziz and Ulrika Jonsson – instead, people waking up in the morning got us lot.

The viewing public don't take easy to change and this transition was to prove the point. They also don't like being told what they will or won't like. Michael Wilson and Fiona Armstrong were deemed to have the 'F-Factor' according to the GMTV publicity machine. But when asked to explain what the F-Factor was, they revealed it had four letters and ended in 'k', which in itself proved to be a bit of a f**k-up. The press seized on it and the public resented being told who they should find fanciable, preferring to be the judges of that themselves. The viewers weren't left to discover Michael and Fiona's chemistry cocktail – they were told about it in advance. In hindsight that was a mistake. A sort of public huff took place and people opted not to watch for a while. Michael and Fiona's fate would have befallen anyone in their position. Me being too minor to promote much in the press benefited by being part of the second wave of presenters to be given a chance.

Michael Wilson and Fiona Armstrong were the right people at the wrong time. Both were not only good at their jobs, they were good company as well. No one took delight at them having to fall on their swords after six weeks. It was particularly embarrassing for me to now have to take over the top slot but Michael couldn't have been more gracious. He took me out to lunch, told me to have no guilt and get on with the job.

Part of the reason GMTV was always in a state of crisis was basically because they had paid too much for the breakfast franchise. The sitting tenant in the form of Bruce Gyngell at TV-am had deemed it to be worth £14 million. The GMTV consortium bid was £34 million and promised everything from regional opt-outs to helicopter eyes in the sky monitoring morning traffic. Pie in the sky, more like. They were on a financial loser from the start, which not only led to changes on the screen in pursuit of the ratings but behind the scenes as well. The aces up their sleeves included the on-screen talent they had assembled, now to be shored up with TV-am favourites Lorraine Kelly and Dr Hilary Jones to help reassure the audience that although things were changing much of what they knew would stay.

The man who stopped the whole thing going down the plughole in those early days was the programme editor, Liam Hamilton. Only once before had I come across someone with such comprehensive knowledge of TV, and that was my editor at *Open Air*, Peter Weil. What Liam didn't know about ratings, viewing habits, presenters and general tricks of the trade wasn't worth knowing. Not only was he a superb administrator, together with Colm McWilliams at Ulster Television and Susan Woodward at BBC Manchester, he was that rarest of breeds – an intelligent, decisive, and almost always correct, gallery editor. Liam knew live television. People like these are air-traffic controllers to my pilot. With their directions and decisions I had no fear flying, whatever the conditions.

As I've said, I've always believed that as a presenter I'm not paid for when it's going right, I'm paid for when it's going wrong, and at GMTV it was – big time! The job itself held no fear for me. It was what I'd done at UTV for four years and on BBC Daytime for five. Getting people to notice we were there and trust us was the challenge. I believed that for people to watch first thing in the morning the items had to be a mixture of very interesting, very controversial or very amusing. Anything else was bland and you can get that anywhere. I also embarked on a much looser form of presentation. People at home are busy first thing in the morning. There are things to do against the clock like shave, brush your teeth, dry your hair, feed your kids, feed yourself, get your make-up on – and that's just the men – find your car keys, rush for the eight o'clock bus or train. If we moved with them, were flexible, reminded them of the time and the weather prospects while giving them the news in an entertaining way, they would find us of use. In other words, make it radio on the telly.

Not many in charge could envisage what I was talking about so I did it my own way. Stick to the script, they'd complain. That's exactly what we were doing wrong, I'd argue. Instead I would use the script as the foundation – but then get off it and come back to it when technically or editorially necessary. The effect is presentation that's informal-looking but is actually very

203

informed because the script is there as the basis for all you are saying. Not only did it look and sound better, it made me come across better than any presenter who chose just to read the autocue. The show that had proved so difficult for everyone to bring to life was mine for the taking. This is what I was born to do.

Like Cristiano Ronaldo on the Old Trafford pitch, I could show off all my tricks and turns and dance my way through a running order the way he can through defences. And it was football that gave me my next idea. Football was sexy again. The Premiership had just come into being and Man United were back from the dead. They were looking for their first top league title win in twenty-five years – and boy did the Liverpools, Arsenals, Man Citys and the like not like that. United were the team the ABUs loved to hate – short for those who wanted 'Anyone But United'.

Again, I drew on my childhood memories of broadcasting. I remember how the legendary Radio 1 and 2 DJ Ed 'Stewpot' Stewart had people shouting at their radios because of his constant adoration of his football club, Everton. Listeners knew it was just a wind-up. Even though they were poles apart, they were poles together as well. They only complained because they liked the banter, the interaction, the fact that they had a stake in the programme and someone was paying them attention. For this sort of broadcasting to work it's got to be a two-way thing. They blew a fuse or two but they liked the fact that Stewpot loved his team as much as they loved theirs. The Blues, the Toffees, Goodison Park, Alan Ball, Brian Labone, Joe Royle, I remembered it all fondly from the seventies. If people were watching GMTV – however few – I wanted them involved too.

So out I trooped each morning. If United had won the night before I never shut up about it. Then the complaints would start. If they lost I never mentioned it – until the viewers phoned in and complained about that too. Then I'd invent some obviously ridiculous excuse as to why we lost, which would wind them up even more. Such was my wind-up effect that one morning the London Weekend Television switchboard, in whose building the GMTV studios were housed, blew up. Rather than being pleased with the response I was ordered by a GMTV Ayatollah never to talk football again. Now since this guy knew as much about TV as José Mourinho does about losing, I went over his head and tried to convince the managing director, a very decent chap called Christopher Stoddart, that rather than rely on the LWT switchboard, we should get an operator of our own.

The result, as they say in football, was that I sneaked an away win. The proviso was that I couldn't give out the phone number, as he would only provide one phone line and one operator. So if anyone wanted to dial in desperately enough they had to go to the trouble of phoning directory enquiries, the theory being that would curb their enthusiasm and keep the numbers calling low. And so it remains to this day. So, if you've ever phoned in to complain or criticise anything on GMTV, that's why, despite the best efforts of Annie or Susan, you hold on so long. Enter a competition though and you'll be put straight through – I hope that's not because they like getting your money much more than your comments.

Talking football meant talking the same language as the people who were waking up with us. It meant talking the same language as the supporters, as any mum who had a child wanting a new kit, or any husband whose mood that morning, like mine, was affected by the result the night before. It worked brilliantly. It started to get the programme noticed, which was a good thing.

Taking on the role of main anchor meant my commitment to GMTV leapt from three to five days a week. I'd be up at four in the morning and was often still in the newsroom at four in the afternoon. The pressure was on to make this programme a success – but again with no family around me in London I could do it. What else was I going to do? Take long lunches and spend the rest of the night in the pub? Not for me. I was too practical and I was in a hurry to make up lost ground. I needed this programme to work for me to get a longer contract and bring about what I really wanted – my wife and kids by my side.

In the meantime, the flying back and forward between Belfast and London continued. And if anyone tells you commuting is easy, they obviously haven't done much of it.

EIGHTEEN

Airport Tales

If it all falls apart for me on TV I know I could definitely get a job as cabin crew, so often have I had to catch a plane. I can recite all that 'doors to manual and cross check' business in my sleep. Sometimes the journey can be made or spoiled depending on who you get to sit beside. Heading from London to turn on the Christmas lights in Belfast in December 2005, pop star Rachel Stevens's journey may have seemed longer than mine, but then the view was better from where I was sitting. Until, that is, the pilot was told to abort his landing because of fog. Such manoeuvres surely involve a gentle upwards curve back to 36,000 feet, but this must have been the sort of G-Force astronauts experience on blast-off. Rachel may well have thought she was heading for hell with nothing to hold onto but me, but let's just say it was one of my more pleasurable flights.

In commuting by plane, it's not the actual flight time that's a problem, it's the getting to the airport, dealing with the delays, killing the time nibbling on all the unhealthy food in the snack bars and on board, realising too late you've forgotten your credit card, driving licence, favourite pair of shoes. Whatever you need, you can always guarantee it's on the wrong side of the destin-

207

ation. Then there are the days when your baggage goes astray or there are no taxis at the other end. I could go on for ever, just like some of the journeys, and forget any talk of it only being an hour's flight. The quickest I have ever been able to do Belfast–London, door to door, is three and a half hours.

Fridays were always my favourite days. I so looked forward to getting home. I remember one day being in 10 Downing Street interviewing Prime Minister John Major, racing to Heathrow, catching the 10.30 shuttle, and at 12.30 being in my jeans at the local council tip, dumping bags of rubbish. Our tip was overseen by a Persian Ulsterman, I kid you not, who wouldn't let me leave until I'd taken some saffron to cook with. I had no idea as to the value of saffron, but from the way he was acting I should be highly honoured ... so I acted just that. I don't think my wife would have been as keen if she knew its origin, but what she didn't know didn't hurt her.

I always marvelled at a man who had fled the madness of the Ayatollahs for the madness of Northern Ireland. My world often seemed a bit mad as well. I'd gone from Downing Street, mixing with the Prime Minister, to mixing with binmen – all in the same morning but in two different countries. Granted, both had a lot of rubbish to deal with in their lives, but often for me the contrasts and balances were strange. Sometimes it was hard to remember who you were and what you were doing. The real downside was being full of good intentions but finding myself so knackered that instead of playing with the kids I would often fall asleep. But at least I slept soundly knowing they were around me.

If Fridays excited me, Sundays just totally depressed me.

Belfast's International Airport was about twenty-five miles away from where we lived. From there it was quicker to take a short cut over the Black Mountain. The short route was along mostly dark, lonely country roads and it was a journey I dreaded, particularly in winter. These days Belfast's new city airport is right on my doorstep and incredibly convenient.

I hired a regular driver called Tom McElhone for that weekly run. The best thing I ever did. Besides being great company, Tom got to know my habits – which usually involved being late. He was a dapper man in his fifties whose cars, like him, were always immaculate. Over the years, he became a good friend. I was always envious of his Sunday night routine. Once he'd dropped me off he would regale how he would be off home to relax with a glass of red wine and a movie, which sounded very appealing. I'd often think as he was doing that, I'd be watching a safety demonstration for the umpteenth time before take-off.

Tom was always on good form but one night he told me his health had been bothering him. He'd been suffering so badly with heartburn he went to his doctor to see what was going on. It turned out heartburn was the least of his worries; he needed major heart surgery.

'They're going to do a triple by-pass,' he said.

I was shocked. He looked so well. 'What, just like that?'

209

He nodded. 'Just like that.'

Clearly, Tom wasn't well and the doctors weren't going to hang about. He'd be having the operation in less than two weeks. In the meantime, he carried on as normal and when he drove me to the airport the following week he was in good spirits. He didn't seem in the least bit apprehensive about what was ahead of him.

'The next time you see me I'll be fit as a fiddle,' he said.

As we parted, he planned to return home, have his usual glass of red wine and settle down to a Western.

A couple of days later, he went in for his operation. His wife had promised to call to let me know how he'd got on, but when she did it was with the saddest news. Tom didn't make it through. He had died during the surgery.

I knew those journeys to the airport would be even harder without him. In so many respects, he had helped make them bearable. I flew back to Belfast shocked and depressed for his funeral and was honoured that his family asked me to speak about him at the service. I ended what I said with, 'So, my friend, I will continue to travel on that road, but it will feel longer and sadder without you. Whenever I make that journey I'll always think of you and the craic we shared.'

Sure enough, every time I go to the airport in Belfast, I do.

Part of my enthusiasm and energy for what I was doing died with Tom. A regular driver is important to someone like me. Love taxi drivers dearly as I do, the problem with getting a different driver for every journey is that they all ask you the same questions:

'What time do you get up at? Where do you live these days? Have you ever met so-and-so? What's so-and-so really like?' Sometimes it's all no problem, sometimes that's your second, third or fourth taxi journey of the day. The lovely thing about Tom was that he knew when I wanted to talk, when I wanted to use the phone, when I wanted to sleep, when I wanted a bit of craic or when I wanted a good old moan. The road was longer without him, but after a few months my brother Brian recommended someone he thought could help me out, and lovely Gerry O'Reilly took over where Tom left off and became my new man behind the wheel. For all those times you got me, not only safely from A to B, Gerry, but on time, thank you.

Whereas Tom often made me laugh, Gerry was very sensitive to my sadness. He could see how I felt every Sunday night, having put my children to bed and kissed them goodnight. If I had to wipe away a tear he would conveniently look the other way. Boy, how I grew to hate the theme music of *Heartbeat* on ITV. For me it signalled time-to-go time every Sunday, and Gerry was always there to make sure I did. Flight BD97 was waiting, and although I would often feel that I was the only person in the world having to do this commute, it was interesting to see over the years who else did it as well. The regulars included civil servants, politicians, property developers, bankers and lads who worked as builders and painters. Then there were the better-known faces, who were less frequent but always a joy to see, like the boxer Barry McGuigan, the footballer Gerry Armstrong or presenters like Gloria Hunniford or Patrick Kielty.

One night I'd been on John Daly's chat show on BBC Northern Ireland and I had to make the last flight back to London for GMTV the next morning. John's producers had assured me we'd be finished in plenty of time. Famous last words. We overran, and I started to worry I wouldn't make it to the airport in time. I wasn't the only one who needed to catch that flight – James Bond did as well, in the form of actor Roger Moore. The show dragged on because it was very complicated but very good. Roger, me and Irish chat-show legend Gay Byrne had to record a version of 'Singin' in the Rain', complete with water effects. Roger didn't so much sing along with us as speak along with us in his very proper English accent. He was absolutely hilarious. What wasn't so funny was that at 9 p.m. we were still recording, which gave us less than twenty minutes to get to the airport and check in for the flight.

To say we were cutting it fine is to put it mildly.

There was only one thing for it; hearing James Bond needed their help, Her Majesty's Royal Ulster Constabulary came to the rescue in the form of a police escort, complete with outriders.

Not only is Roger Moore my favourite Bond, he's one of my favourite people. So off we went, sirens blaring, lights flashing, and although it was like a scene straight out of an 007 movie, he was scared stiff as we tore through the streets of Belfast in a race against time. The more he held on to his seat the more I thought he was larking about but, 'No,' he told me, 'I don't like guns and I don't like fast cars.'

I was too busy laughing to care. I did, though, on that plane journey find out how much he cared about abused and underprivileged children. It didn't take long for him to sense my empathy and it was with great pride that I accepted from him a few weeks later in his capacity as a UNICEF goodwill ambassador the position of UNICEF ambassador for Northern Ireland.

My life seems to dictate that I'm always making a mad dash to the airport for that last flight, and on one occasion being in too much of a hurry almost got me arrested.

In 1995, President Clinton came to Northern Ireland basically to give the message that the Troubles were over. I had the honour to introduce him to 100,000 Belfast folk packed into the city centre on a bitterly cold November evening.

If you've ever managed to get anywhere near an American president, you'll know how tight the security is around them – honestly, it was just like you see in the movies. There were Secret Service agents everywhere, some visible, others out of sight keeping a discreet eye on things, and all in those stereotypical cream raincoats. All I was supposed to do was introduce Clinton on to the stage, but because of the incredible reception he received in Derry he was running very, very late. Boy, do they know how to talk in Derry. That meant my role became stand-in compere/comedian, for which I was woefully unprepared. So not only was it a cold evening, it was a long

213

evening. Time was ticking away and time wasn't on my side because again I had to be back to present the next morning and the last flight was at the usual ten minutes to ten.

I had plenty of time to rehearse my big line – indeed my only line, but a crucial line all the same. 'Ladies and gentlemen, please welcome the forty-second president of the United States of America ... William Jefferson Clinton.' Simple enough, until I came to do it and, you've guessed it – I tripped up. Well, Jefferson Clinton doesn't exactly flow off the tongue, does it?

Just before the president went on I found myself backstage with him and his wife, Hillary, the entourage having dwindled in numbers.

'You're doing a really fine job,' he said, shaking my hand.

'No, Mr President, it's you who's doing the really fine job. We really appreciate you being here,' I replied.

'Well, thank you very much,' he beamed.

I must say, of all the famous people I've ever met, Bill Clinton has got to be the most charismatic. His height, his striking silver hair, the way he's perfectly groomed, his smile, his eye contact, and that homely American drawl – no wonder the ladies were putty in his hands. I nearly fancied him myself.

A few years later I got the chance to meet one of those ladies. Monica Lewinsky had agreed to give me her first live television interview in the UK since President Clinton's impeachment. She was very engaging as an interviewee and at one stage I put forward what I thought would be

Clinton's view on something, to which she inter-jected quite sarcastically with, 'Oh, you know the president then?'

'Well, yes,' said I, 'I have met him – but unlike you I only shook his hand!'

She took the retort the way it was intended and buckled over in laughter.

After getting the president on to his Belfast stage I listened to his and Hillary's speeches. Both were captivating, but she was even more impressive than him – that shows just how good an orator she must be and why becoming America's first woman president is certainly not beyond her. But I had stayed as long as I could and needed to make a bolt for that airport. So off I sprinted across the lawn of Belfast City Hall. If I thought all eyes were trained on the star turns out front, I was wrong. That's the thing about Secret Service agents – they never take a minute off! It was like an NFL game and they saw me as the one holding the ball. One came out of the shadows in front of me and two came running from either side. At this stage I was happy to stop in my tracks and surrender – but they must have thought, 'To hell with it, we're all dressed up – we might as well do something.'

That something involved them all shouting up the sleeves of those raincoats and two of them tackling me to the ground. I think my next port of call would have been Guantanamo Bay had it not been for a very dapper man in uniform, a baton tucked under his arm, who vouched for my character. He was the then Assistant Chief Constable of Northern Ireland, Bill Stewart. The

215

ACC was finding the sight of me spread-eagled very amusing, but our American cousins didn't share the joke.

'No, no, no, boys – I know this man,' he said, which only seemed to heighten their grip on my neck and wrists, obviously fearing I was on some sort of wanted list. 'Honestly, boys, he's a bit of a TV personality here, you've nothing to worry about,' said the ACC. 'He's on our side.'

Another top cop, in fact the top cop in Northern Ireland, was the Chief Constable Sir Hugh Orde, whose rank couldn't help him when he and I were on that last plane out of Belfast the night it was hit by lightning – not once but twice.

Suddenly the plane lurched to one side. Bang! The right wing had been hit. Seconds later there was another judder. The other wing had been hit as well. Of course, him being one of the most important police officers in the world and me being a well-known public face, we tried to act as if nothing had happened. Then the woman behind us started to shriek. Like a banshee she was, and for anybody who doesn't know, a banshee is a ghostly woman who warns of death and wails quite a lot. I think both Sir Hugh and I wanted to wail as well but felt it our duty to look like tough guys and offer reassurance to her and a few of the other passengers. 'Oh, don't worry about this, it happens all the time,' I lied to anyone who would listen. Still, we walked away from it, and any flight after which you can do that is always a good flight in my eyes.

I spend so much time in Belfast airports that I know most of the people who work there on first-name terms: the check-in staff, the guys who man the X-ray machines and the cabin crews. Never let me hear anyone say a bad word about cabin crews. Down through the years they've always looked after me very very well. In the days before budget airlines put paid to the frills, BMI used to offer little champagne bottles to business-class passengers. My travelling companion heading to London on one of his many commitments was friend, solicitor and Belfast notary public Denis Moloney, who like myself rarely lets a drop of alcohol cross his lips. In fairness Denis is much more never than rarely, being as he is a member of the total abstinence society. However, with champagne it was a case of waste not want not, and if we couldn't use it Denis knew some un-likely recipients – the holy sisters at Westminster cathedral. The BMI girls could hardly believe their ears but Denis made such a case for the needy nuns that we left that night with two sick bags each packed full of quarter bottles of red label Piper Heidsieck. If his pleas are as good in court it's no wonder he's as respected as he is.

Two of the holy sisters also wanted to venture outside the convent to meet me – probably to help save my soul. It was with pleasure that I arranged for Sisters Clement and Barbara to see behind the scenes of GMTV and watch the programme go out. I don't know who was more taken aback – the holy sisters at watching S Club 7 close up or my production lot who had to follow my normal daily presenting example and refrain from swearing for a whole programme!

Appropriately, Belfast City Airport departure lounge provided me with the opportunity to end a long-running public feud in my life. Anne Robinson was one of those who would single me out in her newspaper columns for a pop. I could tolerate her 'A-Moon' pet name for me (being a reference to the shape of my face) but the straw that broke the camel's back was an article in which I believed she denigrated me as a father. She made her attack after seeing an interview I carried out with a 62-year-old who was using fertility treatment in order to conceive. To do this she had to go to Rome for the treatment because it was deemed unethical in Britain. This lady said that her age was no barrier to her being a good mother. I pointed out that maybe part of being a good mother was to be there when your children may most need you. In other words, the older she left it to become a mum, the less chance there was of her being around when this child was ten years plus.

Anne Robinson took exception to that and asked in her article: what did I know about being a good father? Was I around for my children? Hadn't I deliberately left them to seek fame?

Believe me, some pretty bad things have been written about me by critics over the years but none hurt me more than this. She could have said anything she wanted about me but I knew I had moved mountains, gone to almost super-human lengths, to be with my children for most of the important events in their lives, and any I had missed, believe me, were no fault of mine. Sometimes I can carry the weight of the world on

218

my shoulders but this piece completely floored me. I crumpled. It broke me. Suddenly everything was too much.

I had had a kicking in the press for having a row with Anthea Turner, for my increasing weight, for allegedly leaving my wife, but this was the final straw. However unjust I believed all the other attacks to be, this one was so far off the mark that it reduced me to tears. Mud sticks, and I couldn't even sue. I sought advice and was warned against taking action because this was just her opinion and, given the facts, it wasn't the most outrageous opinion to have. If I were to sue it would take time, energy, money, and my lawyer thought the outcome was by no means clear-cut, however unjust the sentiment was. I swear if Anne Robinson had been a bloke I would have gone round to the BBC, taken her by the throat and thumped her. There was no way I would have taken that slight from a man. Instead, I lived with the hurt and pondered not so much on the truth of what she was saying, but the perception. Is that what people thought of me? And worse – is that what my kids would grow up thinking of me? It just wasn't true. It didn't take long for me to know that the kids wouldn't and couldn't think such an aspersion would be true either. As for anyone else, well, that I didn't know. So began a sniping war between me and Anne Robinson – primarily directed from me towards her with any chance I got in various interviews. She responded a bit but not much. I even stared her out across the room at a select BBC function, refusing to sit at the same table as her and very definitely declined all offers to ever appear on *The Weakest Link*.

Then, on Sunday, 4 December 2005, in the departure lounge of Belfast City Airport, I was doing my usual thing of having a laugh with the ground staff girls when I noticed that the only other person in the British Midland lounge looked like Anne Robinson. Surely not, I thought – what the heck would she be doing in Belfast on a Sunday morning? It was the day after my birthday, a birthday which I had spent hosting the funeral of my boyhood hero George Best. There were a lot of people in town for that but I knew she wasn't one of them. I could let it go and pretend not to see her or I could confront it head on after all those years to lance the boil. George's death had put me in the mood to do the latter. I pointed towards her and she rose from her seat. Before I could get my words out she spoke across the room, saying, 'I owe you an apology.'

'Too bloody right, you do,' said I.

'No, I do, but you read an offence into the article that wasn't intended.'

'Of course it bloody was,' said I, as she clasped both my biceps. There then ensued a back and forward you said this, no I didn't, you took it the wrong way, I did not, read it again, Eamonn. Then with all sincerity, looking me in the eyes and still holding my arms (maybe because she'd read that I would have thumped her if she'd been a bloke), she said, 'I am really sorry.'

When a person says that to you there's not much more you can do but accept it, and she convinced me with her look, her grip and the way she said it that she genuinely meant it. Suddenly seven years of bile and bitterness towards her evaporated. I could feel it leaving me, dissipating into the ether. And it was a nice feeling. She asked me if I would sit beside her on the plane, and I did. It was one of the quickest and most pleasant journeys I've had in the thousands I've taken between Belfast and London. I could feel straight away that actually I really liked Anne Robinson as a person. She was intelligent, conversational, self-deprecating, humorous, very in touch with Ireland and things Irish and, in short, not the horrible witch that I had decided she was. How pleased I was that that anguish had been exorcised from me, and that she understood better that my children, their welfare and their future were quite simply my reason for existing. None of that would have happened without the flight to London.

If we're honest, flying is something that even frequent flyers like me are constantly worried about. I mean, it's not natural, is it? All that heavy metal kept up there by just two engines. I don't know about you but it's where I always rediscover my religious faith. It's funny how all those prayers you learned as a child suddenly come in very useful indeed on take-off, landing and when turbulence rears its ugly head at 30,000 feet. That fear is one of the reasons I don't like saying goodbye to loved ones at airports. I don't mind if I'm travelling, it's worrying about them in the air that unsettles me.

When my children were younger I'd never let them fly by themselves. I'd always make sure I was with them, and often that involved many,

many extra journeys just to chaperone them back to Belfast with me returning on my own. Journeys I could well have done without but obviously for which I would never have forgiven myself if anything had gone wrong. Now they're older, I have either relaxed my standards or I simply don't love them as much – only joking, nippers! Still, I've never got used to seeing them go.

Airports have always been sad places for me. You just have to look around and it isn't long before you spot upset faces and people hugging each other. If it was a long journey to the airport in Belfast on a Sunday night, I was to learn as the children got older it was an even longer journey seeing them off at Heathrow or Gatwick and returning back to my house in London. How over the years I have cursed that stretch of sea that divides us.

NINETEEN

Jill Dando

All of us who work on telly will have the odd moan about fans. How our privacy is at times breached when you would prefer it not to be. I'm very cool about it. If people didn't like us or like what we do then we wouldn't be on – it's as simple as that. And, anyway, aren't we all fans of someone at the end of the day? One of my closest friends in the business was a fan of the Peter Pan of Pop. Her girl-next-door persona made her, for a time, the most famous and liked telly presenter in the land. It drew thousands of welcome admirers to her but, tragically, it also drew one very unwelcome one.

In 1988, a breakfast presenter who positively dazzled first thing in the morning caught my eye. Jill Dando was the rising star of BBC *Breakfast News* at the time.

I was on *Open Air* in Manchester then but I'd often find myself doing interviews and items in London, and that meant a peek inside the hallowed halls of the TV universe in Britain – BBC TV Centre in London. It's a doughnut-shaped building that is featured in so many programmes, with an address that has appeared in even more. How many times have you been asked to write to BBC Television Centre, Wood Lane, London?

For me back then it was the home of Saturday night entertainment, *Top of the Pops*, and the *Blue Peter* garden, where Petra the dog was buried. These were the days before independent production companies, before John Birt sold off the BBC's silverware, before time and motion studies, and before cost-cutting. To walk the circular corridors of TV Centre was better to me than any magic created by a theme park. There'd be *Doctor Who's* Tardis sitting in one scene dock and Barry Norman's *Film* set, a *Panorama* logo and a *Grandstand* set stacked up until Saturday. All the sitcoms, big costume dramas and entertainment shows with bands and dancing

223

girls were recorded around TV Centre's studios. Even the canteen was buzzing with celebrities and famous faces and you never knew who you might bump into.

I just sat there on my own not concentrating on my meal and breathing it all in – what a way to earn your living, I thought. I'm being paid to visit all this. My daydream was interrupted when a statuesque blonde walked over to me with her lunch tray. 'Oh, I'm a big fan of yours, I've always wanted to meet you,' she said. Two things really surprised me about this incident. The first was that anyone was a fan and the second was that the words were uttered by Jill Dando, who had recently joined the BBC news team and was attracting a lot of attention. I laughed. 'Well I'm a big fan of yours too,' I said.

She sat down, we had lunch together, and it was the start of a lasting friendship. Jill and I hit it off straight away and from then on chatted regularly on the phone and met up when we could.

A couple of years later, we worked together for a while when I presented Sports for BBC *Breakfast News*. Jill's on-screen persona was often very proper but she was a real prankster and took great delight in trying to distract me from reading my bulletins. She knew that there were certain words that would trip me up or send me into a fit of the giggles. A situation made even more likely to happen because of the formality of the breakfast news programme at that time. She knew I had a bit of a problem pronouncing the name of an up-and-coming Croatian tennis player, Goran Ivanisevic, which is not at all pronounced the way it is spelled. I'd want to say Eye-van rather then Ee-van and I always, always got it wrong. To make things worse, Jill often used to slip off a shoe under the desk and, just as I was getting to a tricky spot of pronunciation, rub her bare foot against my leg. Naturally that didn't do much for my concentration. Although tempted, I thought it best not to return the compliment, primarily because she was going out with Bob Wheaton, the programme editor.

A few years later Jill called and invited me over for dinner as she regularly did, but there was a catch. 'Eams, I've got a friend coming round and I want you to keep him company,' she said, sounding conspiratorial. 'It's someone special and I know you'll make him laugh.'

'OK,' I said. 'What time do you want me there?'

'Eleven o'clock.'

'What?' I thought I'd misheard. Jill knew I had to be up at 4 a.m. the following day.

'Come a bit earlier if you like. Half past ten?'

'Half past ten! Who's coming over – a vampire? I've got work in the morning.'

'Oh please, please, Eams. It's important.'

'Who is this guest?'

'I can't tell you.'

'Well, if you don't tell me, I'm not coming.'

'It's Cliff,' she said, barely able to contain her excitement.

She wanted me in tow to keep Cliff Richard amused while she busied herself in the kitchen. The reason he was coming so late was that he was appearing in his musical *Heathcliff* around the corner in the Hammersmith Apollo. Every-

225

body knew she had a bit of a thing for him, even to the extent that the team on the *Holiday* programme had once specially arranged a romantic get-together for the two of them without her knowledge. She was sent to film a Viennese ball in Austria and Cliff turned out to be her mystery dance partner.

'For crying out loud,' I said, 'you don't need me there playing gooseberry then, do you?'

'Please,' she said. 'I'm really nervous about it. Come round earlier and help me get everything ready.'

Jill lived in a lovely white-fronted terraced house in a street called Gowan Avenue in Fulham, and at the time my place was only ten minutes away. We had a nice night preparing the food and catching up on the gossip. She was a fan of Heart FM on the radio and that was the music that provided the atmosphere that carried us through until 11 p.m. when the doorbell went and there was Cliff. Well, actually it was Cliff as Heathcliff as he was still in his stage make-up, complete with sideburns and coiffed hair. Before long Jill scurried out of the room – to go to the kitchen, she said, but I think it was to go upstairs and apply a bit more eyeliner.

Cliff and I got on like a house on fire. The conversation was lively and we were laughing so much that by now, with all the tears flowing, his make-up had run and he began to look more like Alice Cooper. When Jill came back into the room, Cliff was splitting his sides at a TV story I was telling him. Me being me there were a few expletives thrown in to colour things up a bit. Jill

226

was less than amused.

'Eamonn Holmes, how dare you!' she said. 'How dare you swear in front of my guest!'

She had to be kidding, I thought. She knew my form. I had spoken colourfully in front of her before and she had never objected. But it began to dawn on me that she was absolutely serious.

'Apologise for that language or leave this house,' she said.

I stared at her. 'You are joking.' Actually, to be accurate, I think I said, 'You are effing joking.'

But she wasn't. She was clearly mortified, convinced I'd offended Christian Cliff and that he'd be off before the first course was on the table. As it was, he was still wiping away all the mascara running down his cheeks. 'No problem, it's fine by me,' he spluttered through his giggles. And with that he saved my bacon.

I wasn't thrown onto the street after all and the three of us settled down for what turned out to be a lovely evening.

It must have been around 2.30 a.m. when things wound up. All of a sudden I wondered what the correct protocol was for leaving. Was I meant to go first and leave Jill to have a few words in private with Cliff? Would he leave first, so that there could be no hint of any impropriety? If I then stayed behind would he think that her and me were having a thing? While I was still wrestling with the permutations, the Peter Pan of Pop's driver turned up and we all headed to the front door to say our goodbyes.

'This is the picture the photographers would love,' he said, heading off. 'Cliff Richard leaving

227

Jill Dando's house in the early hours of the morning.'

'Yeah, and Eamonn Holmes leaving five minutes later,' I added.

Jill and I stood for a minute or two on the doorstep to assess how the night had gone. She was glowing with happiness. 'It was lovely, a really lovely evening,' she said. 'Everything went really really well, thanks to you.' She gave me a big hug and kiss on the cheek for my endeavours.

I never thought about standing on that step again until a little more than a year later. It was 26 April 1999, a gloriously sunny day, and I was in Belfast on a day off clearing out my garage when I got a call from Jane Lush, the series producer of the *Holiday* programme. What followed was just surreal, even thinking about it all these years later. She told me to turn on the television, that there were reports that Jill had been murdered on her front doorstep. The same front doorstep that I remembered as a scene of such happiness was now the scene of a hideous sadness. Like everyone else, all I could think was why? It made no sense. I'd grown up in Belfast during the Troubles and had survived all that shooting, all those riots, all those bombs, and there was Jill in sedate fashionable Fulham, shot on her own front doorstep.

Although I could shed no light on her murder I was sure the police would want to talk to me. Amazingly it was more than a year after her death before they got in touch.

The woman detective who spoke to me said my number had cropped up when they checked Jill's phone records. I told her the last time I'd seen Jill was at my flat in London not long before she died, that we'd shared a Chinese takeaway and she had left at around 1 a.m. The officer wanted to know the nature of our relationship. I told her Jill and I had been friends, to which she replied, 'Oh come on, Mr Holmes – you visit her home, she visits yours, with no other people present, and you expect me to believe this wasn't a sexual relationship?'

I wanted to quip, 'Unfortunately not,' but my sense of humour had deserted me. My beautiful friend was dead and I wasn't getting the impression the investigating team were any closer to discovering who had killed her.

In July 2001, a 41-year-old unemployed man, Barry George, was convicted of Jill's murder. He was said to be obsessed with guns and celebrity and was sentenced to life in prison.

TWENTY

Separate Lives

In December 2005, the financial details of my eighteen-year marriage were finalised and I, in effect, became divorced from my childhood sweetheart. We had been separated for the previous nine years. I always said I would never divorce her and I never did – she divorced me. It was a point of principle for me that it happened that way. Both our legal teams were

229

quite taken aback at how much we saw eye to eye.
And they were even more taken aback when, after
proceedings, my soon to be ex-wife and I chose to have
lunch together as opposed to discussing the outcome
with our advisors.

My story of separation and divorce is perhaps
different from most. The fact that it has worked
is a tribute to Gabrielle and myself and, although
a significant achievement, it's not something I
ever want to take pride from. Because it worked,
because it was civilised – despite the best efforts
of the media, and particularly the gossip writers.

My marital troubles were to teach me that
showbiz is a world where you can have few
friends and trust few advisors. The news of
trouble in our relationship hit the newspapers
after I had tried to seek professional advice in
handling any such situation. I confided in media
advisors in August 1996 and asked if a split was
to happen how would I release the news and deal
with any subsequent interviews. Horrifyingly,
within days my enquiry was on the front page of
the *Sun* newspaper.

That headline was what finally put paid to my
marriage.

Poor Gabrielle, an intensely private person,
who visibly winced and hurt in the public eye,
had to live her worst nightmare with a tabloid
headline that screamed: 'BREAKFAST TV
STAR'S MARRIAGE BREAK-UP'.

Think of waking up to that. Think of living in a
small churchgoing community surrounded by
relatives, with everybody knowing us, and being

told to go out and get the newspaper because we were all over the front of it. If it was a shock to me, it was catastrophic to her. Gabrielle rarely discussed her business with anyone. I on the other hand was a bit more of an open book, and my open-book approach had directly or indirectly led to this. Seeing scandal with your name on it on every shelf in a newsagent's is not something many people would be able to handle. In fact, you don't handle it; you just get through it the way you get through a bad dream – just hoping you wake up soon.

Except the wake-up call never came.

I brought the papers home. For every national newspaper headline there were another three to cover the Northern Ireland papers. On seeing the *Sun* headline in all its garishness, Gabrielle visibly gasped for her breath, her neck and chest flushed as she held her hand to them. 'That's it, there's no going back – I want out of this.' 'This' was not just the life I had brought her into, but also our marriage. For her, amazingly, there was no comprehension that with an increasing profile on television came an increasing interest from the press and increasing requests for interviews. She tried her best doing certain things but hated them all and to this day is still cursed with publicity photographs from the nineties being printed. Photographs announcing the birth of each of our children, for instance, personally vulnerable times, particularly for women, who naturally never feel they're looking their best after nine months of pregnancy and twelve hours of birthing pains. Pictures she didn't want to be in at the time but which the GMTV press office insisted on.

The *Sun* led with the story on 21 August 1996, and everyone else followed it up. Nothing could have prepared us for the invasion that was that day to come our way and the way of those who were around us.

It was like a siege. We lived in an American-style development of new houses. Open lawns, no fences or hedges, and camped out all over our front garden were reporters and cameramen. This was the garden my kids played on every day. This was the garden their little friends over the road ran across with wild abandon and happiness. This was the garden I had paid a hefty sum to a garden centre to design. It was mine and the press was all over it. For what? This was hurt and stress on a scale I had only experienced before with my father's death, and all these intruders were ringing my front doorbell, long lenses trained against the windows looking for whatever was going on inside. And what was going on inside? Just me, my wife and three very young children blockaded in our own home.

I couldn't get my head around Gabrielle's distance from me and there was no doubt she couldn't get her head around this sort of interest in us.

This was a scary, scary situation, not knowing who to trust, not knowing if your phone calls were being listened to, not being able to go about your day-to-day business, and all the time dealing with the normal requests children have, like, 'What's for breakfast, Mummy?' Who was going to pop out and get a fresh loaf of bread, a bottle of milk or half a dozen eggs? Having the press in our front garden wasn't a world we knew or one that either of us wanted.

While I felt that with the right help and advice around me I could evolve and adapt to this intrusive aspect of my job, I knew by looking at Gabrielle's whole demeanour that there would be no going back and trying to repair our relationship – the press had put paid to that. It was as if she had looked at the marriage contract and said, 'I never signed up for this. It doesn't say anything about all this in here.'

We had never been further apart yet, faced with a common enemy at the door, my only concern was to protect her and the children. If the press weren't going anywhere – f**k them, we were! The cavalry came in the form of one of our many lovely neighbours, Marita McMullan and her husband Eugene. Marita and Eugene had an escape module that was tailor-made for such an occasion – a Winnebago, a huge luxurious campervan on wheels. Normally it was only brought out from behind their house for their excursions to continental Europe, but now it was to form part of the great escape.

Our house was surrounded on all sides by an assortment of reporters, photographers and camera crews – all sides but one. Our back garden may have looked completely sealed off with fences and vast shrubbery, but you don't have children of seven, five and three and all their assorted neighbouring playmates without there being a warren of hidey holes, secret passages

233

and short cuts to each other's houses. So much for being representatives of the media's finest – not one of the crack troop of press corps raised an eyebrow when Marita's caravan on wheels trundled up our small cul-de-sac and reversed into a neighbour's driveway. We let things settle for half an hour then with Gabrielle and I both convinced that this was the best and most dignified exit open to her and the children, we executed the retreat.

This was our Alamo, the difference being that Davy Crockett didn't have a Plan B open to him. Holding hands, and with a suitcase filled with a few essentials, Gabrielle, Niall, Rebecca and Declan went off through the garden up the steep hill at the rear of the house and through a forest of rhododendron bushes. It may have been new territory for Gabrielle but the children knew it like the backs of their hands. Patricia Copeland was waiting at her kitchen back door and Marita at the front of the house where the garage was. The children and Gabrielle got into the Winnebago and lay down. Eugene started the engine, released the handbrake and gingerly drove past our captors. One wrong move, one stall of the engine, one smart Alec in the press pack, would have meant them descending like a pack of dogs on a rabbit. Worse still, Eugene had to pause the vehicle right outside our door to make a right-hand turn back up the hill. Flawlessly, he did his job, and for my wife and children next stop was a bed and breakfast in western Donegal; physically, as far as they could possibly go; mentally, the distress of that day went with them all the way.

234

That left me to face so-called colleagues. But there was no honour among thieves here. A member of the NUJ I may have been but as far as they were concerned I was a celebrity, and celebrities did one thing, they sold newspapers. At that time I couldn't see that. I couldn't see why anybody was overly interested in what was going on in my life and it was another of those occasions that I was to feel huge betrayal.

To this day I couldn't give anyone a definitive reason for Gabrielle drifting apart from me. Why? Because she has never given me one. In all the intervening years I've been left to speculate, to ask what if, to relive things in my mind, including career choices, and ask would it have made a difference? Now after a very long time I am confident nothing would have made a difference.

If I had no answer for the press, it left them with the opportunity of making up their own answer. Top of their reasons was that there must have been someone else involved – and obviously it could only have been on my side. It would fit their imaginary scenario perfectly. Wife at home in Ireland, tied to the kitchen sink with three children around her ankles, while playboy TV presenter husband was out clubbing it. God how they tried to make that story true. One newspaper held court in Belfast's Europa Hotel offering up to £10,000 for anybody who could come forward with the story that would attach me to another woman. While no one could come up with the story, I know of those who sniffed around the bounty promising to do what they could to come up with the sort of lead needed.

It's at times like this when you get to know, not just who your enemies are, but those who are prepared voluntarily and willingly to become your enemies.

Pictures began to appear in the papers of me allegedly 'out on the town'. All turned out to be me at various innocuous film premieres or award ceremonies with the picture trimmed conveniently to cut out everyone else in the party, leaving me and some poor female who I'm sure would have had no desire to be associated with me in the first place. The betrayal particularly hurt in Belfast with sneaky photographers long-lensing me at every opportunity. The only time I've ever seen a paparazzi picture of me on the front page of a Belfast newspaper, I was 'alone with my thoughts' on a mobile phone – except I wasn't alone. I couldn't be. Pictures like this meant that everybody had their opinions on my heartbreak, my confusion. My emotions were being recorded and disseminated for whoever wanted to pore over them. Hidden jealousies came to the fore among people of our own age group and in our social circle. Belfast, like many small cities, has a big 'keeping up with the Joneses' factor. Keeping up was fine, getting ahead wasn't. 'Of course he's been shagging around,' was a quote that came back to me from friends of friends on a number of occasions. Some men may have been complimented; the injustice hurt me really deeply.

Above my work, above everything I had achieved, above my regard for myself, I loved and adored my wife and children. They were everything to me. Everything I did only meant something if it related to them. There was nowhere I wouldn't have gone, nothing I wouldn't have done or sacrificed to make my marriage work and to be with my children. Everything was offered, including giving up my anchor job at GMTV and coming home to work at anything, not even necessarily in broadcasting. I know there is nothing more I could have done or could have given to make my relationship with Gabrielle work. That didn't mean, though, that I could just accept it. Nobody had ever been divorced on my mother or father's side of the family or indeed within Gabrielle's family circle. Not only was there excruciating personal hurt with what was happening, there was also massive moral, religious and social pressure heaped on mine and Gabrielle's shoulders and we had to live out every minute of it in public.

I was a completely broken man. I grieved for the loss of my childhood sweetheart and felt a complete failure. If my first girlfriend, the first girl I had ever kissed, didn't love me, who would? I couldn't see life or a relationship beyond her. She had given us the children we yearned for and whom we both adored, and although I was distraught at losing her I could have forgiven her anything, including the break-up of our marriage if she had made it right again. What I'll be for ever disappointed with both of us for is the break-up of our family unit.

I am as friendly and caring towards Gabrielle as any divorced couple with children can be, and although both of us know that our three children love us equally and hold no malice towards either of us, I still feel aggrieved at not being there every day with my youngsters. I never felt there was anything insurmountable in our relationship, and to this day I feel that whatever our shortfalls we had a moral obligation to be a family for as long as possible – despite our own personal differences.

I never felt those differences were much. If they had been, there is no way that Gabrielle would have allowed me to continue living in the same house for the next two years. Whatever our love for each other, which although damaged was still obviously there, our collective love for our three children was paramount. One of the reasons that the kids came through the break-up so well was that custody or access was never ever an issue. I don't ever recall Gabrielle and I even having to debate it. I saw the children whenever I was free and stayed in the same house. I don't even think the children were aware there was anything abnormal about Dad sleeping on the couch while Mum was upstairs in the bedroom. That was just the way it was. Outside that we had our meals together, we went to the cinema together, we went on Sunday outings in the car, we even went on holidays together for three years. Their happiness was our main concern.

Gabrielle would ease many of my natural apprehensions at being a weekend dad by assuring me that the kids had never known it any other way. I was there on Fridays and Saturdays and Sundays but they continued to be the shortest days of the week. With every spare minute spent with the children, other things went by the by. There was no 'me' time any more. How could I be away all week and come back home and spend five hours on the golf course? How could I spend Saturday afternoon in the pub with my brothers? Not only that but I could feel the condemnation, the sneering, the gossip, the finger-pointing. Everybody was talking about us, we were in all the papers and, ironically, the feeling that no one else was our friend meant that as a family we spent more and more time together.

Unlike me, though, Gabrielle is one of those people who once she has made her mind up has made her mind up. She accepted the separation much more readily than I did. I was always looking for a reconciliation, some straw to clutch at, some glimmer of hope – it was never to come. Magazines and newspapers speculated over how we could be apart yet be together. Sometimes it's hard to keep confronting your pain by being around something you've lost knowing it would never be in your possession again, but it was certainly better than the alternative. I just don't know how I could ever have coped having limited access to the children, knowing that I would only see them come school holidays or every other Sunday.

My anger swells towards people who automatically feel a mother should have immediate access to children in a family and that a father could never love his children the same way. But worse still is my anger towards absent fathers. Fathers who have the option of being around their children, indeed fathers who may even be in a working marriage but who choose to be in the office rather than tuck their youngsters up or play ball with them in the garden. I could never ever imagine having a little mini me out there that I didn't want to be with. More than anything else I have ever had in my life, my children have been not only the most precious gift but the most worthwhile. They are what energise me, motivate me, relax me. I am always at my happiest when they are around. Even if they are just there, not talking, watching TV. There's a warmness to be savoured knowing they're in the same room or house.

There are few things that parents can share with their children. Often their musical taste is completely different from yours, what they watch on TV bears no resemblance to what would interest you. Get into a political discussion and often parent and child are generations apart. But two things stand out for me – one is laughter. I have always lived in houses of laughter. Anything can be healed with a laugh, there is no better medicine. I'm blessed that above anything else I can take to my grave memories of laughing with my children around the dinner table. Memories of holidays not filled with magnificent scenery or balmy evenings but laughter over the most ridiculous subjects and scenarios. Declan, Niall and Rebecca are natural comedians and both their mum and dad love to share a chuckle. Gabrielle is one of those wonderful people for whom laughter and tears come simultaneously, the sight of which creates more laughter for those around. While our three children are naturally appreciative of a giggle, the youngest, Niall, is an out and out king of comedy – a young Peter Kay. More than anything they will ever achieve in life I will be eternally delighted at their ability to laugh.

The second gift I've found as a joy to share with children is sport – football in particular – and it especially helps if they support the same team as you. People think I may have forced my children to support Manchester United. This is not true. OK there was one stage when Liverpool had all those pretty boys playing for them – like Jamie Redknapp, Steve McManaman and David James – when I caught Rebecca sticking up pages from *Match* magazine of these and a few other Reds to put on her bedroom wall. But rather than take a heavy-handed approach I simply pointed out to her that she must have made a mistake. She must have meant to pin up the Reds of Manchester United. To that I may have added some remark about her being cut out of my will, but anyway she went through that little phase very very quickly and it's something we don't ever like to refer to in the family history.

Declan, on the other hand – now that's my boy! On match day Dad and kids are tuned into the same wavelength. 'Who do you think will be picked today, Dad? What about the referee? Isn't it time we bought a new goalkeeper?' We talk as one. When we lose we hurt as one and when we win, well, there's no better feeling in the world. To this day the biggest thrill I have in life is going to a football match with one or all of my children. Even if we are beaten, nothing beats that!

TWENTY-ONE

Car Crash Television

One of the things television loves is presenting twosomes. Even Ruth and I have done it on her programme This Morning. *In TV land couples should equal chemistry. In reality that chemistry can often turn out to be explosive. Famous television presenting couples on daytime or breakfast shows have included Anne and Nick, Frank and Selina, Johnny and Denise, Chris and Gaby, Richard and Judy, Philip and Fern and Des and Mel. One thing I know about all of them is that if any of them ever claimed that they never fell out, never had disagreements, were always in tune with each other – I'd just say 'Pull the other one'.*

Breakfast telly in particular thinks it needs its couples. Two people are supposed to give twice as much personality to the programme. That may or may not be the case. Certainly what they're guaranteed to bring is twice as many problems for themselves and for their production teams. Very few people are expected to work alongside a mirror image – someone who can anticipate the next move and think as they think. Renowned sporting partnerships, like Yorke and Cole in their glory days at Man United, Toshack and Keegan at Liverpool or even Torvill and Dean on the ice rink, bring the medals home. But while partnerships like this attract attention because they work, let's not forget most come a cropper.

Certainly don't confuse comedy partnerships with presenting partnerships. The first set works at getting on with each other, while the other set is just expected to get on with no rehearsal.

Famous twosomes like Morecambe and Wise either appeared in recorded programmes or worked from finely honed scripts. Like Ant and Dec, who are without doubt the best of today's pairings, the skill is to make what has been carefully thought through and practised look completely natural.

There's no such luxury in the twilight world of breakfast television where rehearsal time doesn't exist, many stories and interviews just break that morning, and ad-libbing takes the place of any Bafta-winning prose. Breakfast presenters are expected to be all things: serious when news is happening and comedians when it isn't.

Some presenters are very good at thinking on their feet, and some presenters can't even think whether they're on their feet or sitting down. That can lead to car crash TV, and sometimes the viewers quite like it. Car crash is a good analogy. To give you an insight into what live co-presenting on a current affairs magazine programme feels like, imagine yourself driving. You have the steering wheel but no control of the pedals – someone else has got those. They can decide whether to go faster or slower, when to brake and when not to. You also have control of the gear stick but they've got their hands on the indicators. You control the wiper blades but they can decide whether your lights go on or off. How long could you stick that for? As I said, 'car crash' – unless you're very good and, believe me, even the best get the sequence out of order.

In my time on GMTV I co-presented with Anne Davis, Penny Smith, Lorraine Kelly, Anthea Turner, Esther McVey, Kate Garraway and Fiona Phillips. Add to that a sprinkling of Jackie Brambles, Sally Meen and Sally Eden and it made for a few interesting combinations. Most worked; one famously didn't.

Anthea Turner was unveiled as the new GMTV female anchor in June 1994. I had been the male anchor for a year and a half by then, and had considerable experience in such roles prior to that, so you may be forgiven for thinking that somebody in charge might have asked me what I thought about working alongside her. In the event they didn't. It was a sort of arranged marriage and it was left to the bride and groom to make it work.

The first thing I knew about Anthea joining was when I saw it in the papers. That was to be a bit of a pattern with anything that orbited Anthea's world – sooner rather than later it would end up in the papers and, since I had now made an unplanned entry into her orbit, that was about to include me. I phoned GMTV's Director of Programmes Peter McHugh from Meridian Television where I had just finished another recording of the ITV afternoon programme *TV Weekly* and asked him if Anthea's signing was true. He confirmed that it was indeed the case and asked me what I thought. I pointed out that it didn't much matter what I thought as it was all a bit late now but, since he asked, I felt that editorially it would be a tall order for a girl who had no obvious journalistic track record or experience in our sort of programming. Bear in mind this was not the GMTV of today, which tends to bear more than a passing resemblance to a shopping channel. This was the GMTV of old where there was room for breaking news stories and we were expected to tackle serious issues like the war in Yugoslavia, banned marches in Northern Ireland or local government and European elections. Some of these things of course do not make good TV, but there was still an onus on presenting staff to be up to date with them.

While there is no doubt in my mind that I constantly irritated the hell out of McHugh because I raised the questions others wouldn't, I do think that under the surface he had a respect for my opinions and what I had to say. In the absence of advice, I offered him my full support for an appointment that I certainly couldn't fathom. And that support I gave wholeheartedly – for six weeks – then my patience ran out.

That's because, unlike the viewers at home, I was witness to two distinct sides of Anthea Turner. It shouldn't really have become my problem but I sort of started making it so. By annoying others she started annoying me. I think her perspective wasn't helped by those who surrounded her. Her career had been propelled into the newspapers. Anthea was a media darling,

245

and for the first time I could see how getting your picture in the press translated into getting a job. Some TV bosses love people who are in newspapers and magazines because it makes them well known. They still haven't twigged that viewers tend to like their TV programmes presented not just by well-known people, but mostly just by people who can do them well, and Anthea was at a disadvantage because she was learning on the job.

There's no doubt she brought a large sprinkling of showbiz dust to our little breakfast programme, but I found myself too often covering up for her on screen and pulling her out of holes. Now I was having to worry about two roles instead of just my own. At UTV and the BBC I had been constantly reminded of how important it was to get my writing spot on, ask the right questions, stick to the timings of the programme, hit junctions for adverts and weather bulletins and – most important of all – the end of the programme. After six weeks I knew my world wasn't Anthea's and her world wasn't mine. This pairing wasn't going to work, the bosses weren't going to change it, and for both of us it wasn't to be the happiest time of our broadcasting lives.

It all came to a head after the show one morning in March 1996. I felt Anthea was becoming increasingly diva-like and I don't do divas. I believed she was out of control and I decided I was going to hit her brakes. 'Look, Tippy Toes,' I famously blurted out, 'everybody else in this place might be frightened of you, but I'm not f***ing frightened of you.' The speech I came out

246

with is one that I would equally apply to myself. It's one that I think some presenters should sometimes remind themselves of. 'What exactly is your talent? What exactly makes you think that people like us are more important than anyone else? Do you know what you are? Like all the rest of us you're just f***ing lucky!'

The silence that followed made those words hang in the air. Anthea gave no response – she just went rather pale in the face. It was obvious that she wasn't used to being spoken to like that. I didn't enjoy the outburst and I don't enjoy recalling it, but I believed it then and I still believe it now. She then turned on her heel and took flight in tears straight up to the office of the man who hired her, Peter McHugh. After the tears were dried and Peter Powell, who was both Anthea's husband and agent, was called and informed, I was summoned upstairs.

McHugh hadn't appointed me – he had inherited me as he only joined GMTV after I was put in place by the previous head of programmes, Lis Howell. I always felt that in his eyes I was always the baddie in these situations. I knew that he knew my patience had worn thin with what I considered was the ridiculous situation he had landed the whole programme in by appointing Anthea in the first place. As a consequence we had become an increasing laughing stock in the business.

This was the first standoff of many between me and McHugh. After five years of trying to get my career back on track I had the job that every other prospective male anchor in the country wanted, and I needed it. McHugh also needed me. His viewing figures told him that my future and his were inextricably linked. I believe you should never threaten something you don't mean, and he knew me well enough at that stage to know that I meant it when I said, 'I've had enough – it's either her or me, you decide!'

At that Anthea burst into more tears and I slammed the door.

The rest of the nation was aware of the story a few days later as, amazingly, it made the front page of a daily tabloid. The spin, though, was that the big boss had 'banged our heads together'.

Another powwow was called at which a deal was done. It was agreed that Anthea would go – but not soon enough for my liking. I said I would stick the situation till the summer; they held fast to Christmas. Reluctantly, we had a deal. With the air cleared, on the surface the next six months were very cordial between the two of us. Though there were still those persistent newspaper stories that just kept popping up, slagging me off and questioning the state of my marriage.

What seemed to many to be a dream job was now a living hell. There was a bit of a concerted hate campaign against me in a few publications, I was increasingly sad at home in my personal life, I was living alone during the week, and finding fewer and fewer people I could trust or confide in. On top of that there was the 'Anthea camp' to deal with at work. You can only ever speak as you find and obviously that's what I'm doing. Other people found Anthea to be fantastic company. She had a star quality that many just found irresistible.

Her leaving day was 24 December 1996. Christmas Eve up to that point tended to be a nightmare day for me because of GMTV. Naturally enough, they only cared about their programme, which ran to 9.25 on that morning, but I had to care about being part of the Irish exodus leaving England and getting a seat on a flight back home. Not only would I have been up from 4 a.m. at the end of one of the busiest weeks of the year, but I would have to fight my way through the hordes at Heathrow, sit on the runway for an hour or more waiting for the world to take off in various directions, and once in Belfast do what any dad of three youngsters has to do on a Christmas Eve – get the last-minute pressies, wrap them up, visit Grandma, get the turkey and ham, get the drinks in, mend the Christmas tree lights, get to midnight mass – and then do all those little jobs that Santa's helpers never do, like build the bloomin' toys, which sure as heck need the only shape screwdriver you don't actually have! Then I'd flop into bed about 2 a.m., twenty-two hours after getting up, only to be woken by the three little angels themselves at about five o'clock wanting me to accompany them down the stairs. Did I sleep after my Christmas lunch? What do you think?

So forgive me if it seemed rude to the press but since the flight I needed to be on left Heathrow at 10.30 a.m., I had to leave the GMTV studio no later than nine o'clock to get there on time, and even that was cutting it extremely tight for a journey that could take anything from forty-five minutes to an hour and a half. Everybody on the programme knew I would be leaving at nine o'clock that morning and they knew why, Anthea's leaving day or not. I had bought her a Christmas present, I had said my goodbyes to her and things were very pleasant – until Boxing Day when my hard-earned rest was shattered by headlines of 'HOLMES SNUBS ANTHEA'. Not only the story either, but exclusive pictures in colour of me 'storming off the set'. That was the sort of crap I had to deal with. But if I thought that was bad, worse was in store. New Year's weekend and the Sunday papers made it not a very nice start to the day or the year. The *Sunday Mirror* screamed, 'WHY I HATE "PRINCESS" ANTHEA – exclusive by Eamonn Holmes'. The story in itself was a complete underhand sting. It was always the rule at GMTV that if presenters were slagged off in print it was just one of those things. However if the bosses' names appeared in print then it really was shit-hit-the-fan time. And lo and behold, in this *Sunday Mirror* exclusive there was McHugh's name and my opinion of him.

So I was awakened to one of his usual foulmouth tirades, never pausing for breath or listening for a possible explanation. I was guilty, that was that.

I was summoned back to London for what I can only call a preposterous kangaroo court. I'll explain more about the *Sunday Mirror* story and how it came about shortly but my real puzzlement was that if Anthea was an ex-employee, why was everybody getting their knickers in a twist?

250

Whereas nine months before I was prepared to resign rather than stay presenting with her, I wasn't going to this time. This time all the cards were stacked against me and I wasn't going to leave on the back foot. So the first thing I did was get myself one of the best lawyers in the land, Mark Thompson, who was then with legal eagles London-based Schilling and Lom. Bluster is big at GMTV. I may have had to take a lot of shit but Thompson wasn't going to. He was as precise and cold-arsed as it gets and he made them aware they were on very thin ice if they issued any disciplinary proceedings against me.

That *Sunday Mirror* story generated front-page news for a whole ten days, and how did it come about? From somebody who had worked in the GMTV press office. David Dillon had befriended me on the basis that we talked football. Cups of tea in the canteen on a Monday morning to dissect the weekend's matches gradually turned to dissecting the way the station was run. Of course, there were things that I would have said, the way anybody gossips about anybody at work, but little did I think that they were nuggets of information to cash in for the proverbial thirty pieces of silver. Unbelievably, Dillon was an ex-newspaper hack who had been given a job at GMTV guarding the secrets and image of some of the country's best-known screen faces.

Fine if Dillon had taken the whole credit for the interviews, but the *Sunday Mirror* headline had my name across it – by Eamonn Holmes. The misapprehension was that I had sat down and composed the whole piece. It was me who was

251

getting the flak and yet they all knew who the mole was. Still they continued to castigate me for allegedly slagging off an ex-employee.

The blows were raining down from the press and they were denting me big time. The pressure was unbelievable: the humiliation, the anger, the stress put on everyone around me, the obligation to carry on supporting my family, and at the same time being expected to go on air to wake up the nation in the morning with a smile, then present a live snooker tournament from Birmingham throughout the day and into the night for ITV.

Anthea was very comfortable with her relationship with the press at that stage; for me there was no relationship. I had gone from affable Irishman to blustering Ulsterman. That's another little thing that happens. When they like you you're Irish and when they want to set up a negative picture they describe you as an Ulsterman. The swords were certainly wounding me but let's not forget that old saying – those that live by the sword die by it. The pro-Anthea press was having its moment but how viciously it was to stab her when it no longer had any use for her.

I hung on in there but my relationship with GMTV was never the same again. From that day on there was basically no relationship and I don't feel that was a failing of mine. Anthea may have gone, but effectively I felt that from that time onwards I was finished there as well in the eyes of the management.

Nine years on I hold absolutely no animosity towards Anthea Turner whatsoever, although I still hold animosity towards certain people around her. Over the years papers loved to keep the so-called feud going by pulling out old quotes. When I eventually left GMTV they were at their tricks again. At that point I felt enough was enough and I decided to contact her. We exchanged regards and buried the hatchet. Her life had moved on and so had mine and neither of us I'm sure are the same people we were then. We all grow older, wiser and perhaps more mellow. I know in both our lives that things we cared about then are not the important things in our lives today, GMTV being the prime example.

Never was Anthea Turner even remotely the most horrible person I worked with in broadcasting. Not by any stretch of the imagination. What she was was a media magnet. I know she's genuinely in love and I hope she enjoys her health and happiness for years to come. What's past is past. What did I learn from the whole experience? I learned to be careful with whom I make small talk, that especially newspaper reporters can probably never be your friends, and I learned not to care so much about anything I ever worked on again, because it's like loving something you will never get to keep.

I raised questions about Anthea because I wanted the best for the programme, but I cared more about GMTV than GMTV cared about me.

I may have won the battle but I had lost the war. On screen, though, things more or less looked rosy. I was already the longest-serving anchor of a breakfast show in Britain and was probably at the height of my looks if not my powers. Look at my back, though, and you could count the knives.

So, now the Queen had abdicated, who would the crown be passed to? The answer was crystal clear to me. In our Los Angeles bureau was a blonde reporter – bright, sassy, opinionated, funny, lively and slightly on the edge. She had the X Factor. She was Fiona Phillips.

So many people on TV have the ability to drain energy from the screen. Fiona did quite the opposite. I had always enjoyed the two-way interviews I had done with her over the years. She got the stories, got the quotes and got the laughs. But would she get the job on the sofa? Not if I recommended her! My endorsement of any presenter or member of production was the kiss of death. Being in 'Eamonn's camp' wasn't good. And so it was with Fiona. The decision-makers had to believe she was their idea. Fine – whatever – as long as we got the right person in the job I didn't care. Fiona tells the story very well of how just before the mantle of co-presenter was bestowed on her, she was warned that 'she got on too well with me for her own good', and how she should 'keep her distance'. Thankfully, Fiona never did like being told what to do. So there was a new arranged marriage and this time I thought the 'bride' and I would have a pretty good chance of celebrating a few anniversaries. We got on with the job, which we thought we did quite well. With Fiona it was a new beginning, a whole new ball game, and a chance to do things

254

a whole new way.

One of Fiona's great pluses as well as minuses is that she tends to be unconfined by much of the formality studio presenting brings. At times she was a runaway pony and I relished trying to grab those reins and hitch a ride. Fiona and I decided pretty early on that we wouldn't hide our irritations with each other on air. No more 'nicey nicey', no more doing it like Anne and Nick – this was more like Stan and Hilda, *Coronation Street's* legendary warring husband and wife. It was good for our relationship and the viewers loved it.

Our different styles were united by the fact that we made each other laugh. Whereas the hard-working backroom team who put GMTV together every day couldn't object too much to the orders they were given, we couldn't keep our faces straight at some of the stuff we had to make shine on screen. It wasn't so much the items themselves as the juxtaposition of them. Families on the couch talking, and in some cases sobbing, about how for instance Dad's gambling debts had ruined their life, followed by us enticing people to pick up the phone and part with their hard-earned money by entering our competition as many times as they like. 'Go on, have a go,' the script would say.

Too often there was a lack of vision and direction. There were days you didn't know whether to laugh or cry. Most embarrassing of all was having to interrupt an interview with Prime Minister Tony Blair so we could run a sponsored item on Christmas turkey leftovers and what to do with them. 'Before we deal with a possible war in the Middle East and your relationship with the chancellor, Prime Minister...' Fiona and I linked to it the only way we could by making light of it. 'Can you, Mr Blair, tell us what you did with your turkey titbits?' People used to think as presenters we conspired to make things sound ridiculous – no, they just often were ridiculous. To the PM's credit, he laughed along. In fact, I'm sure everyone at home laughed along too. The only people who couldn't were our producers in the gallery. That's because, poor guys, they knew they had to face the bosses upstairs who wanted our lines played with straight faces. In my experience the bosses upstairs laughed at very little – especially themselves.

TWENTY-TWO

GMTV ... Good Times, Bad Times

The three things people most commonly say to me are:
  What time do you get up at in the morning?
  You look much thinner in real life. And:
  What was David Blaine like?
OK, well, they definitely say two of those things.
David Blaine, in case you don't know, does tricks.

In August 2001, like you, I didn't know much about David Blaine other than that he was an illusionist from the States with a reputation for

256

the controversial and bizarre. In the UK, he was only known for appearing in a Peugeot car commercial as a street performer. Now he was in Britain to promote a TV show in which he planned to make the Tower of London disappear. Very interesting – but not really to me. You see, I don't like magic very much. I'm interested in the supernatural because I can't explain it, but magic tricks just don't do it for me because that's all they are, tricks that anyone can learn. I need a bit of mystery with my magic.

My main interest in Blaine that morning was just to get him into the studio. Suddenly his people announced that he didn't want to hang around any longer and he was going back to New York. Rather than leave a five-minute hole in the programme, I ran out to the corridor and persuaded the producer and Blaine's people that if he would just hold on two minutes we could get him on as the next item. It meant a bit of shuffling regarding the other bits of that morning's programme but with seconds to spare I got his bum on the couch twenty minutes earlier than planned. In the rush and confusion he had created I didn't get to exchange courtesies and find out the basic things like what he wanted to talk about. It was important to find this out because truthfully I hadn't really got much I wanted to talk to him about – not, as it turned out, a good day to lack interest in a guest.

I knew I was in trouble right away when we showed a clip of him doing one of his tricks in the car ad and I enquired, 'How do you do that?'

He stared at me and said nothing. I tried

257

another tack – no response. Utter silence. So far, so bad. Seeing that tricks were his business I asked him curiously, 'Is it a trick to talk?'

He gave a shake of the head that told me 'no' without saying it. At this rate, it was going to be a very long interview. In my earpiece a voice in the gallery reminded me I had three minutes left to chat. The production assistant might as well have said three hours because those three minutes ticked by like the longest three minutes of my life.

I persevered, coming up with questions from nowhere that even impressed me, but obviously not him. It was as if I was speaking another language. I thought perhaps the staring eyes, the moody persona, the silences were all part of the act, so that was my next question.

Blaine shook his head – again no words, just a negative response.

'So it's just you?' I volunteered.

He nodded as in 'yes' and raised his left hand. Amazingly, on his palm was a drawing of an eye. Thank God, something at last to latch on to. 'What's that – what's the eye all about?'

Then followed the moment I'd been waiting for – a word! 'Pro-tec-tion,' he drawled.

'Protection from what?' said I.

'From death.'

Now there was a cheery thought. And I needed that protection right at that moment because I was dying on my feet.

At this point I was tempted to tell him to sling his hook on the assumption that he was jet-lagged, drugged or just couldn't be arsed. But

258

then a thought occurred to me. Perhaps he was ill. For all I knew he might have been a diabetic. I had witnessed this just the week before with the then GMTV weather man Simon Biagi. Simon and I had popped out for a bit of lunch when he gradually became abusive. It started with a couple of swear words and then an insult or two and then three ... he was normally such an easy-to-get-on-with guy that I was very taken aback until he asked me to get him some glucose tablets from his bag. After sucking on these he asked me if he had behaved oddly. 'You could say that,' I replied. And it was then that he explained to me that it was part of his diabetic problem if he didn't keep his sugar levels up. Could this be happening again before my very eyes on live TV with David Blaine? It would be awful if I had a go at him and moments later he slipped off the sofa and into a coma. So, I decided to give him the benefit of the doubt, and pressed on.

'Two minutes on the interview,' said the voice in my ear.

'Well, you've brushed with death a few times before. We're going to see the trick with the ice – tell us what you did here?'

We ran a clip of him frozen in a block of ice. He had spent three days and three nights like that, risking his life in the process it seemed.

Not unreasonably, I asked, 'Is it a death wish you have?'

'No, it's not a death wish. It's just that I love doing these things.'

He really didn't look too well and wasn't making much sense. Where was Dr Hilary Jones

259

when you needed him?

But at least he was talking – sort of. I carried on until, to my relief, the voice in my earpiece told me to wind up. 'I reckon life around your dinner table must be fun. There must be a great lot of conversation about death and the meaning of it … I hope the evil eye protects you and keeps you safe.'

He gave a chuckle, which was about the most animated he'd been all morning, and left.

As I said at the time on air when I finished the interview, 'Different, wasn't he?'

As if getting up early isn't ageing enough, doing interviews like that was guaranteed to add a few years. It's a lonely, lonely feeling trying to keep an interview going when you think the whole country is looking at you. If I was somewhat shocked at Mr Blaine's reticence to speak, I was more shocked that Miss Fy-ona hadn't made one single attempt to interrupt. Getting through an interview without Fiona getting a word or three in edgeways was something of a rarity. So where was she when I needed her? Holding back her laughter, that's where. I was about to wet myself through fright while she was about to do the same through hysterics!

Still, I had to see the funny side, and a couple of years later when he came back on the programme I was ready for him with my own 'evil eye' drawn on my palm. Amazingly, this time he was much more talkative. 'I was just having fun,' he told me, referring to our first tortuous encounter.

'I'm glad one of us was,' I replied.

I went to see him when he did his stunt in the glass box suspended above the Thames at the end of 2003. When he spotted me he scribbled a note on a scrap of paper and dropped it from above. It read, 'That visit on your show was so much fun. See you again.' He also did me the honour of passing his water on to me – drinking water from his bottle, that was, so that we could test it for nutrients and stimulants. By then David Blaine was one of the most famous people in showbiz.

No one had really heard of him before our first interview, but I tell you what, after that day, everybody had heard of him and I'll certainly never forget him. So, was the reluctance to talk one big publicity stunt? It could have been, but what if it had backfired? If I had known I certainly would have worn a better shirt-and-tie combination or thought of funnier retorts since he's guaranteed me appearances on blooper shows around the world for years to come.

David Blaine was an awkward interview to do but at least he was nice. Awkward and not nice is a much worse proposition. For that, movie star Meg Ryan fitted the bill perfectly.

I was despatched to Paris to interview her in 1995 for her latest film, *When A Man Loves A Woman*. In it she played an alcoholic, opposite Andy Garcia. It struck me as a very different role to the ones we had been used to seeing her in.

We set up for the interview in a hotel room. Usually, when you meet your subject for the first time, you get a sense of how forthcoming they're likely to be once the camera starts rolling. When

Meg Ryan appeared I can't say I got the impression she was falling over herself with excitement at the prospect of chatting to me, but never mind.

I had thought her performance in *When A Man Loves A Woman* was a real departure, and began by saying so. 'Is this a new Meg Ryan we're seeing in this film?' I said.

She gave me an icy look. 'And what's wrong with the old Meg Ryan?' she demanded.

In complimenting her, I had somehow managed to offend her. From then on it was downhill all the way. 'No, there was nothing wrong with the old Meg Ryan, it's just that a lot of people thought that this would be a girlie film,' I said. I was thinking of her previous star appearances in chick flicks *When Harry Met Sally* and *Sleepless In Seattle*.

Whatever she was thinking sent her eyebrows into upward arches. 'So there are girlie movies and boy movies?'

'Yeeee-s,' I tentatively nodded, thinking that's what she wanted to hear.

'No!' she snapped. 'There are only movie movies!!'

She also didn't want to discuss anything about previous films, her mother, her father or her then husband, actor Dennis Quaid. Needless to say, talking to her was not one of my career highlights. Before long the interview came to an end and, just when you thought that's the bad bit over, my producer bravely – or foolishly, perhaps – stepped forward and asked if she could have an autograph. 'You see, it's for my boyfriend, Miss

Ryan, he's a huge fan.' Miss Ryan didn't even raise her head. 'I don't do autographs.' I then thought it wiser to slip the camera I was clasping in my right hand back into my pocket.

Back in London, some careful editing and use of film clips salvaged what had been a very forgettable day with someone who was a complete pain in the backside. What we ended up with gave no indication of the glacial atmosphere we had to endure. I managed to make her look very good, which didn't help me when I tried to tell people what she was like in real life.

Because of her ditsy image on screen no one would believe what a cow she'd been. Until, that is, Michael Parkinson had the same sort of experience on his chat show ten years later. It was perfectly summed up with the following exchange.

'You trained to be a journalist – if you were me now what would you do with this interview?' said Parky in exasperation, having reached the end of his tether.

'Wind it up?' suggested Miss Meg.

Definitely a better actress than an interviewee.

Against that, many Hollywood stars are even better than they appear on screen. Dream chats for me have included John Travolta, Donald Sutherland, Martin Sheen, Dustin Hoffman, Sharon Stone and, even nicer than any of those, former agent 007 Pierce Brosnan. If ever there was a man who had reason to be chocolate and eat himself, Pierce was it. Too good-looking by far and with every bloke's dream job, yet I rarely came across anyone better mannered and more giving in an interview situation. He's also great craic off camera as well, swapping stories with me about his schooldays in Ireland under the Christian Brothers. For those who have never had the pleasure, they are the sort of paramilitary wing of the Catholic Church.

Another delight was Catherine Zeta-Jones – not only to interview but to see how well she has done. I knew Catherine around the time she was going out with telly presenter John Leslie and enjoying her first taste of fame in *The Darling Buds of May*. When I mentioned this on air Fiona was rather dubious that I could possibly know someone who had gone on to become a Hollywood star. When Catherine sat on the couch Fiona did one of those disbelieving, 'He claims he knows you well. How well would that be?'

What transpired next was an I-think-I've-died-and-gone-to-heaven moment, as Catherine reached across, held my face and said, 'Oh, about this well–' and kissed me on the lips.

I savoured the moment for as long as possible before turning to Miss Fiona and saying, 'See – told you!'

If only I had known her that well.

Another stunningly attractive lady who featured prominently on GMTV was Princess Diana. There was hardly a day went by that we didn't mention her in relation to the news, showbiz, fashion, health or family dilemmas. She was a perfect subject for the programme that we were, and as I was to find out the perfect viewer as well.

I met her in the autumn of 1993 at a charity champagne reception at the Landmark Hotel in

264

London. The timing could have been better. That very morning the state of her marriage to Prince Charles had come under scrutiny on the programme and in a phone poll we'd invited viewers to have their say. The princess had come in for a bit of flak although, in fairness, so had the prince. I just hoped she hadn't seen it.

When she arrived I was already chatting to a couple of people, one of whom was her lady-in-waiting. Then from across the room came Diana – tall, beautiful, elegant, and with the longest pair of legs I'd ever seen – heading towards me.

Her lady-in-waiting began the introductions with, 'Ma'am, this is–'

Diana interrupted. 'I know who he is.'

My jaw dropped. She gave me a dazzling smile. I melted. 'Oh yes, I often watch you when I'm in the gym,' she said.

For a brief moment, I basked in a warm glow. Princess Diana actually knew who I was. She watched GMTV. Then a terrible thought occurred. 'I hope you weren't watching this morning, ma'am...'

'I was!'

The warm glow turned to an embarrassed flush. 'I just want you to know I didn't agree with what people were saying,' I said.

Diana, however, wasn't in the least put out. By then, I suppose, she must have been used to having what was going on in her private life picked over in public. Instead, she started talking about Northern Ireland and the recent wave of violence there. Just a couple of weeks earlier an IRA bomb had exploded without warning inside a fish shop on the Shankill Road, killing nine people, including a seven-year-old girl. A week later, in retaliation, seven people died when Loyalist paramilitary gunmen opened fire in the Rising Sun Bar in the village of Greysteel. In the space of a single week, twenty-three lives had been lost in sectarian attacks and the mood was very volatile.

'It's terrible what's happening in your part of the world,' she said. 'They won't let me go, you know.'

'Who won't let you go?'

'The Palace. I want to go and show the people of Northern Ireland that I care. Do you think I would make a difference?'

I knew how much a visit from the princess would mean. 'You definitely would make a difference,' I said.

I told her I would be taking part in a peace march in Belfast that very weekend to try and stop the awful cycle of revenge tit-for-tat killings.

'Will you tell them that I do care and I'm thinking of them?' she asked.

I assured her I would. 'That's very good of you, ma'am.'

We had been chatting for a little while and she showed no sign of wanting to move on. 'What about the boys?' I said.

Prince William and Prince Harry had just gone back to boarding school for the autumn term. Diana's eyes filled with tears. 'I miss them terribly,' she confided.

'It'll not be for long,' I tried to reassure her.

'It's very, very hard being apart from them.'

Then, suddenly, her mood changed. She did a twirl and said, 'What do you think of my outfit?'

She was wearing a fitted green velvet suit trimmed with black. She looked gorgeous. 'It's very smart,' I told her.

'RUC green,' she said, referring to its colour. 'It would go down well in your part of the world.'

'Not necessarily, ma'am,' I pointed out to her, thinking of parts of the province where such a uniform would definitely not be well received. She started laughing.

After ten minutes in her company, I saw how anyone could be utterly bewitched by her. But just as I was beginning to think this could be love, that beefcake actor David Hasselhoff walked in and, quick as a flash, off she sped to greet him.

Her lady-in-waiting turned to console me. 'She really liked you,' she said. 'She never spends that long talking to someone if she doesn't like them.'

I was very flattered. Sadly, though, that was the one and only time I got to meet her.

Coverage of her death was to bring the station record viewing figures. It was a great tribute to us all that in those days people turned to us for the news as well as the lighter stuff. There was a great crusading feeling among the GMTV production team to go out there and punch above our weight; to try and compete with all the other news-gathering organisations. From the viewers' perspective one of the things we did best was put the presenters they woke up with every morning, presenters so familiar to people watching at home that they knew the names of their other halves and children, at the centre of the stories which mattered to them and affected their lives. For me those were stories like the Paddington rail crash, the Dunblane massacre and the Omagh bomb.

News of the Dunblane tragedy broke just as we were coming off air on the morning of 13 March 1996. A gunman had walked into the junior school in the small Scottish town and opened fire on youngsters aged just five and six years old. It had all the hallmarks of one of those terrible American-style shootings where someone runs amok in a classroom. Straight away I said we as presenters should get ourselves up there.

Making a dash for Heathrow Airport were me, Lorraine Kelly and a production team, knowing that soon the entire press corps would be streaming out of the capital and heading north en masse and there wouldn't be a seat to be had on any flight.

When we got to Dunblane it was such an incredibly sad scene, sadder than I could have imagined. It was then that my news sense gave way to my feelings as a father. This little community had been devastated by local loner Thomas Hamilton, who had gone into the school gym and sprayed shots at random around the room. In just three minutes he had killed sixteen innocent little children and their teacher before turning the gun on himself.

But work had to go on and we were there to do a job, to explain this story without sense.

At ten o'clock that night I went to the church hall where the police were issuing photographs of

268

the victims. But these were no ordinary photographs, these were class group shots. The same sort of class photographs that I had just got in the post from my youngsters' school. As I looked at the faces of the children smiling up at me, children who had now been murdered, I could easily have been looking at the faces of my own three. They were all in the same age group as these youngsters, all in the same type of school and the same sort of class taught by the same sort of teachers. Any one of those children could have been mine. Declan was then seven, Rebecca five and Niall just three. If any of those parents loved their children the same as I loved mine, how could they ever get on with their lives again? I couldn't hold back my tears.

That night none of us got any sleep. With so many reporters in the town accommodation was scarce to say the least and there was nowhere to stay. I had managed to get a room for myself and Lorraine to freshen up in at the Gleneagles Hotel, some twenty-five miles away. I'd spent my honeymoon there, it was a place I associated with good times, but was now a place touched by immense sadness. The hotel staff were extremely good to us and rustled us up something to eat in the early hours. There was just time to get cleaned up and put on a change of clothes before heading back to Dunblane, ready to go on air at 6 a.m.

The Dunblane massacre was one of the most moving stories I have ever had to cover.

Two years later, on 15 August 1998, I reported on another awful event: the worst terrorist atrocity Northern Ireland had ever seen – the Omagh bomb.

The bomb was left in a car on a Saturday afternoon in the centre of the market town, which was crowded with shoppers. It was planted by the Real IRA, a Republican breakaway group intent on wrecking the peace process. Police had received a telephone warning around forty minutes before it went off, but it was unclear and led to officers evacuating the wrong area, unknowingly directing people towards the explosion.

Twenty-nine innocent souls lost their lives that day and more than two hundred were injured or maimed. The victims were both Protestants and Catholics, men, women and children, people from north and south of the border, a twelve-year-old Spanish boy on a school-exchange trip and his teacher.

In terms of loss of life the Omagh bomb was unique in the history of Northern Ireland's Troubles. Where it wasn't unique was in its senselessness, viciousness and cowardliness. Like Dunblane it was perpetrated against the innocent.

The day itself was a particularly beautiful one, a marvellously sunny afternoon and the first day of the English Premier League football season. I remember it so well. I was sitting with my son Declan following the scores on Sky Sports Gillette Soccer Saturday when the news started to filter through of what had happened. God, how we all thought we had seen the last of this. How it brought back memories of all that people like me had lived through and which we now dared to hope our children would never have to.

It was a Saturday like the one when I nearly lost my mother and father in the Abercorn bombing twenty-six years earlier. The difference for me now was instead of being used to running from the scenes of explosions, my job was to take me to this one, and that's where I was to be for GMTV the very next morning.

When I arrived in Omagh, what struck me was the smell of dust that only an explosion can bring. There was also a sense of emptiness, of sadness, of death. With every step I took there was the crunch crunch crunch of glass from the shattered shop fronts cracking underfoot. Debris was everywhere.

You know if something is really evil when you see hardened professionals in the police and medical services looking as forlorn as the ones I saw. People talk about impartial reporting. What was there to be impartial about here? What was there to be impartial about at Dunblane? These were both sights where you could feel tragedy and the hand of evil.

There was no other side of the coin to show. I saw my job to speak not just as a reporter but as a citizen of Northern Ireland, someone who had to live with this terror in their midst. My story was the story of 99 per cent of decent right-thinking people there who just wanted to get on with their lives. The people of Omagh, the emergency services, welcomed me into their midst. I felt that I was representing the audience who watched GMTV and conveying their condolences. No door was closed to me, and indeed the members of the Royal Ulster Constabulary on the ground gave me such access that it provoked complaints from the other news operations of Sky and the BBC. I knew I was in a privileged position: they were reporters, I was Eamonn. Not wishing to abuse that position or create any fuss, I often declined vantage points, thanking the police for their help but explaining that although I was the only face they wanted in certain areas, it didn't really work that way.

This was one of those occasions, like Dunblane, where you have to be made of stone not to shed a tear. For me, it only took the list of the dead to be published, and the first picture was all I needed to see – that of an incredibly handsome young lad called James Barker. He was of a similar age to my eldest lad and looked quite like him. How would I have coped if that had been Declan? I couldn't have. The victim's mother and father had to. Indeed, at the time of writing they are still pursuing in the civil courts the cowardly bastards who were behind this. Ironically, James's family had moved back from the rat race in south-east England for a better quality of life in his mother's native Ireland. She blamed herself terribly and all she wanted was a better life for her husband and children.

I see some of the other families and survivors from time to time at the airport or when I am in Omagh or at certain events. People like Donna Marie McGillion, a nurse who was very badly disfigured, and to whom it was my privilege to present a *Daily Mirror* Pride of Britain Award the year after the bombing.

But one day in 2005, just when I was least

expecting it, a lady came up and tapped me on the shoulder where we live in Surrey, England. 'Do you remember me?' she said. I was at a loss. If she had not told me she was Donna Marie Barker, James's mum, I wouldn't have known. We sat down and had a cup of tea together and she told me the understandable toll the intervening years had had on her. News programmes move on, lives take longer.

Representing the station, representing the people of Britain and Ireland, representing programming that made a difference, programming that informed, educated and still wasn't afraid to entertain – that was when I was proudest working for GMTV. That's when our programme was a real two-way service, speaking to the viewers and going out there on behalf of them.

It was a privilege to be entrusted with that as a broadcaster. Few people can reach those heights and fewer still do the job properly when they get there. Understandably, it's a job lots of people want and some just want to take it away from you.

TWENTY-THREE

Sleep Deprivation

If I ever write another book it's going to be about the importance of sleep. By the time I caught on to the truth of the term 'beauty sleep' it was too late. My looks had melted like a tub of ice cream left out in the sun. If anybody ever tells me I look well on telly first thing in the morning I pass the compliment on to the make-up and lighting departments. These are the people who see how I really look. It's lighting and make-up who combat the effects of sleep deprivation ... in fairness, so do eye masks, herbal tablets, travelling with your own pillow, quite a lot of lavender spray and oodles of Night Nurse...

Breakfast TV is the right programme at the wrong time of the day. Traditionally it has offered all the variation you could want as a broadcast journalist, with one problem: it's six in the morning when really you want it to be six at night. Given the way my life turned out, it's ironic that I've never been good at getting up early. Sometimes I think I don't live on earth at all but that this is really purgatory and I'm being punished for the sins of a previous life. From my days at school when Father Murray stood at the top of the driveway ready to apprehend the latecomers, which all too often included me, I have had a

274

problem. It's funny how being paid to get out of bed helped ease that problem but I've never been one of those who wake up before their alarm clock goes off.

I think I could only get out of bed with a spring in my step if my bed was on fire – and even then I would still probably 'snooze' the alarm clock a couple of times. But I'm not the only person in the world who has to do it and across the land people have been very keen to share ideas with me, like setting three alarms at a few-minute intervals and having them progressively further from the bed and at progressively louder volumes. The flaw with that solution was my uncanny ability to get out of bed, walk across a room, turn off the clock and get back under the duvet without ever actually waking up.

One student wrote to me, telling me the solution was easy. Before turning in for the night, shower and shave, then put on your shirt, tie and suit, leaving more than enough time for an extra forty winks come the morning. Some other students advised me to seduce and go to bed with an incredibly unattractive member of the opposite sex. They assured me that, on waking, nothing would make me move faster! Just to set the record straight, I've never actually tried that one.

Other suggestions included installing a large mirror over the bed, which would apparently be a good motivator for being anywhere other than there looking at my reflection. The longer I live, the more effective I believe this could be.

But the one that really worked for me was realising what a lucky boy I was to be doing what

275

I was doing. That's what gets me on the go, still slowly mind you, because although the spirit is willing, at 3.30 a.m. you're still asking the flesh to do unnatural things – like move.

I've thought of all sorts of weird and wonderful ways to get to sleep and then wake up again. These have involved various lavender-based oils, ointments and sprays. I've also swallowed herbal tablets by the bucketful and, as a last resort, super-strength cold remedies. Now these are brilliant, they just make the waking-up bit even harder than normal. People often assume that you get into a pattern that can't be broken and that even when you have a day off you can't sleep late. I can truthfully say that, over fifteen years of early rises, that's never been the case for me.

Actually, getting up isn't really the problem. It's more what time you go to bed the night before and how deep your sleep is. The quality of slumber is as important as the quantity. If you've ever had that feeling of a disturbed sleep because you were worrying about the alarm clock not going off, then you will know what I mean. Add to that the concern that you may be interviewing the Prime Minister or the Chancellor of the Exchequer in the morning and you can see how a few tosses and turns ensue. Indeed a combination of those very factors led to the worst bad-hair day of my whole life.

I'd gone to bed knowing I had a big interview the next day with Chancellor Gordon Brown, and for whatever reason I didn't hear the alarm clock. Well, maybe I did hear it and switched it off, but whatever happened, I was late for work.

Up I sprang out of bed and leapt to the bath-room. A quick shave, but no time to wash and dry my hair – at least not if I was going to beat the traffic from SW19 into SE1 where GMTV was located. Better if I washed my hair in the make-up room, but still I couldn't go out looking like Ken Dodd. It was at this stage that I reached for some product. 'Product' to anyone who uses a hair salon is what they try to flog you after a particularly expensive or awful cut, with the words, 'Would you like any product, sir?' Know-ing the girl is usually on commission I tend to feel sorry for her and buy lots of stuff that I don't need nor indeed would ever know how to use, having had more or less the same hairstyle for all of my life. So I have the sort of bathroom that is full of 'products'. Things that make your hair shinier, things that make your hair straighter, things that make your hair thicker ... and things that make your hair stiffer.

Maybe it was because I couldn't get my eyes fully open or maybe I just didn't read the label, but I reached for something that was eventually to make my hair stiffer – a lot stiffer. Right then, though, it did the job. I opened the yellow top and applied the product within liberally. OK, I looked a bit wide boy but my hair was shiny and now flat. On reaching work my main priority was last-minute preparation for Gordon Brown's interview, and that done I assumed a short rinse of my hair and a quick blow dry was all I needed to do before going on air. Late – me? I now had minutes to spare – fifteen of them in fact.

As I leaned over the basin and turned on the

hose I heard a strange sort of cracking sound – like ice before it shatters. On applying the shampoo cupped in my hand I felt that my hair had suddenly gone rock hard. Lifting my eyes up to look in the mirror, all I could see was that my hair had, for want of a better term, crystallised.

'What on earth did you put on it?' asked Simon Jay, the makeup man, appalled.

'Er ... gel,' said I.

'Are you sure it was gel and not wax?' said Simon.

No, I wasn't sure, and as it turned out he was right. It was wax. If you ever drop melted candle wax into water I think you'll get the idea of what I was having to deal with here. Simon rushed to my aid and began to heap on copious amounts of shampoo. There were suds everywhere but every time we rinsed them off the wax was still there. It wouldn't budge.

The chancellor had now entered the building and was shown to a waiting room. I asked Fiona to cover for me but as she wasn't expecting to do the interview and had gone to bed without doing any preparation her initial reaction was not too enthusiastic. She comforted me with the words, 'What the hell have you done to yourself?' I knew what I'd done – I just wanted somebody to tell me how to undo it.

The harder we scrubbed at my hair the more uncontrollable it became. It was a totally ridiculous sight as I made my way to the studio. To try to paint the scene for you, it was flyaway around the edges with an Adolf Hitler lick in the middle. Not a good look, not only first thing in the morning but at any time. Catching a glimpse of myself in one of the off-air monitors, I simply had to own up to the viewers and explain my comical appearance. There was no point covering things up. People all around the land were looking and obviously thinking, 'What happened to him? Whose hair is he wearing today?'

These were the times that TV became truly interactive, not with phone polls and competition questions, but simply with people at home relating to me and me relating to them. I had a problem and they were going to fix it for me. The same solution came in by the hundred – 'Use Fairy Liquid, Eamonn.' Obviously I wasn't as big an idiot as I thought. Seemingly, people around the land apply wax followed by water to their hair all the time, judging by the response. Unable to face the chancellor in my comical state I simply relinquished the reins and said to Fiona, 'You take over, he's all yours.'

That's where Fiona was brilliant. Even when I landed her in it she disintegrated into tears of laughter. She was also able to share the joke with the chancellor, telling him I was so vain I couldn't face interviewing him looking like Coco the Clown. The viewers loved it. It must have been the most watched political interview we'd ever done on the station with everyone waiting for me to reappear. Believe me, it takes a while to find a bottle of Fairy Liquid in a TV studio at that time in the morning. Eventually we did and eventually the wax melted away. I think it took a lot of hair with it but I got back to near normal by 7.30.

All that before most people had even stirred from their pit on breakfast telly. You go from zero to 110 miles an hour all in the first two hours of wakening from your slumber. Think what that would do to a car engine, never mind the human body.

Then there's the body clock. You wake up and you grab something to eat before you go on air, usually the traditional bacon roll and a cup of tea. Three hours later, after the programme and a number of meetings, somebody often says, 'What about a bit of breakfast?' and you're at it again. Lunch can follow soon after and then if you ever do fall asleep in the afternoon, especially in the depths of winter, and wake up looking at an alarm clock saying five, six or seven o'clock, for a few awful seconds you don't know if it's five, six or seven in the morning and you've slept in. As you stumble to the window it's dark outside – but then it's dark in the morning as well. It takes a few minutes to tell the difference.

One of the biggest disturbers of sleep (besides children, football matches, a row with the wife or a DVD from Blockbuster) has got to be eating late. Take it from me, if your shift pattern changes to bring in early morning starts, don't have chicken tikka masala after ten o'clock...

TWENTY-FOUR

Ruth

I've had the pleasure of presenting with many more than attractive women. Some I've flirted with, but I've only gone further than that with one, and I didn't even get into trouble with the other half – that's because she was the other half. Many of you will know Ruth from presenting on This Morning, *one of the satellite travel channels, or reading out your birthday requests on West Country television with her hand up a rabbit called Gus Hunnibun.*

The first time I laid eyes on Ruth Langsford I was dressed only in a bathrobe. She on the other hand had on a vibrant red waterproof jacket complete with hood. That's because she was bobbing up and down on a fisherman's boat on her way to Rathlin Island and I was lying on the couch watching BBC1's *Country File* on a Sunday morning. I took notice of her because of her talent – other men would just spot her as talent. That was me all over, being impressed because she was good rather than being impressed because she was good-looking. And she was both. This is why, if the TV work ever dries up, I should become an agent.

I'm always aware of who's out there in the presenting world, who can do it, who can't, and

281

who's hovering around on the edges ready to break through. As Ruth continued to bob up and down, sea spray flying through her hair, doing a very good piece to camera, I remember being a bit mystified as to why I hadn't come across her before. She had obviously been doing what she was doing for a while but I had never seen her on the network before so I was intrigued, and having marked her ten out of ten – on all counts – I filed her away in the back of my mind. Watching TV on the couch was something I had learned to do very well. My estrangement from Gabrielle obviously meant that although we shared the same house we didn't share the same bedroom.

A few months later back in London GMTV fitness guru Derrick Evans, better known as Mr Motivator – incidentally, another raw talent I had spotted and introduced to telly – was holding a little party night at his home near Wembley. At the time I lived on the complete opposite side of London, in south-west Wimbledon. A near neighbour was GMTV weather girl Sally Meen, who was always a great one for encouraging people to get together and have a bit of fun. So while I had reservations about the trek across town to Derrick's place and having to be back again at a relatively early hour because of the next morning's pre-dawn start, she egged me on and, besides, she needed a lift. That was me – everyone's favourite taxi man because I very seldom drank.

Sally had a friend staying with her from her native Plymouth, a girl she had worked with in telly at TSW, who was coming too. As I pulled up

282

to Sally's house, there was a tall, striking, blonde standing on the street corner. I drew up to the kerb and I remember thinking, 'Wow, now where would you meet a girl like that?' Well, I was just about to. I hadn't formed the connection that this was 'the friend' but it was. Sally locked up her front door, came down the path and joined her. Suddenly I was very keen to go to Motivator's party. Sally got in the front of the car and introduced her friend Ruth, who sat in the back. Anyone who knows Sally will know that she's all talk. She talks very well. In fact, she rarely shuts up. But you know what – I never heard a word she said for those first ten minutes of the journey. I just kept looking in my rear-view mirror and there, perfectly framed behind me, was this picture of gorgeousness. How do I know her? I thought. I must have met her somewhere before. But if I had, how would I have forgotten? Then the penny dropped.

'You didn't do a report a few months ago from Rathlin Island for *Country File*, did you?' Somewhat surprised, Ruth confirmed that she had and that it was her first time in Northern Ireland. If I was thrilled at remembering who she was, she was even more thrilled by how impressed I was with her. It took us nearly ninety minutes to get to Mote's house. In a way it was a lovely journey but I wanted to get there and sit opposite this girl and find out more about her.

If you've ever seen Mr Motivator on the telly you'll know that he doesn't do understated. Dressed like an African prince complete in some sort of robe and hat, he looked a regal picture out

283

of his normal trademark multicoloured track-suits. A condition Mote had was that shoes had to be removed on entering his home. I remember that distinctly because as the evening progressed I found myself sitting on a couch with the not only lovely but now, I realised, leggy, Ruth Langsford, perched so elegantly, her flowing skirt carefully arranged to show off a pair of perfect pins. Suddenly her presenting abilities were becoming less important to me. It was lovely at last to have her to myself. I'm sure my irritation showed every time someone polite and well meaning asked either of us if we wanted another drink or if we had had enough to eat. Although my answer was always a very quick, 'Yes, we're fine,' what I really meant was, 'Yes – go away.'

If there's such a thing as love at first sight then I was prepared for it to happen, until she started waxing lyrical about her boyfriend. Bollocks – always the way. How stupid of me even to think there was a chance that somebody as gorgeous and captivating would be on the market. Quickly my ardour cooled and sensible me began to take over again. Funny how almost immediately I began to notice what time it was. 'Right, Sally, time to go – we've got to be up for work in four hours' time.' That wouldn't have mattered to me if Miss Ruth had entered into some flirting or had been single but I had come back down to earth with a bump and was quite annoyed with myself for having gone all a-flutter.

The journey back was much faster than the journey there. I said my goodnights to the girls and headed home. Next morning at work Sally could see that there had been a little sparkle in my eye towards Ruth. 'Now she was all woman,' I confided to Miss Meen, who, never being one to keep something to herself when she could tell somebody else, got the word back. Over the next couple of years Ruth would come up to London from the south-west and stay with Sally on three or four occasions a year. Sally was always very good at inviting me along to things when she knew Ruth was in town, which was nice of her, but in a way it was a sort of Chinese torture. I really had a crush on this girl and yet she was out of my reach and I was far too much of a gentleman to make an advance or stray into territory that wasn't mine.

Sally, bless her, knew how miserable, lonely and empty my life was outside of when I was with the children, and I'm sure tried to match-make. Ruth may well have found the whole thing amusing but she was very committed to her boyfriend. Then on one of those rare occasions she was up in town I ended up bringing her and Sally to dinner and hearing the fantastic ... I mean awful ... news that Ruth and her boyfriend had split up. She was very weepy and upset about the whole thing and although I should have provided a shoulder to cry on I think I became annoyed that she was annoyed. Jealous would be a better description. And so things drifted on for me and Ruth. She was now single, so was I, and yet nothing happened. I just assumed that she didn't fancy me, or why would she want to take on a bloke who was separated but still married and had three young children? I also, looking back, probably had this other failing in that I just couldn't stop talking about my love for my children and how much I missed them. It was only after we became an item that Ruth told me that far from being a failing, that's what made her love me.

'If you had been a man who denied his kids then you wouldn't be a caring man and the sort of man I knew I could love,' she told me.

If I thought getting together with Ruth was going to bring me short-term happiness, I was to be proved badly wrong. A lot of people were intent on me not having a happy ending. Far from allowing me to move on with my life, the press were mischief-making, trying to out Ruth as some sort of scarlet woman who had stolen me from my wife. As you can imagine, after a few weeks of being followed, having her telephone scanned, having members of the press posted outside her elderly parents' home and both of us constantly being 'papped' by photographers, relations between us were fraught. Neither of us wanted this attention. Neither of us could cope with the skulking about and the evasive measures we had to take. And neither of us knew if we could keep the relationship going.

Ruth was very frightened – I was very angry. I had to find out if there was a future with this girl, and yet because of my celebrity I wasn't being allowed to do so. Any secrecy on my behalf was because the children had never been officially told by their mum or me that we had broken up. What would it have meant to them? Gabrielle and I approached it on a need-to-know basis and over the past couple of years they hadn't had any need to know. Life for a seven-, a five- and a three-year-old was pretty simple, pretty stable, quite innocent – and I had intended keeping it that way until the situation warranted it. The press, though, felt they had a duty to get this information out into the ether around my youngsters before I did. I just didn't feel there was any need to tell them that Ruth was in my life until I knew she was going to be in my life for the foreseeable future. Of course, the less we wanted to be seen together, the more the appetite grew for photographers to prove the rumours. Again there was no shortage of acquaintances ready to provide details of where they thought we were going to be. Again the result was cutting off more people around us simply because we couldn't trust them.

Ruth was photographed filming on location, cars kept vigil outside a London flat she was now renting, and many of her friends in the West Country were approached for any lurid tales about her that they may have had. Even us having a meal with friends in a restaurant led to front-page pictures and headlines. But the most ridiculous scenario had to be us deciding to get away from it all and head as far away as we could – next stop, Cape Town, South Africa, thought I. It was a ten-hour flight and seemed another world away, until, that is, we stepped into the cable car that was to bring us to the top of the magnificent Table Mountain. As we got in, who was standing straight in front of me but one of Fleet Street's most illustrious tittle-tattle experts.

Writing about me has filled many a column inch for him over the years and it would often have saved his publishers much in legal correspondence if he had ever felt like checking some of the facts with me. I'm sure it was just a coincidence that the *News of the World* that Sunday ran a front-page lead in their Irish edition talking about me and Ruth on safari 'making love under the stars'.

In the absence of a picture of us doing this they printed one of a cheetah instead, which made the story half right because we did visit a cheetah compound, but anyone who knows Ruth will know that she doesn't do tents, so the rest of it was a bit of tabloid hype.

Despite the efforts and curiosity of many, Ruth did meet my children soon after. We both knew the relationship would stand or fall by their reaction. I can only report it as the start of a beautiful friendship between them all, challenged only by the news two years later that Ruth was expecting our baby Jack. When I told Declan, Niall and Rebecca, I was really shocked that they seemed shocked, and I realised that I suppose they had never even contemplated they would ever have a rival for my love and attention. It was a small hiccup that lasted only a day or so and was partly smoothed out with the help of Gabrielle's blessing for us.

This meant a lot to the children and to me. Since then I could never ask for more of a bond, love or affinity between them and their new half-brother. I have four children, each has three siblings, and both Ruth and Gabrielle have an everyday involvement in that. The children's acceptance of Ruth was a pivotal point in our relationship, and so was their reaction to Jack. Equally important were Ruth's patience, tolerance and understanding of my circumstances. I am as proud of her as I am of my children, all of them, and if we work as a unit and as a family it is because of the love and laughter between all of us. There are seven of us, including my ex-wife, who make these relationships work. That is the family we are; some roles are bigger than others, depending on the situation, but there is a flexibility and fluidity that puts the children's happiness as the main priority. Some may find that strange. I call it blessed.

Ruth Langsford came into my life and gave it purpose once again. She gave it direction, she gave it love and she allowed me to love again. With the grace that surrounds her naturally in life, Ruth became one of our family and added to it – not only with herself but with little Jack.

Come his birth, Ruth was determined that I shouldn't miss a second – whether I wanted to or not. Indeed, the very morning he was to arrive into the world I was on my way out the door to wake up the nation with GMTV. What Ruth interpreted as 'ghost contractions' I felt were something much more imminent – and good job too. At the last minute I pulled out of presenting the programme and instead persuaded Ruth to let me bundle her and that little overnight case she had so carefully packed into the car.

This is the sort of circumstance that shows how differently men and women think. Ruth didn't want to go to hospital for fear of the whole thing being a false alarm and her looking like a panicky first-time mum. As a man, fear of a false alarm was completely outweighed in my mind by the possibility I would be left all on my own boiling water in the kitchen the way they do in cowboy movies as Ruth screamed through labour pains. Better safe than sorry. Of course I didn't tell her this. I convinced her, having been through all this three times before, that I knew all the signs. In fairness, it didn't feel like a dress rehearsal – and it wasn't. What it was was the longest car journey of my life through the rush-hour traffic between Surbiton and Kingston Hospital. How that traffic snaked along and how Ruth's contractions grew in intensity and frequency. Labour is perhaps not the best feeling a woman will ever go through but it's often underestimated what it takes out of a man!

When we got to the hospital, she opted for gas and air. As things would take a few hours from there on in, I naturally went wandering around the ward – much to the delight of many of the expectant women. Well, I say it was delight, but there's every chance that most of them were in another world because of pain-killing drugs. The room Ruth was in was so hot and the duration of her labour was beginning to drain my reserves a bit. I'm not sure what began to annoy her the most – me not being in the room or hearing me laughing so much with the nurses outside. So, I was continually summoned back to her bedside – in and out of that room I went like a yo-yo. Then a special request: one mum-to-be's last wish before birthing was to hold my hand. I was happy to oblige but between doing this and dispensing words of comfort to those around her, I was beginning to feel like that priest they always wanted me to be at school. Having done God's work, God was in turn good to us and Jack was born, not only healthy but at around five o'clock, giving me plenty of time to get back home in front of the telly before Man United's Champions League match against Lille. Before I left there was the little matter of the baby's name. Jack was actually to be Alexander until I made the mistake of abbreviating it in front of Ruth. Not having had any drugs, the penny dropped immediately.

'That sounds like a football manager. I hope you're not turning out like one of those sad people who name their children after footballers?' she thundered.

'Moi? Of course not, dear.'

From there on in the Jack and the Alex were swapped round. But he was still named after two wonderful men – my Granda Fitzsimmons and the greatest football manager there has ever been.

If Ruth thought having Jack was hard, getting him out of the hospital without some sneak photographer invading our lives was harder. We didn't object to a photograph, we just objected to the whole world seeing him before our family circle could be gathered together to see him first. The length those buggers went to with their long lenses and their white vans with blackout curtains bordered on the pathetic. We couldn't even understand what all the interest was. Every time I called at the hospital, there was a snapper in the car park or in a corridor. Come the day Ruth and baby were discharged, the staff at Kingston backed up their excellent patient care with an excellent escape route. Little did we know until it was too late that it would take us through the hospital morgue. It was another little reminder that fame comes at a price.

TWENTY-FIVE

Man United and Me

There are a lot of things in life I could do without – football's not one of them. It's a reason for being high and it's a reason for being low. Sometimes it's just a reason for being. Over the years I have found it a huge comfort blanket – an escape from what is going on in the rest of the world or the rest of my life. In case you don't know, my team is Manchester United. There's a banner draped within view of my seat at Old Trafford that proclaims, 'One religion – MUFC', and that about sums it up. Let me let you in on a secret. Do you know how I manage to get up so early day after day? It's simple. I have a Wayne Rooney alarm clock – guaranteed to go off after an hour!

People think Ireland is divided into orange or green. Actually the predominant colour is red – Man United red. OK, there might be a little bit of Arsenal and Liverpool red in there too, but

292

United are the dominant red. People from the Emerald Isle love their English football, basically because we have no outlet of our own as the game isn't played to a very high standard at home. The other reason is that, as in so many other walks of life, Ireland has supplied some magnificent players to the beautiful game down through the decades.

King of those has to be George Best.

Belfast in the late sixties and seventies was known throughout the world as a trouble hot-spot. It was a small city that didn't have its sorrows to seek – they were all around. Civil unrest, religious intolerance, economic depression, high unemployment ... and despite all that we had the best footballer in the world. Not only had he the trophies, the skill and the looks, on top of it all he had the name – Best ... European cup winner, the fifth Beatle – and he was from wee Northern Ireland. He was one of ours. Whatever our differences we could unite behind George. With the genius that was Best, how could you not support Man United? He had a record about him in the charts, 'Belfast Boy', he had the long hair that everyone wanted, and he had the shirt outside his shorts that we were all clipped round the ear for trying to copy at school. He even made greed good. We all wanted to be as greedy with the ball as he was but we weren't him – he was a class apart.

Old Trafford then became the mecca for many people throughout Ireland to pay homage at the feet of the Great One. These were the days before cheap flights. These were even the days before expensive flights! Most of the few flights out of Belfast would have gone to London, and I had certainly never heard of anyone who had even been on an aeroplane. The route to Manchester lay by boat – the boat to Liverpool. What an adventure that would prove to be.

The year was 1972, I had never been anywhere outside Ireland, and neither had my dad or brothers. The initiative came from our family doctor. Dr Paul McKeown wasn't only our GP, he was a dear friend from childhood of my mum and dad. It was typical of my dad that as a man without an exam to his name he kept company with and felt easy with someone of the standing of Doc McKeown. The academic gap wasn't a hindrance because for Dad it was all about people and, credit to Dr McKeown, although a wise and learned man, he was without airs or graces.

The experience on the boat was all new and very exciting, leaving Belfast in the dark and waking up docking in Liverpool some ten hours later at seven o'clock in the morning. If the docking manoeuvre looked difficult it was nothing to the manoeuvres it took to set foot on English soil. All was going well on our football safari until we came to a security check. This was another complication of the Troubles. The Prevention of Terrorism Act was in full force and anybody was subject to its restrictions without very much explanation. Basically if the cops didn't like the look of you they didn't have to let you into the country, and there was something about our party that they didn't like the look of.

I think the disagreement may have been over identity. Now there was no point asking my dad for passports for him and us – we didn't have any – so while we were somewhat confused and befuddled as to what was expected of us, when they tried the same objection with Dr McKeown he unleashed the wrath of his intellectual capability. Now there was the difference I was talking about. Dr Paul knew he had that intellectual capability, he simply chose to speak on everyone else's level until he needed to step up a gear, and this was it – hairdryer-force on the men from the Home Office.

'How dare you prevent me as a citizen of the UK from moving freely within this country, with no reason or justification?'

'Under the Prevention of Terrorism Act I must remind you sir that–' came the reply from the plainclothes officer.

Before he could complete his sentence Dr Paul was throwing more than the book at him. 'I must remind you, officer, that I am a medical doctor and a physician to the British Board of Boxing Control. I am also on the medical ... blah blah blah.'

I can't remember what he said but whatever it was he said it very well. I could hear judges' names, a reference to the Hippocratic Oath and vouching for 'a man whose children I have brought into this world' (that would have been us). Eventually I think he just wore them down. After half an hour they were glad to see the back of him. From Liverpool it was a train journey into Manchester and then my first sight of an orange bus – orange and white buses everywhere around the terminal in Piccadilly. It's funny the things you notice and the things you remember, like black and green taxis in Portugal the first time I went there, or cream taxis in Corfu. With Manchester it was buses. We only had red buses with cream insets in Belfast and most of those usually had black smoke pouring out of them so popular were they for barricades. The bus took us to Old Trafford and even though the capacity then would have been half the 70,000 it is today, I had never seen so many bodies gathered together in one place in my life. For us out-of-towners it was a scary experience. Little could I have dreamt that day how this place would become such a fixture for me in the future and these crowds define so much of what I am.

The match was Manchester United against Newcastle United and the second problem arose when we realised that the tickets were for United's famous Stretford end. Bear in mind I was twelve and my brother Brian eleven, and this was in the days before seats. It wasn't so much standing room only as swaying room only. It was noisy, it was packed, it was very frightening and I'm ashamed to say the whole experience was somewhat overwhelming. But those were the days when you could walk up to the man at the turnstile and say, 'Could we swap these for other tickets?' – which amazingly we could. He issued us tickets for a smaller enclosure at the other end of the ground behind the goal – much more comfortable, but we were surrounded by Newcastle fans.

Although they were the enemy and mixing fans like that would never be allowed today, it was all great fun and very carnival-like, except they kept chanting this funny phrase which none of us could understand: 'Howway the lads, howway the lads,' which I understand today roughly translates as 'Come on, the fellas in the black and white strip'.

In those days there was a little white picket fence that went round the outside of the pitch at Old Trafford with Shell petrol adverts stuck to it. We were so close to the corner flag and the goalposts you could hear the dull thud of the ball when it was kicked, you could hear the players shout instructions at each other, you could examine Bobby Charlton in detail flicking his strings of hair over his bald spot. We were so close we were within touching distance. And there alongside Denis Law with his blond feathered haircut and collar turned up, and Willie Morgan jigging about on the wing, was the man we had all come to pay homage to – Georgie Boy!

I had only ever seen anything like this on television before and here it was like a drama being acted out before me. The colours were so vivid, the red and white of United, the black and white of Newcastle, the noise, the smells, the passion, the pain – God, how I love football. Today, I have my own seat in the ground and every time I settle down in it I think of the day when I had to stand with the opposition. As my father shared that day with me, so every time I go with my children I savour the flavour of not only what's happening on the pitch but the closeness between father and child for those ninety minutes.

Having a closeness to one particular team is one thing, but few football fans could enjoy the luxury of actually knowing the manager of their side. That was another of the big benefits being on TV brought my way. Alex Ferguson joined Man United on 7 November 1986. Like him, I was a newcomer to Manchester as well, having only been there a month before his arrival. Little did I think that one day not only would I know Fergie but that he would have a cup of tea in my kitchen!

My first meeting with the boss was in 1994 as a result of Cilla Black. Cilla was presenting a programme called *Surprise, Surprise* and was looking for an escort to bring two young lads who had had quite a hard life to Old Trafford for a behind-the-scenes tour. I know the boys were thrilled to be going – but so was I. The once bare trophy cabinet was beginning to fill up quite nicely, and the team was studded with star names like Bryan Robson, Ryan Giggs, Mark Hughes, Peter Schmeichel and, of course, Eric Cantona.

Whatever fearsome reputation Sir Alex now has, one of the main things I have always noticed about him over the years has been his fondness and affection for children. He reminded me of my dad in that respect. He made those two young lads feel very important that day. Nothing was too much trouble for them or for Cilla's production team who were making the film – even though Cilla is one of United's arch-rival Liverpool's most famous supporters. On that very subject,

298

Fergie's first words to me as I approached him on the training ground were, 'Thank God there's somebody on TV that sticks up for United.'

Music to my ears, as obviously my efforts to spread the Red gospel every morning on GMTV were not falling on barren ground. It's always nice when someone better known than you knows who you are, not only personally but also professionally, because it makes the job easier. Well-known people can attract better-known names to whatever show they work on, and get better interviews because the interviewee knows the type of person they're dealing with – whether they are straight down the middle, quirky, serious, or likely to take the piss. But the boss wasn't just being nice or flattering – he was dead serious. Taking me aside he clenched his teeth, spitting out, 'These days to be on BBC sport it seems you have to be a paid-up member of the Liverpool supporters' club.'

You could see where he was coming from. The BBC's main football pundits were former Liverpool players Alan Hansen and Mark Lawrenson, their head of sport Brian Barwick, subsequently to become chief executive of the Football Association, was an avid Liverpool supporter, and there were various other commentators, presenters and reporters whose refusal to declare which team they did support only compounded Fergie's conspiracy theory.

Another of the impressive things about Sir Alex was that once he had given you the thumbs-up he was loyal to you as long as you were loyal to him. It was something I identified with easily from my years at school where it was a virtue, or vice, that was instilled in us. I've known Sir Alex since that day and although we must see each other three times a year at various things it's not a relationship I would abuse. People immediately think that because I'm a high profile United supporter I must have free tickets whenever I want them. Not the case. I do have two season tickets at the Theatre of Dreams but they're paid for by my own money. One of the United directors, Michael Edelson, very kindly invites me as his guest to the directors' enclosure and a meal in the boardroom once a year on my birthday, and every time I see Sir Alex he tells me to call round for a drink after the game. But I always feel he has enough people hanging round him, and usually there's a plane to catch or breakfast television looming in just a few hours' time.

Football in general and United in particular have always been my relief, my way of escaping. Though I stop short of saying my way of winding down – most times it's quite the reverse. But for those ninety minutes nothing much matters but how often we can put that ball in the back of the opposition's net.

One of my biggest regrets about being away from Belfast so often is missing out on the gatherings we used to have as neighbours for Man U games. A group of ten or so of us would simply decamp into one or other's house on match day or night and, given the amount of games United play that are televised, that's a lot of decamping, a lot of beer, a lot of crisps and snacks for anybody to put together – but always great fun in the company of Jim Clark, Donal Delahunt, John O'Doherty, Conor Herlihy or Stephen Prenter. All grown men, all with more than responsible positions in the Civil Service, banking or finance, and all reduced to schoolboys for ninety minutes.

The big date in the calendar is always Man United versus Liverpool and it was my turn to host proceedings. I had just installed one of those giant projector screens in my house in Belfast. The effect is fantastic. The room is blacked out like a cinema, the walls and shelves adorned with United paraphernalia, everybody is gathered on the couches or leather bean bags strewn around the floor and the scene is set for baying at the enemy. Three days before the big encounter I walked into the airport lounge at Heathrow to find Sir Alex Ferguson waiting to board the plane to Belfast where he was on one of his regular visits to see John White and John Dempsey, who run Northern Ireland's biggest Manchester United supporters' club. Fergie beckoned me over and we checked in seated side by side. These are the sorts of experience that money could never buy: to sit with someone who is one of your all-time heroes, gauging their opinions on certain players and why this happened and why that happened. On landing it just got better. I live literally three minutes from Belfast city airport and the boss asked me how I was getting home. I said, 'I'll just grab a taxi.' To which he replied, 'No, no, the two Johns are picking me up and we'll drive you home.'

And that's what happened. On the way I thought I had better phone Ruth, who I knew

301

was making lunch for me, and try and warn her who was about to arrive. I was worried simply because sometimes if you don't see a person in the context you're expecting to see them, why would you recognise them? My big fear being that if Fergie arrived at the door Ruth would think he was the taxi driver. So, in code, I phoned her. 'Yes dear, you know, the boss... Well...'

'What boss? Your boss?'

'Yes – my football boss.'

'But you don't play football...'

'Never mind that, he's coming to the house.'

'What house?'

'Our house. In about three minutes.'

'What are you taking about?'

She hadn't a clue, and I didn't want to look as if I was all excited that Fergie was coming to visit. Well, the look on her face when we walked in, standing there stirring beef stroganoff over a hot stove with rice steaming away in another pot. 'Oh,' goes Ruth, on seeing who's arrived. 'Oh indeed,' said I, knowing I was now getting one of those looks that said, 'Why didn't you tell me? Look at the state of the place.' The boss declined lunch but had a cup of tea during which I kept saying to Ruth, 'Where's the camera? Where's the camera?'

'I don't believe it – you're not going to disgrace yourself by asking for a picture, are you?'

'Too bloody right I am,' said I.

This is where women have an innate ability to hit where it hurts. 'Look at you, you're pathetic, you're all excited like a child.' If this was designed to put me off it didn't work.

Ten of my best mates were going to be in this very house in three days' time paying homage to Fergie's Red Army and I reckoned that gave me just enough time to get the pictures taken, developed and put in frames for all to see. As a matter of fact I was even beginning to think about one of those blue plaques that they put up outside houses saying things like 'Florence Nightingale lived here'. There was already one six houses away from mine saying 'C.S. Lewis lived here' ... yes, *The Lion, the Witch and the Wardrobe* man himself. The one I could put up would be a different colour – red and white – with 'Fergie had a cup of tea here'. I got the camera and I got the picture, despite Ruth's protestations, and I had my choice of backgrounds: Fergie against our front door, or Fergie with our cooker as the backdrop. Needless to say, come Sunday the boys were suitably impressed.

In December 2004 I was asked to take part in the Christmas celebrity version of *Who Wants To Be A Millionaire?* Taking part in the show had always been a problem for me because it was a main Saturday-night rival to the Lottery quiz *Jet Set*, which I present on BBC I. But this time there was no conflict of interest, as *Jet Set* wasn't due to return until some time in mid-January 2005. The *Millionaire* producer asked me who from GMTV I would like to partner me. 'I don't want anybody from GMTV to partner me,' was my immediate response. Now, looking back, that's an obvious example of how I just didn't want to be associated with their whole set-up any more.

'Well, who do you want?' they asked.

'Sir Alex Ferguson.'

'Oh, no chance, he would never do it,' they said.

'Have you ever asked him?' I queried.

'No, but he would never do it. He doesn't do things like that.'

I wasn't so sure. 'Well, let me ask him and we'll see.'

I put the request in with the boss's secretary, Lynne Laffin. 'Oh I think he'd like that,' she said. 'He's nuts on quizzes.'

A couple of days later the phone rang and it was the boss. You always have to be careful about these sorts of conversations because sure as heck it could be some DJ on some local radio station somewhere putting on a voice and taping your every reaction but, in fact, it was the boss. 'I'd love to do that. Do you know I win that million every week?'

And with that I was about to play in a Fergie team.

Who Wants To Be A Millionaire? is recorded in Elstree Studios in Hertfordshire, and come the big day, as we waited in the equivalent of the players' tunnel before coming on, it was the boss who was the nervous one, but boy did he want to win, and it was great feeding off his competitiveness. 'I've been getting the boys to test me when I've been on the coach going to matches. I haven't told any of them what it was about but I've made quizzes compulsory for the past few weeks.'

When we went out there we got off to a great start. Question after question right and we didn't have to touch a lifeline. Then we got to question number eleven for £64,000. Whatever happened we knew we would take away a minimum of £32,000, but with the way we were going it could easily have been the million. 'For £64,000,' said Chris Tarrant, 'in the sitcom *The Good Life*, what was the name of Tom and Barbara's pet cockerel? Was it A – Rasputin, B – Trotsky, C – Lenin or D – Marx?'

Well, I looked at the boss and he looked at me. He hadn't a clue and neither had I. I tried to think this one out logically. It was a sitcom. The pet is bound to have had a comedy name. There was nothing comedy about Lenin or Marx. It was a cockerel. What does a cockerel do? It trots, sort of, and Rasputin reminded me of that song by Boney M of the same name, and that lead singer of theirs – he certainly knew how to move. So putting all that together we decided to use our 50:50 lifeline and take two wrong answers away. That left us with Trotsky and Lenin.

'Well, it must be Trotsky,' said the boss.

'No, no, no, not necessarily,' said I.

'We can't be sure. We should use another lifeline – ask the audience.'

They of course obviously hadn't a clue and went on the theory I'd come up with, voting 97 per cent Trotsky and 3 per cent Lenin. Was that enough to choose? The boss thought yes. I thought, let's use the third lifeline and phone a friend.

The boss said, 'Who should we phone?'

'Someone you can sack if they get it wrong,' said I.

He decided on Choccy, Old Trafford's striking legend Brian McClair, who was then in charge of United's youth team. So we phoned Brian and waited with baited breath for his answer – but it didn't come, he hadn't got a clue.

'Useless,' mocked the boss. So we were on our own. Fingers crossed the audience were right. 97 per cent thought Trotsky and guess what – 97 per cent were absolutely wrong! Chris stretched it out as he does. 'You were playing for £64,000 ... and you've just made that ... £32,000!'

Gutted, sick as a parrot, a game of two halves, the ball didn't go our way – all those football clichés just rolled off my tongue. Now I knew what defeat on the pitch must feel like. The boss took it badly, although not at first. We paused backstage to receive a pat on the back from Sir Paul and Lady Heather McCartney, but once we got back to the green room Fergie phoned everybody he knew – everybody on our Phone-a-Friend list, and everybody who wasn't as well.

'Not one of them – not one of them – knows the answer,' he railed. 'What sort of question was that?'

I was loving this. That's how much victory mattered to the man. You know your team is in safe hands when you've got a guy like that in charge. For the next three weeks the phone calls came twice a week starting with, 'Eamonn – it's Alec here, I've phoned fifty people.' Then it was, 'I've phoned a hundred people...' Then it was, 'I must have phoned two hundred people and nobody knows the answer to that question. I tell you they must have been bloomin' Arsenal supporters to set that one.'

What a man! But we still left with £32,000 to help bring football to disabled or disadvantaged youngsters or them to football.

Football is a common language and religion. Wherever I go, whoever I meet, football can often be the common talking point. More people strike up conversations with me relating to kicking a ball than they do about TV. I've never done an interview with politicians Gordon Brown or John Reid without having to snap out of some football ponderings to say, 'Anyway, about the inter-view...' Brown is a Raith Rovers supporter and Dr Reid a Glasgow Celtic man and both know the subject well.

Showbiz stars are the same. Knowing my allegiance makes them want to declare theirs. My red zeal even reached the ears of film star Kevin Costner, who was determined to goad me through much of our interview about how much superior he believed his beloved Arsenal were to Man U. Costner had become a Gooner during the early nineties when he was in Britain filming the Robin Hood epic, *Prince of Thieves*. He first saw them play at Aston Villa during a break in filming and now tunes in or goes to games when-ever he can.

The Costner, Brown and Reid experiences, together with the people I'd bump into on the way to or at matches, got me thinking. Thinking about the great conversations and banter I'd had sharing cabs from Manchester Airport with Ulrika Jonsson, Angus Deayton and Richard

Wilson – all United supporters on the way to Old Trafford. Having a drink in the bar at Maine Road with Noel Gallagher, who'd probably be prouder to be called a City supporter than a rock star; exchanging abusive text messages with Radio 1's Liverpool-supporting DJ Colin Murray – there had to be a show in this. I began to ponder: entertainment and well-known figures talking about sport, and sports stars talking about entertainment. I wanted sports talk with a smile on its face, and it wasn't long before BBC Radio 5 Live would put a smile on mine by making it happen.

The much-coveted Saturday morning slot between nine and eleven had just become free on Five Live with Adrian Chiles moving to BBC 2's *Match of the Day 2*. With his strong West Midlands accent and devotion to West Brom, Adrian was instantly recognisable to listeners and was very popular and respected. He'd be a tough act to follow. Number Two at Radio 5, Moz Dee, was the man to get in touch with me. He and station controller Bob Shennan had spoken to me before about joining Five Live and I really wanted to but, realistically, it would have meant sacrificing too many TV commitments and, compared to radio, they were the ones that paid the bills.

Being offered the Saturday-morning slot was both good news and bad. Good, because it was new ground, a venture into radio and a means of reinforcing my sport interest and connections, plus the BBC wanted my name attached to the station. That was a strange feeling as it was happening at a time when GMTV were trying very

308

hard to do the opposite – take my name down a peg or two. Radio 5 Live is a tremendously prestigious station. It works because it does exactly what it says on the packet – 'news and sport from the BBC'. It was what I was about, what I wanted to do.

It was, however, also slightly bad because at the same time I was doing GMTV four days a week, *The National Lottery Jet Set* for around twenty weeks of the year and my 'Man of the People' column every Sunday in the *People* newspaper. Did I really need another early morning start and an extra long day for forty Saturdays of the year? I had to ask the question but I already knew the answer – of course I did!

If you're in broadcasting for the long run you've got to be very lucky or very industrious and, never having won much in life, I tend not to trust in luck too much.

It was July 2004, and only ten months were left on my GMTV contract. I was totally disillusioned with the set-up there and if ever I was to give myself a chance of breaking free I had to build up as many alternative work outlets as possible. And anyway, at my age I was well and truly developing a face for radio! With Bob and Mos completely supportive of how I wanted to shape the programme, the deal was done.

So much of my working life had been in sport. From the two years at Ulster Television to *Sportsround Northwest* at BBC Manchester, BBC *Breakfast News*, darts, snooker and tennis for BBC Sport, snooker, darts and *The Sports Show* for ITV, it had never gone away, but rarely had it

309

been so enjoyable as it was with radio. Gone were the restrictions TV brings in terms of time and topics. With Beverley Turner and Colin Paterson on my team in the studio, we talked about everything to everybody in sport and showbiz who would talk to us. From commentators to competitors, singers to soap stars, all united by the communion of sport. The whole show was put together by an independent company. Run by Keith Bunker and Isobel Williams, it's called *Bite Yer Legs*, Keith being a big Leeds United fan and 'Bite Yer Legs' being forever associated with legendary hardman Norman Hunter. With infectious enthusiasm Keith and Isobel introduced comedy sketches and competitions, often using their own voice talents on tape.

This is when working isn't a chore. This is when it's a privilege to work with people who are knowledgeable, enthusiastic and passionate. Thankfully, the audience picked up on that as well. In just one year we added one hundred thousand extra listeners to the 9–11 a.m. slot, making it the most-listened-to programme of the day on Five Live. Despite the negative attitude towards me at GMTV, the figures, production content and quality of guests we were attracting here helped buoy up my flagging esteem. There was still life left in the old dog yet.

TWENTY-SIX

The National Lottery

Does anybody have a typical Saturday any more? My ideal would involve cleaning the car, going to a match, out to a movie in the evening and maybe a Chinese to finish off the day. Nowadays, there are fewer and fewer matches on a Saturday, and so many more of us have to work. Far from being a leisure day, Saturday has become my longest working day of the week. Not that I can really call it work, involving as it does two of the most enjoyable programmes I have ever been on. Up I get at six o'clock to report for seven at BBC Radio 5 Live for my weekly show, which starts at nine. I'm off air at eleven, then after a short debrief it's down two flights of stairs and into the BBC Television Centre for my half-past eleven lottery meeting. At this we finalise scripts and quiz questions before rehearsals get under way for that night's big show. They say about the lottery that winning it could change your life. Well presenting it certainly changed mine.

The National Lottery Jet Set is the only live quiz show on terrestrial telly. As a viewer you can feel what that means. There's an edginess and excitement that comes through the screen, and anything can happen in that half hour – including somebody at home winning millions of pounds,

311

or somebody in the studio jetting off on the trip of a lifetime.

There's never been a single Saturday night when I've been presenting *Jet Set* that I haven't felt the hairs rise up on the back of my neck as the theme music starts to play. This is big time – the hotspot of the week as far as the schedules are concerned and the pinnacle of most presenters' ambitions. So what am I doing there? Fair enough, I always wanted to be a journalist and report from various locations around the world, but I didn't think that the Television Centre in Shepherd's Bush at eight o'clock on a Saturday night would be one of them. When I was a youngster, that was the domain of Cliff Richard and Cilla Black, of Val Doonican, who used to sit on a barstool in Shepherd's Bush theatre, the reverse shot showing the clock on the balcony. I would cop a look at it just to test whether the show was really live or not. It was the time of evening Bruce Forsyth made famous with *The Generation Game* and in which Noel Edmonds was king of the castle in Crinkly Bottom for all those years. And now for almost half the year I am there as well.

The *Jet Set* offers a dream life to someone, and it had given me the same. Yet amazingly, although I have become well known for hosting a string of quiz shows, it was a hard area to break into. No one would consider me for them initially on the basis that 'Well, he just doesn't do them, does he?' It was a real chicken and egg thing. To get a quiz show you had to be doing a quiz show, and going back to my roots at Ulster Television was to

312

be my breakthrough.

UTV had commissioned a long run of quizzes called *All Mixed Up* from local independent production company Wild Rover. Philip Morrow was the boss there and he wanted to give the whole project the most polished look he could. Whereas by 1998 most people back home wouldn't approach me for too many jobs on the basis, they assumed, that I would be too busy or too big to bother, Phil did, on the basis that if you don't ask you don't get. There was a motive behind his madness. Although he may add to his production costs by hiring me as opposed to a local presenter, his plan was to use the finished show as a sort of advert to tout round bigger television companies as an example of what he could do.

In that, he was absolutely right. I firmly believe that work leads to work. When you're hot, you're hot and when you're not – you're not! Based on what I was earning per show at that time, the fee Phil could offer me was well short of what I could get elsewhere, but I wasn't achieving anything elsewhere in terms of quiz or game shows. So although this was to be a showreel for Phil's Wild Rover ambitions, I felt it could also be the same for me. All the advice from everyone, including my agent, was, 'How could you be bothered?' But things change in television all the time and it's so important as a general presenter to keep yourself relevant.

My ambition as an anchor was always to be the next Des Lynam, but it was clear to me now that there wasn't going to be a next Des Lynam.

Sports presenting had gone in lots of different directions. Sports jocks were in vogue, in the form of ex-players and competitors hosting shows, as were sports babes in the form of very good-looking girls who knew their stuff but would also provide a big draw factor for blokes. Since I was neither of those, I could see the writing on the wall. So where would the regular work come from if I was to jump ship from GMTV? Certainly from nothing Des Lynam was doing because the goalposts had changed.

Des had been great for me through the years. Not only was he my presenting God, he had also thrown presenting scraps off the table, which I had dined on very well indeed. I first met him close up and personal for a profile piece we were doing on the *Open Air* programme. It involved looking at what Des did away from broadcasting, which turned out to be a bit of cycling on a mountain bike. So off we went along the banks of the River Thames around Barnes, stopping off at the great man's local pub for the bulk of the interview. Rarely has a filming day been more pleasurable. Des not only knows his job inside out, he also commands a healthy comical cynicism off screen which ranks him in the league of Terry Wogan and Northern Irish broadcasting legends Jackie Fullerton and Gerry Kelly. All wickedly funny and all, like myself, not adverse to the odd cuss word making them even more colourful off the box than on it. If ever I had to choose the company that would make me laugh to tears or inspire me, these men would be it. Probably a mere coincidence that we are all

314

from the same country.

After our bike outing I went on to follow Des when he gave up BBC 1's *Holiday* programme and *How Do They Do That?* I know for a fact he recommended me for GMTV, a role he was offered but turned down, and on the quiet he's told me that as soon as he's had enough of *Countdown* – it's mine! It's a pleasure being in the company of class, and that's what Des is. Often I worry that I'm not learning any more because there is no one to learn from. Des came on my radio programme to talk about his autobiography and just by him speaking I learned. That's how good he is.

For the next two years *All Mixed Up* became the top-rated programme on Northern Irish TV screens, but more importantly it gave me my break into the bigger quiz arena in Britain, although not in the way I expected through Phil's showreels. Unbeknown to me, the lad who worked the big screen graphics board we used did many of the other quiz programmes for both BBC and ITV. Phil knew about him and had brought his expertise on board as part of the better look he wanted. His name was Chris Goss, and his next job was to be with the BBC in Manchester. At that time the Wednesday night lottery format was being jigged up from its normal five-minute slot to a fifteen-minute slot. The production team had come up with an idea to be played on Wednesdays called *The Third Degree*, but they hadn't got a presenter. When Chris Goss suggested me the usual answer came back, 'But he doesn't do quiz shows.'

'Oh yes he does,' said Chris, 'I'll get you a tape.'

As I said, work leads to work, and with that roundabout journey I landed my big break into quizzes with *The National Lottery Third Degree.* The toughest part of the show was not doing it, but getting there and back. GMTV still ruled my mornings, Manchester was four hours' drive from London on a good day, and three and a half hours back on a good night. Going to Manchester for football was one thing – missing out on Wednesday-night football and having to work in its place just two miles away from the Theatre of Dreams was another. That's the sort of hard work and commitment that's required in TV to morph into your next reincarnation on the box. Lots of television presenters at my level would have thought the Belfast job beneath them, they would have thought the Manchester job beneath them and not worth the trouble, and in common with so many they would find themselves very quickly out of work. Believe me, as in most sports or walks of life, the harder you work, the more you practise, the luckier you get.

And then the luck started to roll with another BBC Manchester Daytime quiz called *Pass the Buck,* bringing me to the attention of the BBC 1 controller of the time, Peter Salmon. Peter phoned my agent and asked her if I would be interested in a Saturday night lottery show. Is the Pope a Catholic? My huge excitement, though, was to be countered with a huge fright when Peter revealed that the new show would have to be ready to go in just three weeks' time. Bloody hell! That was hardly enough time to get myself a couple of new suits, shirts and ties. Obviously I was not the first choice for this project, and on meeting the production team my panic increased when they told me that the main reason for my appointment was my reputation for holding a live programme together. Without naming names they intimated they had been through a number of presenters, none of whom could keep the programme on track for its allotted time. The reason for this lay in a few flaws that were obvious to my eye. Like a doctor being sent to revive a patient, or a physio called to get a player ready in time for the Cup final, I quickly saw where the problem areas were that I had to change.

'I need to see the pilot tapes you have recorded so far.' Nobody wanted to do that to protect the identities of the other presenters who had tested for the programme. 'Bollocks to that,' I said. 'Do you want this programme sorted or don't you? We haven't got time to worry about whether I know who's been offered the job ahead of me or not.' I got the tapes and spoke to the producers about where I felt the show was hitting problems, and so began the most trusting and pleasurable relationship I have ever had with a series of highly talented and very nice TV people – from the programme originator, David Young, to my first producer, the delightful Suzi Lamb, followed by Michael Mannes, liked by everyone and with due reason, mischievous Andy Rowe and Mr Saturday Night, Barrie Kelly. All the series over the years were supervised by the executive producer Phil 'the wise old owl'

317

Parsons, who loves the wise bit of my nickname for him, but not the old bit. These folk formed the nucleus of a beautiful and sharp working relationship. *Jet Set* was born, it took off, and together we've helped to make it a winner, becoming as it has the BBC's most popular and longest-running lottery show. Up to now, thank goodness, it hasn't hit turbulence yet.

I have, though.

Like the night the girl in the final could hardly hear what I was saying because she was on the other side of the world in Melbourne, Australia. The question I asked was, 'Which German word means *whirlpool* and is the name of a pastry dessert containing apple?'

'Could you spell that word for me, Eamonn?'

'Whirlpool – W-I-R-L-P-O-O-L – whirlpool.' This, bear in mind, from the man who presents *Hard Spell*, the search for the nation's best young speller! The answer in case you don't know is strudel. The live element always throws up hilarious situations.

Question: 'What's the furthest planet from the sun?'

Answer: 'That'll be your anus, Eamonn.' It took me a while to say 'CORRECT' to that one, due to Phil Parsons's hysterical shrieks of laughter in my ear.

Question: 'What's the name of actor Tony Curtis's famous daughter?'

Answer: 'Fern Britton.'

Question: 'Which bird is pictured on the national flag of Mexico?'

Answer: 'Jennifer Lopez.'

I promise – I'm not making this up.

Although all the fun and frivolity gave me a rollercoaster ride, the scariest night of all was a Wednesday in April 2005 when the draws were moved to 10.45 in the evening. OK, I know I had had an early start with GMTV and it was the end of a very long day before the start of another very long morning, but I had one of those motorway moments – you know when you realise you've been driving with your eyes closed but you don't know for how long. Whether it was a second, ten seconds, twenty seconds ... you just don't know and you wake up with such a fright, your heart beating fast. Well, it happened to me on national TV in front of six million people on a Wednesday night. The studio was hot, Alan Dedicoat was explaining what was about to happen with the draw, the balls were released and made a very comforting sound – a bit like a tumble drier whirring away – and the next thing I knew Alan's voice was saying, 'Eamonn!'

My eyes sprung open. Where had I been? How long had I been there? Had anyone noticed? Was I snoring? I got us off air much to everyone's hilarity. Maybe people were right. Maybe I was doing a bit too much. Something would have to go, and it was just about to in the form of– GMTV!

TWENTY-SEVEN

Nearing the End at GMTV

If nothing else at GMTV, at least I got a laugh – even when I wasn't supposed to. One of my career inspirations, Dustin Hoffman, *from the movie* All The President's Men, *was to be one of my last big name interviews there. How fitting was that? Life was coming full circle. Even more fitting was the title of his new movie,* Meet the Fockers – *boy was he coming to the right place!*

Meeting Dustin Hoffman brought memories of the New Vic cinema in Belfast from thirty years earlier flooding back. It's rare that I would ask a guest to sign something for me but, on the morning of the Hoffman interview, I was up at four o'clock searching for my DVD of *All The President's Men*. We had recently moved house and there were boxes everywhere still to be unpacked. I rummaged through them, cursing for not having made time to look the night before. I made a bit of a mess, tipping things out onto the landing, and, in the process, came across a few things I'd forgotten I had. Of course, I couldn't find the one thing I was after. No autograph, then.

Before going on air, I went to Dustin's dressing room to introduce myself. Inside, the Oscar-winning actor, dressed only in his underpants, a collar of tissues at his neck, stood with his personal make-up artist who was applying what was necessary.

It's not every day you find yourself chatting to a Hollywood star in his undies. (Although a few days earlier I had also walked in on *Hotel Rwanda* Oscar-nominated actress Sophie Okonedo in hers. Her only embarrassment being that her bra and pants didn't match – can't honestly say that I noticed.) Hoffman didn't seem bothered in the least. I suppose he's used to having people around him when he's on set or in his trailer but, even so, he was incredibly approachable.

He also had the unmistakable charisma that seems to go hand in hand with being a movie star. There was a serenity about him, a kind of other-worldliness, that was impressive, and I wasn't the only one to pick up on it.

Charles Kennedy, the then leader of the Liberal Democrats, was another guest that morning. In his position at the helm of the third biggest political party in Britain, he was well used to mixing with people at the highest level and taking it in his stride. When he met Dustin Hoffman, though, it was clear he was just as much in awe as I was.

Hoffman wanted to know what Charles Kennedy's political agenda was for the rest of the day. Aware that he was planning to return to the Commons for Prime Minister's Questions, I said, 'Oh, he's doing the same as you – he's off to meet the Fockers.' Hoffman laughed so much I thought his undies were going to fall off.

When I told him that *All The President's Men* had inspired me to become a journalist, he said, 'Yeah, but who did you want to be, me or Robert Redford?'

Stupid question. I wanted to be Robert Redford, of course – didn't everyone? – but I couldn't tell him that, could I? 'Oh, I wanted to be you,' I gushed.

He told me the film had boosted the numbers studying journalism at colleges in the United States by around 30 per cent, each student no doubt fancying themselves as the next Bernstein or Woodward. I wasn't the only one, then.

In the studio, we chatted about *Meet the Fockers*, a movie of which the title alone is enough to make me laugh. Heaven knows how they got away with it. It's a very funny film but it's also quite a departure from the kind of work Hoffman was doing at the start of his career, with films like *The Graduate* and *Midnight Cowboy* – both of which earned him Oscar nominations. Maybe we all start out with noble intentions and somehow get sidetracked as time goes on.

I know I had. All those years ago, in the darkness of the New Vic cinema, I had dreamed of being a crusading journalist in the Watergate mould. Robert Redford with dark hair. Instead, here I was presenting the daily mix of showbiz, gossip, news and competitions that is GMTV. The irony wasn't lost on me. Still, to end up on the sofa with one of Hollywood's most respected stars, an actor whose work had been such a source of inspiration, wasn't all that bad.

As Dustin Hoffman chatted easily about the

Fockers, it crossed my mind that in a few days I would be saying goodbye to all this. Then what? Good question.

Off air, during the commercial break, I went to thank Dustin and found him with his publicist watching a recording of our interview, his forehead creased in concentration as he scrutinised his performance. 'What was I like?' he asked me. 'Did I get enough comedy into what I said? Was there enough satire?'

Dustin Hoffman, so approachable and casual, was also an absolute perfectionist – and the great thing was he still cared, even about a relatively minor interview like this. That's why he was still going strong in his sixties. Amazing that even an Oscar-winning Hollywood star of his stature still worries about being good enough, doing a decent job, giving the best performance. Attention to detail obviously applies to everything he does, including a few minutes of light banter on a small programme on the small screen.

Maybe I hadn't turned out to be Robert Redford, but I had still managed to co-star with Dustin Hoffman.

TWENTY-EIGHT

End of an Era

The legendary Man United captain Roy Keane was at Old Trafford for twelve and a half years – exactly the same amount of time I spent as 'captain' of my club, GMTV. United and Roy parted company because he felt he knew how to run the team better than his bosses. Whether he was right or wrong, it was how he felt, and whether I was right or wrong, it was also how I felt at GMTV.

As a presenter you get lots of gigs in TV and few jobs. GMTV was my job. Understandably, but wrongly I suppose, I felt a certain ownership of the programme. It's like seeing a girl as your wife when she only wants to date you. When I left, the story that did the rounds was that my departure was down to the early starts and lack of serious content at the station. Some columnists pointed out that despite my criticisms I had still been happy to take my pay cheque – of course I had. It didn't mean that I didn't constantly try to change what was being broadcast.

It didn't mean that I didn't constantly hold out a dream that one day things would change, not only on air but behind the scenes, and that the little group that held the key jobs and made all the decisions would change with it. GMTV was, and is, an eighties-type programme in the year 2006. I feel sorry for so many of the talented people who work there who, like me, want to produce the best telly but can't. In my latter years there, there was an attitude of, why change, why evolve when we had no competition? The truth was closer to few at the top knowing how to evolve, how to push the boundaries. Many were remnants from TV-am and still did it the way it was done twenty years earlier. Worse than that, the last few years saw a pruning of personnel and production resources and an increase in sponsorship, competitions and the duration of advertising breaks. Correspondents were trimmed to such a degree that if news stories break in Ireland, Scotland, Wales, the south-west, the north-east, or the east of England, the only people available to cover them are two reporters based in Manchester and whoever happens to be on call in London. Add to that the bureaus in Glasgow axed, Belfast closed down and no one in Wales.

As a station it was making more money but I could see in so many ways how you, the viewers, were being short-changed. We used to give you so much more and I believe we still could have and still made the right money to keep the board happy. Real talent in TV is to be able to grow an audience with relevant and imaginative programming. Anyone can cut costs and say they're making money as a result. As a station it was stagnant and shrinking.

What was happening there before my very eyes was also being allowed to happen in other ITV regions which, like GMTV, were being freed of many of their public service commitments. The drip-drip effect of this is that your area, your region, your voice, might not be heard. Less regional representation means less talent from Scotland, Ireland and Wales, and everywhere in England getting a platform. It means fewer political issues and personalities getting an airing, it means fewer new bands having a show-case, fewer reporters and presenters having somewhere to learn their trade, and ultimately you the viewer knowing less, and as a result caring less, about the area you live in.

I don't miss GMTV because the programme was lacking in purpose, direction, belief and ambition. I don't miss it because it was becoming like Groundhog Day with the same interviews with the same people. I don't miss it because the ad breaks were becoming longer than the interviews and, in an increasing pursuit of yet more income, we were turning into a shopping channel selling holidays and competitions, and almost every single item, including the weather and the TV preview, was sponsored.

Morale among those who worked hardest and were paid least was very low. If most staff in the place thought they were treated with disdain, believe me, most presenters were treated worse than that. I was treated worst of all because I earned more than anyone else – including the bosses, none of whom had hired me. Unfortunately for them, they had inherited me. I ask you, in which other industries do the subordinates take home more than the bosses? Football, maybe –

but there can be few others. As you can imagine, if you earned more than your boss, that might create a little friction. But it worked both ways. If the programme was doing well all their jobs were safe, and I was one of the reasons the programme was doing well. My work ethic, though, meant that I found it hard to stomach some of the work practices. I believe you have to lead by example. I had worked my way up from the bottom to the top. I could do any of the jobs in production so I didn't need lectures on how hard people worked or what they were paid. I had been there, done it, got the T-shirt, done all the jobs it took to climb the ladder.

My position became totally isolated with the loss of the head of press and publicity, Sue Brealey, who, like me, was no admirer of the management techniques. Sue was incredibly capable intellectually and was a rare species there in that she spoke her mind. She was my only defence shield and could see a lot of what was going on. As a result, she would often put me right regarding the latest gossip and do her best to deflect untrue press tittle-tattle. When she left I was on my own.

That put me in a nightmare scenario. Imagine, for instance, if you worked for bosses who were rarely in the building at the time of day when business was done. Hard to contemplate, but that's the way it was. As a result I had sometimes felt compelled to point out that it might be a good idea if certain members of management would more than occasionally get themselves into work before nine o'clock. Maybe not the best career strategy, but call me old-fashioned, I thought with GMTV there was a big clue in the title. In case you don't know, the initials stand for 'Good Morning TV'. If you saw a boss before nine there was a fair chance royalty or Tony Blair was due in the building.

Not only that, but it was always the University of Hindsight. Criticism is fine when it comes from people who are actually there to see the alternatives and realise what is happening when it is happening.

One of the things I'm convinced really got up their noses was that audience research often said people woke up to me when it should have said people woke up to GMTV. That had to be fixed, and one of the ways of doing it was to create the GMTV 'family'. In short, everybody was upgraded in terms of profile, and I was downgraded. The way they went about it was hilarious. For instance, the tenth anniversary celebrations in 2003, when I was removed from the front of the official picture and placed at the back. Short of putting me in the building next door they couldn't have put me any further away. This is the first time I have ever commented on that picture publicly or privately. They could have pulled my fingernails out on the day and I still wouldn't have offered an opinion, because I saw it as part of a pro-active humiliation procedure. With Lorraine Kelly, I was the only surviving presenter from day one, and felt a bit of recognition centre stage marking the tenth anniversary line-up would have been a decent thing. No reaction came from me but amazingly the newspapers got my thoughts anyway... If I wasn't going to give a story, there was always someone neatly placed with press contacts to do it for me.

Fiona Phillips's husband Martin Frizell was controversially promoted from reporter to editor in 1999, and therefore became the boss of both me and his wife – not a scenario they'd recommend at Harvard Business School. He didn't mess around making his intentions clear from the start.

A few weeks later he invited me to breakfast at the very upmarket, olde worlde eating house Simpson's on the Strand. The purpose of our little get-together was to tell me that he was winding me down from a five-day-a-week commitment to four. This I don't think had the effect on me that was intended. I was visibly delighted. 'But I've been trying for this for years,' I said. 'What's brought about this change of heart?'

He answered that he had found 'a real family man'. Now he was getting my hackles up. I took this to be a reference that I was no longer deemed to be a 'family man' since my wife and I had broken up. My replacement was to be former professional tennis player Andrew Castle. Once again, I was surprised at the direction the programme was being taken in, Andrew not being a journalist. Proper apprenticeships were very important to me. It had taken me twenty years to get to this stage and now apparently you could walk into the same job from a completely different world. I like Andrew and in the intervening years he has handled himself very well but back then, with all due respect, his strengths lay in different areas. However, mine was not to reason why and, with a burgeoning workload and weekly dashes to and from Ireland, I had a lot I could do with that extra day.

While I was happy to accept a four-day week I was not happy to take a pay cut, nor was I expecting one. Two weeks later a letter arrived from the personnel department informing me that this was to be the case. What was extremely irritating was that up to that stage GMTV had been happy to use me and whatever skill and popularity I brought to the programme without ever conceding on the time-off factor.

I had asked, I had begged, I had pleaded for a four-day week, but had been told, 'The audience expect to see you there every morning, and that's where you'll be – five days or no days.' I remember telling this to Chris Evans, who at the time was our great rival with his *Big Breakfast* on Channel 5. Chris was bewildered as to how I had managed to stick the pace for so long on five days a week. When I told him what they had threatened, his advice was to threaten them back. 'Tell them three days or no days – that's what I did, and that's what I got,' he said. I didn't have Chris's confidence, so I had gone on to sign the five-day-a-week contract. I always remember being so disappointed with myself when, on reluctantly accepting their terms and putting pen to paper, one of my bosses chipped in laughing, 'Look at it this way. A contract like that mightn't make you happy, but at least it lets you be miserable in a better class of place.'

They got their way then, but this time round

there was a clause in that same contract that was to come back to haunt them. It stated very clearly that I was contracted to present five days a week. It wasn't me who was changing these conditions – it was them. I wasn't breaking the agreement – it was them. As far as I was concerned, I had agreed to work five days, and if they didn't want to use me for five days they would still have to pay me.

After a couple of weeks of to-ing and fro-ing with agents and lawyers, they realised they were in the wrong. It became obvious that Andrew's appointment was being funded by the money they thought they could save on my deal and – here's the twist – Andrew had now signed up so they couldn't back out without it costing them a year of his salary. They had just handed me an annual 20 per cent pay rise for three years. Not since the day I sat in Rory Fitzpatrick's office at Ulster Television in October 1980 had I, through no negotiating skill of my own, received such a whopper of a windfall.

By now you're probably beginning to build up the picture. They had reason not to like me and I had reason not to like them. Realising that my luck couldn't hold forever I stepped up my search for work elsewhere.

Petty rivalries between presenters were not discouraged on the basis that divided presenting talent was easier to control and manipulate. One of the ways this was exacerbated was by reducing dressing rooms to the size of loos. Not only that, but each one was to house a number of pre-senters. I was demoted from having my own room and shoehorned in with John Stapleton, Andrew Castle, Ben Shepherd and Dr Hilary Jones. Although the area was the size of a toilet we didn't actually have one, or a wash basin, so nowhere to do your ablutions and freshen your breath before and after programmes. The boys were no trouble at all and very easy to get on with – with the exception of Stapleton. In my previous dressing room I was able to adorn my walls with my sacred Manchester United paraphernalia. In a deliberate act of antagonism and aggression, John Stapleton felt it was his right to do the same with his scabby Manchester City bits and bobs in our new abode! Only now can I put it on record in these memoirs what puerile behaviour I felt this to be for a grown man and respected professional in his mid-fifties. Indeed, looking back, I feel this contributed greatly to my decision to move on... Well, it didn't actually, but it could have – if I didn't like him so much!

If the boys were cosy, the girls were positively claustrophobic. There were six regular female presenters plus occasional newsreaders such as Jackie Kabler and Amanda Sergeant, who were split between the two remaining cubicles. Think of the skirts, blouses, shoes and old pairs of tights that were strewn everywhere between that lot! It was unfair that these girls had to work such unsociable hours and often be judged on their appearance with the bare minimum of basic facilities.

Being more senior, Fiona and Lorraine got one room between them and their various outfits. Kate Garraway also qualified for residency in this room but chose the more claustrophobic option of huddling in with Penny Smith, weather girls Claire Nasir and Andrea McLean, and the guesting newsreaders. If anyone believes television is glamorous, just do the behind-the-scenes tour at GMTV.

The dressing-room contrast that I experienced at most other TV stations was immense. It was always nice to have flowers in a vase, a little welcoming note or a bottle of mineral water, but that's not what I was looking for. At GMTV, we presenters felt how they treated us was how they valued us and the attitude towards dressing rooms was symbolic of what we felt was the company philosophy – treat them mean and keep them keen. And it certainly did that for me – made me keen to get the hell out of there! That meant increasingly building up that work portfolio outside the place. It also meant working round the clock, but the more I worked elsewhere the more empowered I felt. My eggs weren't all in the one basket and they knew it. The more independent I became over the years, the more they appeared to resent me for it. It was the most fantastic standoff. We eyeballed each other, they longing to be rid of me for not toeing the line, me wanting to tell them where to stick their job, and each of us time after time backing down from the brink because the moment was probably not quite right yet on either side.

The resentment from management was totally understandable – in fact I would have been failing miserably if I had not been winding them up. Resentment from certain other presenters,

333

though, I hadn't banked on.

When I joined GMTV in August 1992, everyone was on what was called an exclusive deal. That meant they could work for no other broadcaster. Having had my fingers burned after losing my job at BBC North West two years earlier, it wasn't going to happen again. The best position to be in when negotiating any contract is them wanting you more than you want them. And so it was for me at that time. The result was I was the first presenter on either GMTV or its predecessor TV-am to be freelance. That was the way it stayed for the next two years or so. Another exception was made when Anthea Turner joined in 1994.

So I continually set terms, conditions and levels of pay that many of my colleagues enjoy today. It earned me the nickname of 'Red Ken' from one of the bosses, but I was still good value for them. Those terms and conditions were essential to who I am today and allowed me to set down other foundations as a broadcaster in sport, quiz shows, radio and newspapers. Not only that, they gave me extra time to be with my young family in Belfast. When I was in England I would happily work twenty hours a day but come Thursday or Friday and that trip back home, I was exclusively theirs and they mine. Because they weren't with me during the week I could set a work pace second to none, but when they were off school my contract allowed me to be off with them.

It took years to build up that situation. In the early days, GMTV claimed me on one too many special days for me to leave anything to chance.

It was good for the other presenters because it gave them something to look forward to in terms of standing in. I never felt the holiday arrangements were unreasonable compared to any of the rest of them because they all lived in London where those that had children could, for instance, collect them from school and tuck them up in bed at night. Because of the daily schedule, that was something I could only look forward to come the weekends, which went all too quickly. Some saw it differently though. I dread to think of the amount of wasted hours in my life spent getting to, waiting in or travelling from airports. Time that other folk spent on the golf course, in the gym, at the cinema, down the pub, sleeping or complaining about me not being there. TV presenters do that a lot – complain. Often blaming everyone: the press, the industry, their age, their sex and especially their agents as to why they are not getting as many programmes or as a good a contract as somebody else in this case, me.

Whatever the problems under the surface, the viewer isn't aware of too many ructions thanks to the professionalism of the people who put the programme out and present it on screen. Troopers like the stunningly gorgeous Penny Smith, always a tonic to start anyone's day, John Stapleton, the pro's pro, and as nice a man off screen as he is on and Lorraine Kelly, whose day-in day-out appearances for both GMTV and TV-am have earned her a place in telly's hall of fame. And then there's Dr Hilary Jones – whatever medicine he's on, I'll have some of it. In my twelve and a half years there I can never recall Hilary looking off-form or off-colour. A practising GP in real life, his surgery extended not only to the television screen but also among us presenters. A few reassuring calls to my mum in recent years were always a better tonic for me than medicine, but if they could bottle Hilary's bedside manner the country would be a healthier place.

It was also heartening to watch the blossoming of youngsters Ben Shepherd and Jenni Falconer who found their feet together as a great pairing on the Friday programme, *Entertainment Today*. If the dice rolls for them they look destined either as a team or separately to become really successful broadcasters for years to come. My admiration holds no bounds when it comes to weather girls Andrea McLean and Claire Nasir, who, together with reporters like Richard Gaisford, Sue Jameson, Alan Fisher, Jackie Kabler and so many others, went to bed in the afternoon or evening not knowing which part of the country they would have to broadcast live from the next morning.

Off screen, hats off to the camera boys, sound and lighting technicians, the guys in the graphics department, production assistants, autocue operators and the directors in charge of them all. Guys like Michael Metcalf, Simon Morris and Andrew Stedman – people who put their hearts and souls into what they did. If I was the pilot of the plane, they were the people who filled it with fuel, made sure there were no technical problems and plotted its course. Then there was the daily routine of being 'miked up', when microphone and earpiece wires are run round my body, down the back of my shirt and attached to my waistband – not on the face of it a pleasant experience, unless carried out by Miss Lorraine in the sound department. To everyone, especially floor managers Robby, Miss Sharon, Nobby, Margaret and Samina, thanks for the memories. A thoroughly grand bunch of boys and girls who had to make sense of some weird instructions they were given from above. They were the heart and soul of what you would see on your screens every morning, the sort of people you wanted there when you hit turbulence. Unsung heroes like producers Deborah Kelly, Helen Costello, Mark Kiff and Zoe Bloomfield always did their best in adverse circumstances and, what's more, in a place of few official laughs they provided plenty of unofficial ones.

In the end, though, among the higher echelons I had no one to look up to, no one I respected as a leader. When my contract was up on 27 April 2005, I could see nothing changing and expressed my disillusionment.

As a result, an initial pay increase made to me on a new three-year salary deal was withdrawn and I was not encouraged to continue. Astonishingly, the managing director had the cheek to ask my agent if I would stay on for a week beyond my contract to present the general election coverage on 5 May. Needless to say, I told him via her the answer would be no.

It was the end of an era, the end of twelve and a half years, and the end of what I believed was as good a partnership as you would find anywhere on the screen in the form of me and Fiona. But, although the public agreed with me, GMTV didn't. Their own shortsightedness prevented them from promoting and believing in us the way other companies believed in Phillip and Fern, Des and Mel or Richard and Judy. Looking back, in truth, I actually don't think Fiona believed in it one hundred per cent either.

With ten weeks to work through between the announcement that I was going and my last day, mine must have seemed like the longest goodbye in history with all the press coverage it received. It would have been much better all round to let me go straight away, but there was obviously more publicity mileage in drawing the whole thing out. Anyone who's ever worked a notice period will know that 'no-man's land' feeling. Where was the incentive for me to continue presenting a show I no longer believed in? Oh, that's right – they were paying me! (Always a good reason.)

Then, just as it looked as if I was facing a ten-week prison sentence, the programme experienced a rebirth, much to the jubilation of the production team and presenters alike. It would be nice to think it was in direct response to criticisms I had aired in the press, but no. My final weeks were to be dominated by Charles and Camilla announcing their wedding, by the general election being called and by the death of Pope John Paul II and the election of his successor. The result was that not even GMTV could have the gall to screen a little caption with the words from our then regular sponsors, 'The Pope's funeral. Brought to you by Clinton Cards – Cards for all occasions.' Bet your bottom dollar they will have thought about it though.

Gosh, those weeks were great. It was almost like the old days, with a rush of items bringing viewers the news in an easy-to-understand and interesting way. Behind and in front of the camera the staff could hardly believe it. There was a renewed vigour and sense of purpose. It would mean the scheduled feature 'Britain's Best Shed' would have to be shelved until after I had gone, but we all thought that was a price worth paying. Sadly the trend in too much of TV these days is about creating revenue rather than creating programmes.

So, where are the giants in the industry these days? The people with the new ideas? The ones who can bring the next big thing? The ones in tune with the audience, as opposed to the stock market? Answers on a postcard, please. I spent my boyhood looking for heroes and finding them on the football pitch, on the athletics track, on the golf course, in the movies, in politics. I spent my manhood looking for them in TV and struggling with the search.

After 3,000 or so early rises, 27 April 2005 was to be my last – well, for GMTV anyway. Everyone was smiling until I spoke to them and then, invariably, eyes would well up – but not mine. Under torture I would show no regret at leaving that day. Some of the biggest tears ironically came from one or two who had stuck a knife in my back. It was like a funeral and I had the occasional say in certain items on the order of service. For instance, I wasn't going to have my children used, a tactic which would have guaranteed tears from me. Good news for their viewing figures, but at this stage I owed them nothing. How could you feel fondness for a company who, come the final day of its longest-serving presenter, used a showreel on air that I had to pay for with my own money? Six months earlier, sensing the end was nigh, I had put together my 'best bits' on DVD, which I paid them for – fair enough. What I didn't expect was to see the same highlights played out on air as their tribute to me!

But that aside I did have a trip down Memory Lane with my co-presenter from day one, Anne Davies, a farewell message from the fantastically gorgeous young classical diva Katherine Jenkins, the boss of the country, Prime Minister Tony Blair, and the Big Boss of Manchester United, Sir Alex Ferguson. But while I remained statesmanlike throughout it all, Fiona, bless her, went to bits. Our on-air 'marriage' was about to be dissolved. Just as in real marriages we hadn't always seen eye to eye, we had good times, we had bad times, we loved each other a lot and we loathed each other the odd time too. Neither of us could deny though that there was something special there. It's a pity it had to end.

So many of you watching at home thought it was a pity as well. I was humbled and stunned when the website people presented me with 8,000 goodwill messages. It wasn't only the end of an era for me, it was also a significant day in many people's lives. Not because I was anything special. Just because I was there. There every morning as folk went to school, university, work. There when people welcomed additions to their family into the world and there when bereavements happened and there was no one else to wake up to. People wrote to me and told me that they remember me from when they were youngsters and now they are married with children. I was there most days and now I wouldn't be. It was a great privilege to be welcomed into not only people's homes, but also their lives. In fact so much correspondence did I receive that I set about creating my own website, *eamonn.tv*, to keep in touch and let people know what I'm up to.

Quickly after the programme the studio was transformed and a few modest little drinks and snacks were served. Thank you to everyone who turned up and thanks most of all to my presenting colleague John Stapleton who gave a little speech. In truth, it wasn't a little speech, it was the biggest speech of my life, being they were the finest words I had ever heard about myself. It was the best sort of speech because it was the sort of one that, if you had the brass neck, you would write about yourself but be too embarrassed to actually ever read out. In fact, my only complaint about the whole thing was that the bugger didn't leave me a copy of his script. They were nice words from a nice man and a man who knew even without such an oration he would always command my respect and admiration.

Fiona tried to say a few words but couldn't get

them out. After a while I found her in her dressing room and we said what we had to say. For the past three years I had been entering and leaving the building via the tradesman's door. I saw no reason to change my routine that day. For years I knew that the end would be like this – leaving quietly by a side door exit. I took one last look around my tiny excuse for a dressing room, lifted my good luck messages and last couple of Man United mementoes and closed the door. The parting words came from Susan on the switchboard as I passed by her. 'The viewers will miss you,' she said, 'and so shall we.'

And with that I could have had no finer exit line.

TWENTY-NINE

Sky Launch

My diary was completely empty on leaving GMTV. I had no idea what would happen or where I was heading. I remember Fiona saying to me, 'The sky's the limit for you after you're out of here.' Although she meant it, I was far from convinced. But I've always thought there was something of the white witch about Miss Fy-ona. And, as it turned out, she was spookily spot on, in more ways than one. I didn't so much reach for the sky as Sky reached for me. From having nothing in the offing, the eight months to the end of 2005 turned out to be my busiest time ever in twenty-

342

five years of broadcasting. Thank God for that!

For years *Who Wants To Be A Millionaire?* had been the nation's favourite telly quiz show. Now its makers Celador had the idea of bringing the nation's favourite telly quiz to the nation. *Who Wants To Be A Millionaire Live* was the TV show as everyone knew and loved it but instead of playing for money, contestants in theatres around the country would play for prizes, and instead of Chris Tarrant they would get me. It was very well produced by the events team at Celador under Guy Freeman, and the seven weeks' work in Torquay he offered me took care of the summer. They don't call Torquay the English Riviera for nothing. I don't know what the summer was like anywhere else but in the south-west it was hot and sunny – fine if you're on holiday, but not brilliant when it came to getting bums on seats in the Princess Theatre. It was very good work but it wasn't on television and you only get work elsewhere like this if you are on television in the first place.

That was quickly followed by what must rank as my best job ever, an offer of eight weeks in panto at Belfast's magnificent Grand Opera House. I say my best job ever because, even though there were two shows a day for two months and panto is notoriously gruelling, I didn't even have to be there – I was a hologram! I had only ever heard of this once before, in fact I had seen it with my own eyes, when that doyen of stage and screen, Sir Laurence Olivier, was projected onto a huge globe throughout the West End run of Cliff

Richard's musical *Time* in the mid-eighties. My role was to be the magic mirror on the wall in *Snow White,* you know the one from which the wicked queen seeks constant reassurance – that old line, 'Mirror, mirror on the wall, who is the fairest of them all?' There was a strange sense of déjà-vu about that scene ... surely it wasn't reminding me of some co-presenter somewhere in my past?

Part of the reason I was cast was because John Linehan as May McFettridge was topping the bill. Most people in Northern Ireland believe I'm May's lovechild and the script played out our relationship to the full. With matinees running into evening shows day after day, John would periodically phone me to let me know how knackered he was and how he hated me still looking as fresh as a daisy. Ah well, if it was good enough for Sir Larry, it was good enough for me.

After taking up a few guest slots presenting the BBC 1 morning-time fly-on-the-wall medical programme *City Hospital,* I was offered a full-time job anchoring the programme from Peter Hayton and Chris Riley at Topical TV, who made it. I had worked with both these men fifteen years earlier on an ITV afternoon programme called *TV Weekly* and while it was nice to renew that working friendship I knew in my heart it wasn't really what I wanted to do. It was a tough decision to turn it down because it was an interesting and very well-made piece of television, and they were nice people to work with. But the decision was made easier after an approach from Nick Pollard, the head of the prestigious Sky News channel.

Under the leadership of Sky Controller Dawn Airey, the whole network had big plans. Regarded as the number one twenty-four-hour news channel in Europe, after sixteen years they were moving to the next generation. If that term conjured up an image of *Star Trek*, to me it was confirmed when Nick brought me to see his new £10 million Sky News Centre. Even though it was still being built I felt as if I was standing on the bridge of the *Starship Enterprise*. Nobody in British television in the summer of 2005 had a set-up like this. I had been around for a very long time in the TV game, yet taking the tour with Nick brought back to me the excitement I felt when I first walked into a TV studio. Not only was it a long time ago, but in terms of technology Studio 1 at Ulster Television in 1980 was pre-Ice Age. Then I had never even been in a studio before. Now, it was as if that was still the case. There had been nothing that looked anything remotely like this before. Not only was I being offered a new job, I was being offered a new position in the market and, even though it would be seen by a smaller audience in Britain, I wanted to give it a go. New challenges, new areas, new frontiers, have always brought the best out in me. This was to be a new-look Sky News and I was to present the first programme on its launch day – the breakfast show, *Sunrise*.

To be in at the start of anything is incredibly stimulating. To be involved once is a privilege. To be involved three times has to be the luck of the Irish. I will never forget the first morning of BBC Daytime in October 1986, watching with incred-

345

ible awe and pride as disparate parts of Auntie Beeb came to life together, London, Bristol, Belfast, Birmingham, Manchester and Glasgow joining up and moving like a powerful dinosaur waking from a long sleep. With that, daytime TV was born and I was there. Then on New Year's Day 1993, being the first voice as GMTV was launched to the nation. And now the honour and responsibility of being at the helm of the next stage for one of the world's most respected news channels.

The audience for Sky News is a select one. In addition to the general public, it's a station watched by politicians, captains of industry, news junkies, newspaper people and the television industry itself. Those eyes would be on me come launch date. Worse than getting up in the morning, and even worse than coming to terms with the new technology (if that was possible), was the round of publicity that came with the re-launch. Just as with any new media venture, like writing this book, the tools for getting the message out there are radio, television and press interviews. Never before had I had reason to do as many as this.

At one stage because of technical hiccups the launch date was in severe doubt but, regardless, I was still committed to a conveyor belt of inter-views with various publications throughout Britain and Ireland. You would think talking to people about yourself is a relatively simple and painless task but it seems everyone who writes these days is an amateur psychologist. Whether they said it to my face or whether they left it until

346

publication date to print their thesis, there had to be some ulterior reason for me wanting to get up at 3.30 in the morning again. The answer was much more basic – this was guaranteed work and, amazingly, guaranteed work pays guaranteed bills like the mortgage. Feature writers often find it hard to believe that TV presenters just need a job like everyone else. It wasn't a case of me picking up the phone and saying to Sky, 'Gis a job'. The offer has to come the other way round.

Some had their doubts as to my suitability for a hard news job. They were entitled to them – the main thing was I didn't have them. I have a simple view that the same skills are required in all areas of broadcasting. No matter how different programmes seem to be, in essence they are all the same. For instance, you may not think it but the attributes required to host *The National Lottery Jet Set* are basically the same as those required to host a live news programme. Both require scripting, both require thinking up questions and both require dealing with satellite links around the world. Believe me, if you can host *Grandstand*, you can host the general election coverage. In terms of presenting skills there is no difference between saying, 'Manchester United three, Blackburn Rovers two – that win stretches United's lead at the top of the table, so, let's take a look at the way the teams stand...' and on election night saying, 'Well, that win for Labour in Birmingham South means the momentum is now swinging their way ... if repeated throughout the country the parties would stand like this...' The best presenters share the same skills. Steve Ryder could swap jobs with David Dimbleby and vice versa.

I had inspiration and precedent to draw on from one of my great broadcasting heroes. No one ever seemed to question Sir David Frost interviewing the Prime Minister on a Sunday morning and introducing *Through the Keyhole* on a Sunday night.

The re-launch of Sky News was a particularly precarious operation. The launch date was scheduled for the last week in October and, given that rehearsals were not smooth, at times that date seemed a tall order. New technology is a temperamental thing and the only way the ghosts in the machines can be exorcised is to constantly test them. With the existing news service occupying so much of the manpower needed for these tests, that was proving hard to do. Amazingly, for a while the Sky operation was in effect running not one but two twenty-four-hour news channels until the switchover could take place.

The old-look programming would continue being produced and transmitted from the old studio until two minutes to six on the morning of Monday, 24 October 2005. Then the operation that had served so well for a decade would cease to be and the baton handed over to the new state-of-the-art Sky News centre just yards away across the road in London's Isleworth. Physically it was a short hop, but in terms of technology and the ambition of Dawn Airey and news chief Pollard, it was a world away. Everyone was nervous, including me, and I had good reason to be, especially with those ruddy hand-held computers. Surprisingly, so too was my co-host, Lorna Dunkley. Even though Lorna had presented the old *Sunrise* programme so well for a couple of years, she was unusually quiet. I assumed she was her usual cool, calm and collected self until I asked her to put right something on my hand-held computer thing. As she reached across with her stylus I couldn't help but notice she was shaking like a leaf. Acting the gentleman, I tried to reassure her, bluffing that I was dead calm. That's where these sorts of pairings stand or fall. You've got to believe the person beside you will get you out of a hole if the proverbial hits the fan. I had supreme faith in Lorna, but at moments like that your partner has to hear you saying that to them. It's about sharing trust.

The production team was ace and I immediately hit it off with my extremely capable and likeable producer, Neil Dunwoodie. My only doubts concerned the capabilities of the space-age computer system that brought all the pictures including news reports and backdrops to the screen. That's what I call them – they call them anamorphics. There were still a lot of gremlins and a lot of the technical folk felt they needed a bit more time to familiarise themselves with things. If the computers went down, the pictures would go down, as would our capability to access details of scripts or information on any breaking news stories. The presentation and interviews were the least of my worries. Lorna that morning would not only be my presenting partner but also my computer tutor. In the event, when the clock hit six there was nothing else to do but keep our fingers crossed and get on with it. Thankfully, three hours later, we touched down without a problem. The new Sky News *Sunrise* couldn't have gone better and just continues to get better. It was a wonderful experience and a wonderful insight into another different branch of broadcasting.

Above all, it confirmed to me that the things I enjoy most about what I do are being involved in the day's agenda and interviewing, being able to ask someone the questions that viewers want asked. Sometimes I even get the answers! Even better was feeling that quite often people actually wanted to be interviewed by me – that's a tremendous compliment. I also found that politicians were quite up for a bit of teasing and fencing because they knew who I was. That's a good relationship to have with an interviewee and with people watching at home – both get what they are expecting. So good were the presenters there, like Kay Burley, Jeremy Thompson, Anna Botting, Martin Stanford and Julie Etchingham, that I certainly had nothing to pass on to them about interviewing and presentation. All I could do for some of the audience who followed me to Sky was to try and bring a style to *Sunrise* that was at times different to the rest of the day's schedule.

Once again, my previous experiences in the workplace led me not to put all my eggs in the one basket. Unusually for Sky News, they allowed me to have a non-exclusive deal. We knew it was the right thing for us both. I had spent twenty-five years getting to the point where

I was a household name. I knew it was a position few broadcasters hold so I was keen not to move from a general market to an exclusively specialist one. Besides, freed from the negativity of GMTV, I was really enjoying experimenting with some of the projects that were coming my way. Channel 4 was introducing me to a whole new audience with comedy programmes like *The Friday Night Project* and *Eight Out Of Ten Cats*. Ant and Dec signed me up for their Saturday night *Gameshow Marathon* and there were offers aplenty from all sorts of talk and panel shows. But nothing was to compare with being given the chance to be a singing legend on ITV's *Celebrity Stars In Their Eyes*. When asked by my children, 'Why?' I answered, 'Well, I had to give it a go, didn't I?' I just had to feel what it was like. Even though it scared me like nothing else had ever scared me on TV before, that old St Malachy's ethos of 'give it a go' kicked in again.

For ten years the show's executive producer Jeff Thacker had bombarded me with requests to be somebody, and for ten years I knew my limitations. But now I had a new 'what the heck, devil may care' attitude. Jeff and his team were lovely people but they really were such fibbers. As usual, I would come up with the excuse that: 'I'm only a pub singer – everybody else on that show can really do it.'

'No, no, no,' said Jeff. 'It's all changed these days. It's not serious at all. And besides, you'd be doing me a real favour 'cause it's my last series.'

Always one to help out an old mate, I put my reservations on the back burner and conceded nothing else to Jeff other than I would do a voice test for him. Little did I know that when they get you this far – they've got you!

I had worked at The London Studios on the South Bank where GMTV was based for more than a decade but I never knew that there was a little room on the ground floor that housed the musical director Ray Monks and his piano. It was like another world. Within this hi-tech tower block was a little room that time had forgotten, devoid of computer screens and photocopiers. As Jeff led me around a maze of corridors we must have entered Ray's hideaway through a wardrobe door because it was as if I had arrived in the land of Narnia. But there was no time to take in the atmosphere. Jeff's tactic is to keep moving and for him to keep talking. He and Ray thought I would be very well suited to being Matt Monro or Perry Como. It's funny how you see yourself, isn't it? I was thinking more like Elvis, albeit in his latter days.

'No, no, no, no, no ... Jerry Springer has already beaten you to that,' said Jeff.

I found myself saying, 'Well, what about Johnny Cash?'

Jeff's tactics were working well. Now it was me who was asking him if I could appear as someone on a show I hadn't even wanted to do. Spookily, Ray just happened to have a whole set of Johnny Cash song sheets to hand. Surely they couldn't have known that next to Elvis, the Man in Black was one of my all-time music heroes? I had a penchant for 'Folsom Prison Blues', 'A Boy Named Sue' and 'I Walk The Line', but oddly enough 'Ring of Fire' at two minutes thirty seconds long just fitted their programme running order perfectly and, even more spookily, they just happened to have a backing track to it available. As Ray struck up the piano and I timidly began warbling, a very nice lady appeared and started running a measuring tape across my shoulders and up my inside leg. Now either I was being measured for a costume or this was my lucky night. This is where Jeff is so funny. 'I know you haven't agreed to do anything yet but since the wardrobe mistress just happened to be in the building today, and you're always so incredibly busy, I thought why make you come back for any future fitting if you decide you want to take part?'

He's all heart, that Jeff Thacker. But the coup de grâce was still to come. After one rendition of 'Ring of Fire' Ray's piano fell silent and he looked up at Jeff. The two of them shook their heads, confirming, I assumed, what I already knew about my vocal talents. Assuming they were about to say, 'Thanks but no thanks,' I began to feel ever so slightly hard done by. Instead, they just said, 'Natural, you're a natural.' Going from the brink of dejection to acceptance in the space of three seconds I stupidly bit their hands off and swallowed the bait. The next thing I knew was that I was in the Granada Studios in Manchester having a wig put on my head and being dressed like a card sharp on a Mississippi river boat.

'Tonight, Cat ... I am going to be ... Johnny Cash!'

Various rehearsals in the shower had convinced me that maybe I wasn't too bad after all, and there's no doubt that the talents of the make-up artists and wardrobe people bring the whole illusion to a different level. Just as in golf, where I believe if you dress the part people believe you can actually play, here the more they trussed me up in that black waistcoat and frilly shirt the more I was convinced I could bluff my way through. And what a lovely crowd of people I was appearing with. Former *Blue Peter* presenter Yvette Fielding as Annie Lennox, Mark Charnock and Dale Meeks, who play Marlon Dingle and Simon Meredith in *Emmerdale,* as The Blues Brothers, Debra Stephenson – Frankie in *Coronation Street* – as Kate Bush, Radio 1 DJ Colin Murray as Mark Knopfler, and me as Johnny Cash completed the line-up. All of which was fine until I watched them one by one limbering up in the corridor outside the studio. The difference was these people could sing and dance. Most of them, if not all, had been to stage school and had been somebody in *West Side Story* or *Annie.* Me? I had appeared in *Alice In Wonderland* in Holy Family Primary School when I was seven as – guess what? Bloody Alice! And there was no singing involved either. My confidence draining away wasn't helped by the last-minute introduction to my own personal choreographer.

'What do I need you for?' I ungratefully asked.

'For your dance moves,' came the reply.

'The Man in Black didn't dance,' I pointed out.

And with that the lady pointed out that my stage presence may be somewhat stunted as a result. I could feel Johnny turning in his grave at the very suggestion. I had been privileged to see the man himself close up in concert in the Grosvenor Hall in Belfast in the late seventies. Nobody came to Belfast in concert in the late seventies – so starved were we of live acts that to have seen The Glitter Band or Lieutenant Pigeon would have been a privilege, but to witness a legend in the flesh was a privilege of which few of us were worthy. If I was going to pay homage to Johnny Cash I was going to do the best I could. The singing mightn't have been true to him but sure as hell the footwork was!

Directed by Stuart McDonald, the stage setting was incredible. The honour of taking part in *Stars In Their Eyes* is that you know that even if the person you are impersonating turned up to perform there would be no difference between the facilities laid on for them and those for a mere pretender like you. So, with the full backing of a trumpet band and flame effects that could roast toast, for two and a half minutes I really did – in the words of the song – fall into a burning ring of fire. The words also go on to say, 'I went down, down, down and the flames got higher.' Which about summed up the overall state of my performance. But you know what? Again, it was one of those things that I would never have got to experience if I hadn't have been Eamonn Holmes off the telly. So Jeff Thacker, even though you are a fibber, in the immortal words of Dick Emery, 'You are awful – but I like you!'

Like buses, suddenly all these jobs came along at once. After signing for Sky, the BBC made different offers to me to host *Star Spell*, *Hard*

Spell, a sudoku quiz, a four-night special in the build-up to Children In Need called *Bid TV* and, best of all, the return of my favourite programme of all time, *The National Lottery Jet Set* – brought back specially to be part of the armoury the BBC were using to fight back against ITV's excellent Saturday-night line-up of Ant and Dec and *The X Factor*. On top of that were my weekly commitments to my Sunday 'Man of the People' newspaper column in the *People*, my weekly Saturday-morning show on Radio 5 Live, and my Sunday show on Magic 105.4 FM. Anything else that came along had to be fitted around these main fixtures – including writing this book. It was hard getting the balance right but with a lot of good people around me, especially my other half, Ruth, my wonderful secretaries, Anna Moorby and Caroline Hollinrake, and my driver, Vince O'Sullivan, we got and continue to get there. GMTV were obsessed with anything that might rival their brand, and now I could see why. I had been around on people's screens for so long that I had become a brand of my own – a one-man brand!

What it did mean, though, was that people were coming across me rather a lot on the telly and their radios. Trying not to doze off around mid-afternoon was always the hardest part of keeping it all going and it wasn't a workload without its penalties and concerns.

But when it comes to being a successful broadcaster I believe there are two speeds – full speed and no speed. It's one of those quirky occupations that can often depend on profile, meaning that work leads to more work and less work can lead to no work. Given the options, I have always been one to choose the 'more work' route. But in my game work means profile and visibility. In no other occupation would people say, 'You were working five days last week,' and mean it as a criticism. That's what most people do – work a minimum of five days a week. But when everybody is watching you doing it, for some reason they think it's a bit much.

For me broadcasting is what I do, so I take jobs the way a taxi driver accepts fares. And often that is as glamorous and exciting as the game plan gets – working on programmes to pay the same bills everybody else has to pay: the house, the car, the kids, the holidays, the tax. And, of course, the divorce.

THIRTY

Best of Times

Ever since I was a youngster I had wanted to do two things when I grew up: become a professional foot-baller, and read the news on the telly. However badly you may now think I read the news, let me point out you've never seen me play football! So, with only one of the two choices a career path option, I was left to dream about the other. When I was ten, eleven and twelve, I wanted to grow my hair long, wear my football shirt outside my shorts and my socks round my ankles. I thought the only way to play football was never to pass the ball. Why? Because of George Best, the Belfast boy who was to become the best footballer in the whole world. Youngsters like me worshipped the ground he walked on. How could I know as I practised ball tricks and jigs as a kid that as an adult I would be entrusted with hosting his funeral and, instead of reading the news, I would be making the news.

My job at Sky News meant that when George Best's death was finally announced it was hardly a surprise. Working on a rolling news programme means that you cross many, many times to the scene of the story, in this case Cromwell Hospital in West London, where the final stages of George's life were being acted out. The news at 1 p.m. on Friday, 25 November 2005, wasn't a shock but it was sad. Sad because like many people mourning it marked not only the end of a life but, for so many of us, the end of an era and the end of a period of our lives that we would never see again. My immediate concern was when the funeral would be – and how would I make it?

Funerals are very important to Belfast folk. My father believed it was important to attend those of people you had known, not just those whom you were related to. Recently, I hadn't been very good at attending them. Just a fortnight before I had missed my uncle Christie's burial. He was my father's last remaining sibling and work commitments had prevented me getting back to Belfast from London. I always hate using work as an excuse. Everyone's work is important – it's just that mine is perhaps more inflexible than many other people's. When a studio is booked, a large production team involved or a live transmission scheduled, you really can't say, 'Sorry, I can't be there,' unless the bereavement is very close. I still remember the pressure put on me by the *Holiday* programme to get back after my father's funeral in April 1991. Just because they were ready to get back to work didn't mean that I was. Co-presenter Anne Gregg wrote me a letter at the time, part of which was to highlight the importance of how 'the show must go on'. Although kindly meant by Anne, I thought it then and I even more firmly believe it now – 'Bollocks!' There is a greater duty, a greater responsibility, to the bereaved and to yourself.

I knew that getting to George's funeral was going to give me problems. The main obstacle was a concentrated week of sudoku programmes that had a quick recording and turnaround schedule, but then came good and bad news. George would not be buried on a weekday but on the weekend of Saturday, 3 December. That was good news because it wasn't during a full-on daily working schedule, but bad news because it was on my birthday and Ruth and I had planned to go away. My first weekend off since the summer. When she heard the news Ruth knew that I would feel I should be there and was very understanding about cancelling our weekend.

One hurdle surmounted, but two more then popped up in its place. Both Sky News and BBC Radio 5 Live made requests for me to work for them on the big day. I said that I felt I wanted to be at the funeral in a personal capacity but obviously, as a professional, I could feel the pressure to turn up and do the job. Stalling for time I asked for a day to think things over as to whether my role should be personal or professional. I knew my four brothers, like tens of thousands of others from Northern Ireland, wanted to be there and all I wanted to do was stand alongside them shoulder to shoulder as a member of the public. Then at half past ten on the morning of Monday, 28 November, my phone rang. It was a message from the funeral organisers, Castlereagh Borough Council, on behalf of the Best family, asking me to host the proceedings. What a privilege! George's dad, Dickie, sisters Barbara, Carol, Julia and Grace, his brother Ian and son Calum had asked for me to represent the family, saying I would have been George's choice.

As an interviewer whom George trusted it was an honour, as a fan it was an even bigger honour, but the biggest honour of all was being able to represent the people of Northern Ireland in saying goodbye to our most famous son. Everyone around me including family and people I worked for knew how much this meant. The few days leading up to the funeral were packed as only I can pack them – *Sunrise* on Sky News, five programmes a day for a new *SudoQ* series on the BBC, my newspaper column for the *People* and, to top it all, hosting an evening at the British Academy of Film and Television Arts in London celebrating the work of, and interviewing on stage, Dame Julie Andrews. While all these things are tremendous, nothing would compare to holding together proceedings for George's send-off. To cap it all, I caught a heavy cold complete with cough.

In between everything else were the incessant requests for TV, radio and newspaper interviews relating to Bestie's life. Such was the pressure that week that at one stage it wouldn't have been much of a surprise to those around me if it had turned out to be a double funeral. In the end it was nothing quite so serious – but I did end up in need of medical attention. Not for high blood pressure or stress, but because coming off the plane to Belfast I went over on my left ankle. Waking up on Friday morning, the day before the funeral, I couldn't put any weight on my left foot at all. I hobbled around for half the day cursing the injury and hoping no one was going to ask me to lift the coffin the next day. So serious did the swelling and inflammation become that 1 sought help at the physiotherapist's. An examination showed that my ankle ligaments were well and truly strained and the foot had to be strapped up. Great. On the most important engagement of my professional life so far I was going to look like Hopalong Cassidy. Oh, it still hurts today just thinking about it. Parliament building at Stormont where the farewell was to take place is enormous, with more stairs than you ever want to see with a strapped-up ankle. So there I was on the Friday, limping about doing a rehearsal and turning up for interviews with the assembled media circus. Funny how when you limp so many people think you are play-acting!

If my foot was bad the weather was worse. It didn't just rain in Belfast that weekend, it poured – monsoon standard. Not even that, though, stopped 100,000 people lining the route of George's cortege. In a country that often couldn't rise above its differences, George Best united us in grief the same way as he did in joy. It didn't matter if you were a Catholic or Protestant, George Best was simply just one of us, and I was just a fan who got close.

Maybe it was the amount of painkillers, maybe it was sheer nerves, but come the moment to lead the proceedings I felt no pain. I'm sure George had been in this sort of situation himself – having to play strapped up and with a few tablets inside him. As the coffin came to rest before me it was adorned with floral tributes and dotted with hundreds of large water droplets. They could have been tears, they certainly looked like them and goodness knows there were enough being shed for him. The close family members were clearly very distressed and emotional at this stage. I was OK, I was holding things together very well until I looked down from my podium to the messages on the wreaths, the close messages that weren't intended for public consumption. My eyesight was a worry for the first time that year. I was beginning to have trouble with things close up but at four feet away these little cards, black ink running like mascara in the rain, were in perfect focus and my eyes began to well up. Now not only were my headlights suspect but I needed wipers as well to see anything.

Over twenty-five years I've got used to the idea of a TV audience. No matter how big, it doesn't scare me any more. The whites of people's eyes – that's a different matter, and there they were in Stormont's Great Hall, all looking in my direction. Politicians, including the secretary of state for Northern Ireland, Peter Hain. Footballers past and present, including legends like Denis Law, and the man who won the Champions League trophy for Man Utd in 1999, Ole Gunnar Solskjaer. Sven-Göran Eriksson was there, as was the boss, Sir Alex Ferguson, representatives from showbiz and public life, fans and, most importantly, the friends and family of George. Now wasn't a good time to freeze. I said what I had to say and left the real talking to the people who knew him best. I think we, and by that I mean Northern Ireland, gave him a good send-off. We laughed a lot and we cried a little too, but most of all we were all aware that as a talent we would never see his like from our shores again. Thanks for the memories, George, and thanks for being one of us.

What Makes Me ... Me

So, that was my life so far – well quite a lot of it, and as best as I can remember it. It's not meant to be held up as a better or worse life than anybody else's, but it's mine and it's what makes me, well, me.

I have lived forty-six years, twenty-five of them on the telly, got married, got divorced, been a father four times and seen thirty years of civil disturbances in my homeland of Northern Ireland.

You can't go through all of that without learning a few things:

I've learned that we're all products of our environment and the parents who raise us – but however good or bad, don't be limited by either. Take what is positive and use it to find your own place in the world.

I've learned that the world can be a viciously cruel place, but the important thing is not to dwell on the punches that knock you down, but put your energy into getting back up again.

Probably because of growing up during the Troubles back home and reporting so much tragedy on the news, I've learned that there's much to be said for living each day as your last. I've learned to be nobody's doormat, but I've also learned to be respectful and never to strip anyone of their dignity.

I've learned that true wisdom comes from listening, and being able to do so is a reflection of a confident person.

I've learned to treat others as I would wish to be treated but I've also learned that, when they don't, be prepared to stand up to them.

I've learned it's wise practice in today's world to work for yourself rather than anyone else.

I've learned that the harder you work, the luckier you tend to be.

I've learned I need heroes to look up to or escape with at the movies or on the sports field.

I've learned the importance of not only playing sport but playing it for as long as possible in your life.

I've learned that you are what you eat.

I've learned, perhaps too late, the importance of sleep.

I've learned the benefits of drinking lots of water.

I've learned to have more patience, particularly with myself.

I've learned it's wrong to blame children for the sins of their parents.

I've learned that opinions are the cheapest commodities on earth. Just because everybody has some, it doesn't mean that you have to accept them.

I've learned not to shun responsibility.

I've learned it's nice to have money and the things money can buy, but it's more important to make sure I don't lose out on the things money can't buy.

I've learned that time is one of the most precious gifts to be able to give anyone.

I've learned that the more people criticise me, the more determined I am to prove them wrong.

I've learned that the best way out of difficulty is not to avoid it but to go straight through it.

I've learned that with love and the strength of someone who believes in you and supports you, any of us can do more than we ever thought possible.

I've learned that friends like you to be successful – but not too successful.

I've learned that showbiz is more biz than show

and that any business without a conscience is a bad business.

I've learned that if you have a talent it's your duty to make the most of it.

I've learned that if you don't follow your dreams you will never know if you actually had what it takes ... and surely it is better to have loved and lost than never to have loved at all.

I've learned the importance and value of saying sorry, thanks and I love you.

I've learned that dreams can come true.

And, most of all, I've learned that my family is the most important thing in the world to me – they are my life.

But on top of all this I have learned that I am impatient and I have taken too long to learn all these things. Although I have the outlook of a twenty-six-year old, the mirror tells a different story. If my life has got you thinking about yours all I can say is – get out there and live it!

The publishers hope that this book has given you enjoyable reading. Large Print Books are especially designed to be as easy to see and hold as possible. If you wish a complete list of our books please ask at your local library or write directly to:

Magna Large Print Books
Magna House, Long Preston,
Skipton, North Yorkshire.
BD23 4ND

This Large Print Book for the partially sighted, who cannot read normal print, is published under the auspices of

THE ULVERSCROFT FOUNDATION